IN THE SHOES OF AN INVESTIGATOR

The True Life Adventures of a Private Eye

ELDON O'BRIEN

Wasteland Press

www.wastelandpress.net
Shelbyville, KY USA

In The Shoes of an Investigator:
The True Life Adventures of a Private Eye
by Eldon O'Brien

First Printing – September 2013
ISBN: 978-1-60047-868-0
Library of Congress Control Number: 2013941854

This book is a work of nonfiction and is based on actual cases
investigated by the Author. Certain names, characters, places,
and incidents have been changed and/or used fictitiously.

Printed in the U.S.A.

0   1   2   3   4   5   6   7   8   9   10   11   12   13   14   15

To my wife Catherine, who caused my past to blossom into such a brilliant present and who gilds the path into our future.

The author and his wife and their ten children, June 17, 2013

TABLE OF CONTENTS

INDEX OF CASES

The Camelot Years

Camelot is the magnificent kingdom of the legendary King Arthur. It has been the subject of poetry, romance, music and theatre. In 1967, *Camelot* became widely known when it was the subject of a film version of a Broadway musical, based on King Arthur. In the beginning, *Camelot* was innocent, unmarred by human error and blessed by Mother Nature.

As I look back on my past, from grade school, high school, college and early adulthood, I see my own *Camelot* – a world sparkling with promise filled with potential and propelled by never-ending hope. In the movie, there is a song that goes (something) like this: "The rain may never fall 'till after sundown; by 8:00 a.m. the clouds must disappear. In short, there's simply not, a more congenial spot, for happily-ever-after-ing, than here in *Camelot!*" Now, I invite you to walk with me through my *Camelot*.

For the O'Brien family, San Jose, California was our *Camelot*. The sun was always shining and I even had my own Knights of the Round Table, only they were dressed in baseball uniforms and not in shining armor. Permit me to share with you some of my memories of growing up in San Jose, my magical place. I hope you enjoy reading these stories as much as I enjoyed living them!

Baseball and the Nickel Matinee

Summertime in grade school meant only one thing to me: baseball. Our Naas Candy team played every day at Herbert Hoover High School. On Thursdays, my dad would give me a quarter for mowing the lawn. Then my friends and I were off to play baseball all morning. We would then eat lunch at the Holland Creamery where a tuna sandwich cost ten cents and a chocolate milk shake was five cents. Afterwards, we would ride our bikes to the Hester Theater to see a nickel matinee. We would watch Tarzan swinging through the trees or laugh at a Laurel & Hardy film, but the scariest of all was when Boris Karloff or Bela Lugosi came on the screen. We'd scream, peeking between the seats in front of us, trying but failing to maintain our "cool." When it was over, we would all buy a Baby Ruth candy bar with the nickel we had left over. Those were the days!

If You Flunk, It's Off To War!

Just before Christmas in 1943, I was in high school at Bellarmine Prep. The whole world was at war and the Draft Boards were sending everyone over 18 to fight the Germans in

Europe, or the Japanese in the South Pacific. In our senior class at Bellarmine, we had seven students over 18 and in danger of getting drafted if they flunked out. Howard Emory was one of them and he sat next to me in our Physics class (he spelled Physics with an "F"). He had to pass the class or he'd get drafted.

The day of our final physics exam, the one that would determine whether he flunked or went to war, Howard asked me if he could copy my answers and I agreed. On the day of the exam, Howard was seated next to me on my right and our teacher, Father Cronin was at his desk at the front of the classroom reading the *Mercury Herald* newspaper. All went smoothly. Father Cronin never looked up from his newspaper and Howard copied all my answers. Finally, the school bell rang and we all stood up and placed our exam papers on Father Cronin's desk. Howard was home free!

But when the papers were graded, Howard learned of his one fateful mistake: Not only did he copy all my answers, he even COPIED MY NAME! Poor Howard, he went off to war and I got suspended for one day. He never was the sharpest knife in the drawer but after the war he was discharged and became one of the richest members of our class. To this day we refer to him as the "Mayor of Irvington."

My Desk Can Fly!

It was a sweltering day at Bellarmine Prep. We had only two weeks to go before graduation but today we had to put up with the smell of rotten eggs (sulfur), tar and the boring voice of Mr. Kane, our chemistry teacher. Johnny Schirle, my catcher on the baseball team, was seated in front of me and there was a row of windows on our left. All the windows were open to give us at least a breath of fresh air. Unfortunately, the fresh air smelled of hot tar and sulfur because workers were putting a fresh layer of tar on the roof.

We all sat in old desks with wrought iron legs, hardwood desktops and old-fashioned holes for the inkwells. Johnny watched as the empty bucket was lowered to the ground where a worker filled it with hot tar. Then the worker would give the rope two yanks and a worker on the roof would pull the full bucket of hot tar up to the roof. Johnny and I watched the bucket go up and down and up and down.

Then Johnny got a great idea. When the empty bucket was lowered past our open window, he grabbed it, pulled it in and put the bucket on the classroom floor. He attached the hook to the iron leg of my desk. Then he gave two yanks on the rope and out went my desk, books and all through the open window!!

It made a noise that shook the entire building. Mr. Kane was sipping a cup of coffee when he heard the terrible explosion and he spilled coffee all over his white shirt. And what did Johnny do? He slipped over to an open desk in the second row. And guess who got blamed for the flying desk? Me!

A Battleship On Dry Ground

The war was nearly over when I was assigned to Midshipman's School at my alma mater Notre Dame. For me it was just like coming home only this time I was not on a baseball scholarship but in a Navy uniform, taking a 90-day Officer's training course to become an Ensign in the United States Navy. If you flunked any of your courses, it was off to Great Lakes training as an ordinary seaman. The courses were hard because the Navy had all the Ensigns they needed to bring Japan to their knees. The word around school was that there was an expected 60% flunk-out rate but to encourage us, we all had our photographs taken in an Ensign Uniform for our anticipated graduation.

One of our classes was Navigation where we were to navigate a battleship through many longitude and latitude turns (on graph paper) from our dock in Hawaii to our dock in Guam…easy, or so I thought. After making all those turns, the battleship was supposed to arrive at the dock in Guam, right? Well, my battleship ended up six miles inland on DRY GROUND! As a result, I flunked Navigation and had to prepare to go to Great Lakes. I learned later that day over 56% of the class flunked one subject or another and we were all headed for Great Lakes as common ordinary seamen.

I packed all my gear and walked down to the Grotto to say a prayer. The Notre Dame Grotto is an exact replica of the famous Grotto in Lourdes, France where Saint Bernadette talked to our Blessed Lady. I knelt down and I guess I was crying. Then I heard a voice calling me. I turned around and there was an old priest seated on a wrought iron bench. He was waving for me to join him. He asked me why I was crying. I told him I had just flunked out of school because I parked a battleship on dry ground. He didn't understand but then he asked me if I had been caught cheating or if I had done anything wrong. I said, "No, all I did was park that dumb battleship on dry ground." He sat thinking and after a full minute he said, "My son, ten years from now you will realize this will have been the best thing that could ever have happened to you." That made no sense to me. I just shook my head in disbelief and walked away.

Now, it wasn't even six months before the old priest's prophecy came true. The new Ensigns who graduated were all sent to Japan as the war ended and they became the "army of occupation," spending the next two years in Japan. Meanwhile, I ended up playing baseball with Bob Feller and a host of major leaguers. Johnny Groat and I were the only players not in the majors. Then I was transferred to Pensacola where Don Hoak (of the Pittsburgh Pirates) and I were the co-captains of a team that won the Naval Air Corps championship. We were discharged in 1946 while the new Ensigns didn't come home until 1948. The old priest at the Grotto was right when he said my flunking out was the best thing that could ever happen to me. Oh, and by the way, I pitched batting practice to Ted Williams before he was sent overseas for flying a plane through a hangar.

The Fifth Martini is Free

The war was over and back to Notre Dame I went on the GI Bill, with the tuition paid and $65/month spending money. Notre Dame had a standing rule: no alcohol and you must be in your rooms by 10:00 p.m. or you will be expelled from school. But we were returning war veterans so Notre Dame made an exception. We were allowed an overnight stay, one weekend a month. We would all get onto a South Shore train in South Bend and head into Chicago for the weekend.

It was a Saturday afternoon when eight of us left Notre Dame with $65.00 in our jeans, looking for an overnight in Chicago. We knew we could stay at the Palmer House Hotel where the night manager was a Notre Dame graduate. We were given a room on the 11th floor and we drew lots to see who would sleep on the only bed while the rest of us would sleep on the floor. We dropped off our bags in the room and headed to the mezzanine bar, known for its martini "special offer" - after your fifth martini, the rest of your drinks were free. Now that offer didn't impress most of us because five martinis is a heavy load to carry. But when you have a group of eight veterans who are now "real men," there is always one guy who can't resist a bargain.

Charlie Higgins was his name. He was an ex-Marine who spent the war in the South Pacific and he had a chest full of "glory bars." He drank his five martinis while the rest of us were still on our second. Charlie was seated over at the end of the bar and it wasn't long before he was passed out with his head resting on the bar. We picked him up and deposited him on the only bed in the room. We crossed his arms like they do in a funeral parlor. We turned off the lights and went to dinner and a show.

It was after 2:00 a.m. when we wandered back to our room. Charlie hadn't moved a muscle; his arms were still crossed over his chest. We turned off the room lights and went to sleep on the floor.

The next morning, we awoke at 9:30 a.m.; all but Charlie, he was still asleep. We did our best to wake him up, put on bathrobes and went down to the steam room in the basement to sweat out some of the cobwebs from our throbbing heads. Charlie was gradually joining the human race with painful groans of extreme pain. We sat him in the corner and promptly forgot him. The temperature in the room was103 degrees and the steam made it hard for us to see or hear each other. Suddenly, there appeared Charlie running in panicked circles, stark naked, screaming at the top of his lungs, "MY GOD, MY GOD…I'M IN HELL!!!" So much for free martinis, Charlie!!!

St. Patrick's Day and The Winchester Mystery House

And now, for the final and best *Camelot* story of them all. It was on Saint Patrick's Day, March 17th 1950, when the Ancient Order of Hibernians had their annual dinner/dance at the Saint Claire Hotel in San Jose. My dad and a few of his cronies, George Walsh "The Irish Taylor," Ted Rodgers and John McEnery of the Farmers Union Hardware Store were giving me a bad time because I had no date for the biggest party of the year. They dared me to ask Cathy Kiely, who was operating the telephone switchboard at the Hardware Store, for a date to the party. I thought I'd show these old timers how an "Irish Lad" from Notre Dame operated. I walked right out of the coffee shop and next door to the hardware store. And there she was…WOW! I mumbled something like, I was Eldon O'Brien and I wondered if she would like to go to the Hibernian dance with me on Saturday night. I almost fell over when she said, "Yes!"

Years later, I learned it was all a set up. It turned out Cathy knew my Dad and I guess I looked like him. Anyway, that was the beginning of a beautiful friendship that has lasted over 60 years. I proposed to Cathy at the Winchester Mystery House three months later saying, "We should get married and buy this old house with over 100 rooms and we could fill every room with our children"! It was not the best proposal by far, but it worked and we were married on September 9th 1950.

After a honeymoon in Santa Cruz, we rented an apartment in San Francisco. I joined Brown Brothers Adjusters and a new chapter in our lives began.

"Don't let it be forgot, that once there was a spot, for one brief shining moment that was known as Camelot.

My Adventures in Chicago

Even One Drink is Too Many

All winter, I worked the telephone desk at Kellogg Insurance Company taking all claims on the north side of Chicago. It was warm in the office and I was out of the snow, wind and ice that makes Chicago famous (or is that infamous?).

My Claims Manager, Bart Reynolds, told me if I wanted to be one of the best adjusters in the company, I could learn from the six men who had their offices against the back wall; the ones whose windows overlooked Lake Michigan. These men were assigned the really big cases with the most severe damages. They were called the "Hughes Team" named for their leader, Art Hughes, and they went to lunch every afternoon at the Blarney Stone Grille across the street from our office.

Art Hughes had over twenty-seven years' experience as an Adjuster, handling the biggest and most expensive claims for the Company. Bart told me I should go to lunch with them and ask any questions I might have, but he warned me to never ask the same question twice. I took Bart's advice and before long, I was joining the Hughes Team for lunch at the Blarney Stone every day.

They always ordered a Martini before lunch and of course, I joined them. After all, I was an ex-naval air corp. man and could hold my liquor (*I thought*). Also, they always took an hour-and-a-half lunch. I sure learned a lot during these long lunch meetings…and I drank a lot of Martinis.

It was in early June and I had just returned from my usual lunch with the Team, when Bart called me into his office. He told me he decided I was ready for my very first *outside claim*. This meant I would be adjusting a claim in person, rather than simply over the phone and passing it along to an outside adjuster.

He said we insured a brand new Cadillac owned by Mr. Stanley Collins, the retired President of the Chicago Transit Company. While Mr. Collins' wife was at a supermarket in Evanston, she left her rear window open and someone threw a lighted cigarette through the window where it ignited the upholstery and the Cadillac caught fire. Before a fire crew could control the fire, the car was a total loss.

Bart said my job was to see Mr. Collins immediately and verify the recent purchase price of the Cadillac and settle his claim. I grabbed my brand new briefcase and was on my way to the Collins' home to adjust my very first claim. Boy was I in for a big surprise!

The address was on Lake Shore Drive in the most expensive area of Evanston, where every home was a mansion and every mansion faced Lake Michigan. The Stanley Collins Estate was right out of the movies. It had a long driveway that led to a huge mansion. The front door was at least ten feet-high and when I rang the doorbell, I was greeted by a butler.

I introduced myself to the butler and handed him my card. He said I was expected, however, Mr. Collins was with a guest so I was asked to wait in the library. Books covered three walls from floor to ceiling and the fourth wall was a huge bay window with a breathtaking view of Lake Michigan. In the corner of the room was a gigantic hand-carved mahogany desk with a high-backed leather Judge's Chair. I expected Cary Grant to walk in the room at any moment.

Finally, Mr. Collins, a little man, hurried in, shook my hand firmly and sat in his Judge's Chair. He barely was able to see over the desk piled high with unopened mail. He was maybe 5'5" and at least 70 years old. He had a frown on his face as he shook my hand and I wondered why.

He looked at my card and after a short pause said, "I do not know you Mr. O'Brien, but I do smell the odor of alcohol on your breath. So, I am unable to tell whether you are drunk or stone sober. However, my Cadillac is very expensive and I do not choose to discuss this matter with you under these circumstances. I suggest you return tomorrow morning and we can conclude the matter then. Good day!"

And with that, he got up and walked out of the room. The butler showed me to the front door. I was embarrassed and half sick to my stomach. All the way home to my apartment, I resolved to never, ever take a drink while I was working. That humbling scene in Mr. Collins' library taught me a lesson I would not soon forget.

The next morning, I returned to Mr. Collins' home and within an hour we settled the case on the veranda overlooking Lake Michigan. The butler even served us coffee and croissants!

A Bookkeeper Gets Even

It was early January, when Bart Reynolds my Claims Manager, told me we had to go upstairs to see Mr. Kellogg the President of Kellogg Insurance Company, in his private office. I thought I was going to be fired for sure after my humiliating experience with Mr. Collins, the President of the Chicago Transit Company. That was the case Bart gave me (my very first outside claim) where Mr. Collins' Cadillac caught fire and when he smelled liquor on my breath, he made me leave and come back the next day to adjust his claim. (*See, Even One Drink is Too*

Many). I learned a lesson about drinking and working I shall never forget but right now, I was sure I was going to be fired.

On our way up the elevator to the Executive Offices on the 11th floor, I felt like a dead man walking to my execution. Bart never said a word to ease my pain -- maybe he felt sorry for me. Finally, the elevator doors opened and we stepped out. We were on the Executive floor where only a handful of employees ever entered this sanctum of the most powerful men in the company. The walls were adorned with walnut paneling and the high ceilings were encrusted with elegant molding. Suddenly, a secretary rounded the corner, smiled and announced, "Mr. Kellogg will see you now." His office was huge with a large bay window overlooking Lake Michigan. Jack Burke, my old baseball buddy from Notre Dame and the one who offered me the job at Kellogg Insurance Company, was seated in a leather chair next to Mr. Kellogg's desk. He winked at me as he introduced me to Mr. Kellogg.

Bart and I sat on a couch opposite the two most powerful men in the Company. I had a lump in my throat the size of a baseball but at least Mr. Burke was friendly which helped cut the tension. Mr. Kellogg ordered coffee for all us and opened the conversation saying he had just learned of a major bond loss that would cost the Company millions of dollars. He explained we provided the McCarthy & Johnson Construction Company with a $6 million fidelity bond on their key employees at their home office here in Chicago.

Since the end of World War II, McCarthy & Johnson had grown into one of the largest construction companies in the nation. They specialized in building federally-funded apartments for returning veterans and their families. The two partners started the company with 12 employees and now they had over 600 on their payroll. Each partner had an income of over $1 million per year while their trusted bookkeeper's salary increased from $25,000 per year to $85,000 per year. Apparently that didn't satisfy him.

Mr. Kellogg went on to explain that just after Thanksgiving the bookkeeper decided to "get even" with the partners. He told Mr. McCarthy, who was bidding a 200-unit apartment complex in San Francisco that he had to cash in substantial amounts of stocks and bonds to prepare a financial statement for the federal government. He told Mr. Johnson, who was in Boston on vacation, the same thing. Within days, he had accumulated well over $4 million in cash and negotiable bonds. Then he set fire to the office files. He rented an airplane and flew his family to a small island off the coast of Argentina.

Mr. Kellogg said, "According to the FBI investigators, the bookkeeper and his family are living like kings in an old castle with two swimming pools, a boat house with an expensive yacht and a fishing boat." The bookkeeper was smart, too: the first thing he did when he moved to the island was bribe the local government officials to pass a law not recognizing the sovereignty of any other nation. This meant that so long as he stayed on the island with his family, he could not be arrested and extradited to the United States.

"Now, for the purpose of this meeting, gentlemen," Mr. Burke said, "we have a plan and we need your help. You, Mr. O'Brien, would pretend to be a rich playboy who has gone fishing with your father, 'played by' Art Hughes. You will experience sudden engine trouble and will be forced to land on the island. It is possible, if you have to wait a long time for the repairs to be completed, you could go fishing with the bookkeeper, who is an avid fisherman. Then you could 'accidentally' go beyond the three-mile limit*. He could then be arrested and extradited, and we would be in a position to recoup our bond loss of well over $4 million dollars. I admit it is a long shot, but it's worth a try." *(Protection from extradition under the new sovereignty law extended from the island shore to three miles out into the ocean.)

Wow! This was a far cry from being fired! I agreed to the plan. I could play the rich playboy (on an expense account of course). Mr. Kellogg said he would give the idea some serious thought and confer with his Board of Directors. He cautioned us to keep this conversation confidential and told us he would make his decision within the week.

A week passed and I had my passport and immunizations. I was all ready to debut my acting "skills" and catch the "bad guy" who stole all of our money. Two weeks passed, still no word from Mr. Kellogg. Finally, Bart went upstairs to inquire about the delay. He returned shaking his head. The Board had rejected Mr. Kellogg's plan as too expensive; and what was to prevent Art and me from staying on the island and living like kings on Kellogg Insurance Company money? Incidentally, the bookkeeper's daughter was just about my age and it seemed apparent that the insurance company was not about to trust me, despite the fact they had no reason to doubt my professionalism.

End of story? Well, almost.

You see, I learned a valuable lesson: insurance companies trust no one, not even their own employees! In addition, they are loathe to forgive and forget. About a year later the phone rang in Mr. Kellogg's private office. It was the bookkeeper calling from a payphone right here in Chicago. He offered to return half of the money ($2 million) provided he and his family would not be charged for the crimes committed and they could return to the United States. Mr. Kellogg rejected his offer and the bookkeeper returned to his island. For all I know, he's still there.

My Diamond Compact is Missing

Chicago was warm and humid in September 1948 when I joined the Kellogg Insurance Company. I spent the first six weeks at Northwestern University in Evanston, Illinois learning about insurance coverage and how to estimate automobile damages. There was even a fancy graduation ceremony and we were presented with a diploma declaring to the world that we were certified Insurance Adjusters. Only two of us were from the Kellogg home office in Chicago. The rest, about thirty, were from Kellogg Claims offices around the country. In early November, I turned in my company car because I was offered an "inside" job as assistant to the Claims Manager. The best part was that I didn't have to deal with the cold, wind and snow if I worked in the office, so I jumped at the opportunity.

Bart Reynolds was my boss. He was a great guy, married with six kids, and he had a fantastic sense of humor. He worked his way through Northwestern University Law School and passed the Illinois bar but chose to be an Adjuster for Kellogg Insurance Companies. He was 43 years old when he was offered the Claims Manager's position in 1946. Now, he was in charge of 36 outside adjusters who serviced the greater Chicago area. My "inside" job was to handle all incoming claims on the north side of Chicago. We had another adjuster handling the south side. If the claim was major we would check with Bart and he would assign the claim to an "outside" adjuster. If it were only a minor claim we would handle it over the telephone.

One afternoon, a young lady called and told me her purse had been stolen at the parking garage of the Palmer House Hotel. She had her personal property covered under her parent's

Homeowners Policy. It sounded like a simple claim. She said the purse was worth about $20.00 but inside the purse was a compact encrusted with diamonds and valued at $21,000. She said it was a gift from the King of Sweden and that she had an appraisal by a Jeweler in Evanston confirming the value at $21,000. She offered me a copy of the appraisal if needed.

I told Bart it sounded to me like a phony claim and should not be paid. Bart made a phone call to the insurance agent and learned the family was extremely wealthy and they did have relatives in Sweden. Then Bart told me to call the American ambassador in Sweden. I called and asked the ambassador if the King knew the family and if so, did the King give their daughter a diamond-encrusted compact? I told him the diamond compact had been stolen. He said he would call me back after he spoke with the King's office. The next afternoon, he called me and said the King did know this family and yes, he did give the young woman the diamond compact as a present for her eighteenth birthday. Bart just smiled and signed the settlement check for $21,000.00.

When She Had To Go – She Went!

It was Christmastime. I was on the telephone desk at the home office of the Kellogg Insurance Company in Chicago. A new case came in that day and it is one I will never forget. In fact, it became a feature article in our *Kellogg* monthly newsletter.

A mother and daughter lived in San Francisco. They had just purchased a new Cadillac and decided to visit relatives in

Chicago over the Christmas holidays. They drove from San Francisco to Salt Lake City. Around 5:00 the next morning, they got back on the road and drove onto the Salt Lake Flats Highway. There were only a few cars on the road.

The daughter was driving with her mother in the right front seat. She was travelling at around 80-85 mph on the straight level roadway. At about 7:30 a.m., her mother saw a small town in the distance. She told her daughter to stop at a service station in the town so she could use the restroom. Her daughter nodded as she slowed down from 85 to 25 mph, the speed limit in the town.

When the Cadillac slowed from 85 to 25 mph, the reduction in speed caused the mother to believe the car had stopped as they passed the first service station on the right. She instinctively opened the door and...got out! She fell hard onto the street where she bounced and tumbled several times before stopping on the side of the road. I guess she had to go real bad! She was taken to the hospital with several broken bones and cuts but fortunately, she was not badly hurt.

Hey, when you have to go, you *HAVE TO GO!*

PS: We paid all of her medical expenses under the policy clause that covers "entering or alighting from an automobile."

My Adventure in San Francisco

A City Bus...On the Sidewalk?

The wedding was over, the honeymoon in Santa Cruz was over, and now Cathy and I were living in an apartment on Pacheco Street in San Francisco. My bachelor days had ended and I was working for Brown Brothers Adjusters. It was a good job and a great place to live. Every morning, I would jump into my Nash Rambler, drive downtown, park my car and walk three blocks to the Russ Building on Montgomery Street where Brown Brothers Adjusters had their home office.

It was a magical time for us. We lived on top of a hill overlooking the Pacific Ocean. We would take long walks in the evenings when the sun was going down. San Francisco had wonderful restaurants and great theaters. I had a new job with a briefcase full of interesting cases to work, and best of all, Cathy, my new bride.

Our office handled all the claims for the insurance company who insured the San Francisco Municipal Bus Company. One morning, Art Brown gave me what appeared to be a simple pedestrian case: An elderly lady was standing at the corner of Montgomery Street and Pacific Avenue, waiting for the light to change. Suddenly, a bus attempted to make a right-hand turn from Montgomery Street onto Pacific Avenue. He cut the corner and the right rear wheels of the bus went onto the sidewalk knocking the lady to the ground. She was taken by ambulance to the hospital, x-rays were taken and the emergency room doctor confirmed there was no fracture to her left hip. She was released the same day. The police cited the bus driver for violation of the pedestrian right-of-way.

My job was a simple one (or so I thought). I picked up the police report and verified the citation. I was familiar with the scene of the accident because I walked it myself every morning. Pedestrian traffic on Montgomery Street was always heavy with people waiting to cross Pacific Avenue on the pedestrian "walk" signal. The bus drivers turn right to park in front of the Bank of America building and discharge their passengers. Obviously, the bus driver was at fault for cutting the corner and driving up on the sidewalk.

The elderly lady lived in an apartment house just two blocks from our Brown Brother's offices. I decided to walk up to her apartment and introduce myself. I rang the bell and a nice-looking lady about 70 years old opened the door. She had snow white hair, was wearing slippers and she walked with a cane. I introduced myself and gave her my card. I asked her about the cane and she said her left hip continued to hurt but the doctor told her there was no fracture and the pain would slowly go away.

I told her the bus company would pay all of her expenses but we should wait until she was released from her personal doctor before we settled her claim. In the meantime, she signed medical authorizations so we could get the emergency room records and the doctor's report. I went back to our office and sent for the medical reports. About a week later, the reports came in with a bill for x-rays and treatment totaling $586.00. The report said the x-rays were negative for any fracture of the left hip.

A month went by and she called me saying she had been released by her personal doctor and she was ready to settle. It was an easy case. All I had to do was total up her medical expenses, include the cost of the x-rays and add some money for pain and suffering. She signed a Release of All Claims for $1,758.00. I made my report to the insurance company, sent her a check and closed the file.

End of story? Well, not quite.

Now I can tell you why this simple pedestrian case has haunted me all these years. A full year went by, Cathy and I moved to Eureka and I was made Claims Manager of the Brown Brothers Office in Eureka. Once a year, I had to make a trip into San Francisco and meet with the insurance company Claims Managers who hired us in Humboldt County. My job was to meet with them and listen to their gripes about our bills being too high, etc. As usual, I parked my car in the same lot on Montgomery Street and walked the three blocks to our Brown Brothers home office.

On this particular morning, as I passed a small grocery store on my right, I thought I saw the nice old lady who had been hit by the bus. She recognized me but I had to do a double-take because now she was in a wheelchair and she looked like she had aged at least twenty years. I approached her and she told me a long and very sad story. About a year after I settled her claim she was still experiencing pain in her left hip. Finally, she could stand the pain no longer so she called her son who took her immediately to the hospital. A new set of x-rays showed a compound fracture of her left hip. An orthopedic surgeon had to replace her entire hip socket but because of the long delay since the accident she was now confined to a wheelchair and was unable to walk. Her life savings of over $85,000 had been spent on medical bills.

It was clear her emergency room doctor had misread her x-rays and failed to see the fracture. She said she went to an attorney who told her the one-year statute of limitations had run and she could no longer sue the doctor or the hospital for medical malpractice. I told her I would talk to the Claims Manager who insured the bus company and see if her claim could be reopened. In many ways, I felt responsible to this poor lady who would spend the rest of her life in a wheelchair due to the emergency room doctor's error. I should have called for an independent medical exam and had a doctor take his own set of x-rays. After all, she was hit by a bus and thrown to the sidewalk. I should have taken more time before settling her claim. She gave me her phone number and I promised to call her after I talked to the Claims Manager.

We had a big fancy luncheon at The St. Francis Hotel that day with all the major insurance companies in attendance. Art Brown had all of his Claims Managers from up and down the state, including me. I finally found the bus company's Claims Manager and asked if I could meet him at his office after the luncheon. He agreed and when we got back to his office, he asked his file clerk to bring in the closed file. I told him we had settled the case too soon and now the lady is confined to a wheelchair for life. Was there any way we could reopen her file and help with her expenses? He just gave me a cold stare, shook his head and said, "The release has been signed and the claim has been paid, so you can tell the old lady we can't reopen her file. My responsibility is to the insurance company and not to her. It is my duty to see claims are settled as cheaply as possible and that is just what we did."

That evening, I had to make the painful phone call to the woman in her wheelchair and tell her it was impossible to reopen her claim. She said she understood...but I didn't. Over the years since that accident, the laws have changed somewhat but not much. The insurance companies still evaluate their own claims and act as a judge and jury on the persons who are injured. Sometimes, signing a "Release of All Claims" can be the nail in your coffin if you are the one who has been injured *(see, "An Adjuster at a Crossroads.")*.

My Adventures in Eureka

The Richardson Grove Cameraman

In Northern California, Highway #101 is known as The Redwood Highway because it wanders through Redwood forests from Garberville all the way to Eureka. In the summer, vacationers from all over the country clog the Highway to marvel at the gigantic Redwood trees. They grow over 100 feet high and up to twenty feet in diameter. Richardson Grove is about sixty miles south of Eureka, and in a beautiful valley with a café on one side of the highway and a crosswalk leading to the Visitors' Bureau parking lot on the other side of the Highway. Truckers hauling lumber and Humboldt crab to San Francisco are painfully aware of the volume of tourists who crowd both sides of the Highway in the summer and of the many resulting accidents that occur.

Our office in Eureka handled all the accidents for the Callison Freight Lines Insurance Company. Ray Callison called one day and told me one of his trucks loaded with Humboldt Crab lost control and hit a Redwood tree in Richardson Grove. We insured the truck and the cargo (the crab). Ray said he was sending a replacement truck to the scene and he suggested I meet him there. I agreed.

When we arrived, nothing had been moved. The truck was still wrapped around a huge Redwood tree and although it was an obvious total loss there was no damage to the giant tree. Crabs were crawling all over the highway. Ray had his driver, with the help of willing tourists, load the live crab into the replacement truck and he called for a tow truck to haul away the wrecked truck.

I walked over to the café and found the truck driver sitting in a corner booth with a cup of coffee; he was badly shaken. He had a sore jaw and some bruised ribs from his truck hitting the redwood tree. He told me a story I'm sure I will never forget.

He said he slowed his truck down to about 30 mph as he entered Richardson Grove because he was aware of the tourists who were usually crowding both sides of the highway. Suddenly, he saw what appeared to be a dead body lying on the centerline. He had only a fraction of a second to decide what to do. If he swerved to his left or his right, he would hit at least eight to ten tourists. So, he decided to "straddle" the body because he figured it was dead anyway. When he thought his trailer had passed over the body, he lost his nerve, hit his air brakes and his truck jackknifed into the Redwood tree.

He forced the truck door open and ran to the body that was lying on the centerline of the highway. He couldn't believe his eyes! There was the "dead body" standing up, brushing himself off, and adjusting a camera that was wrapped around his neck! When the truck driver asked him what he was doing, he said he was lying on the centerline in order to get a good angle for a picture of one of the tall Redwood trees!

End of the story? Well, not quite.

The truck was a total loss and it cost the insurance company $46,500. And remember, the Humboldt crab that was loaded into the replacement truck, alive and in good condition for their long trip into San Francisco? Well, now it can be told: Some idiot thought it would be wise to ship them with ice so they would not spoil on the way. Because of the ice, the crab all froze to death and it cost the Insurance Company another $34,000. That idiot, by the way, was me.

A Railroad Crossing...Death Awaits

It was summertime. The kids were all out of school and we were busy packing for a long overdue vacation (our first in over six years). Cathy and I told them we were headed to Disneyland and would spend a whole week in the Magic Kingdom. I was just closing up my office when the phone rang.

It was an old friend of mine who was now the Claims Manager for a national insurance company. He said his company insured a husband and wife who were killed last night at a railroad crossing just south of Garberville, California. Their four children were staying with their grandparents in Santa Rosa, California and now they were orphans.

He wanted me to get the Highway Patrol Report and check out the railroad crossing to see if the Railroad might be responsible for causing the accident. I said we were leaving on vacation and I would be driving right past the railroad crossing late this evening so I'd take a look at the scene. I asked my staff to pick up the Patrol Report and arrange for the family's Ford Station Wagon to be towed to Garberville and stored until my return from vacation.

We left our home in Eureka at 9:30 p.m. with Jim, Tim and Mary in their pajamas and Margie (14 months old) in her crib. It was 420 miles to grandma's house in San Jose (about a seven-hour drive). We planned to drop Margie off with her grandparents and then drive another 400 miles to Disneyland. With a little luck, the kids would sleep most of the way to the Magic Kingdom.

But first, I planned to check out the railroad crossing to see if the wooden cross arms were broken. It's a sure-fire way to prove whether the railroad or the driver of the car is at fault in an accident. If the cross arms are broken, it's strong evidence that it was the driver's fault for trying to beat the train to the crossing and hitting the wooden cross arms that were down blocking traffic. But if the cross arms were not broken (still raised), then the Railroad would be at fault because the cross arms failed to come down and warn the motorist of the approaching train; or the train was speeding and got to the intersection before the cross arms were activated. Simple.

There was only one place on Highway 101 south of Garberville where the Highway passed over the railroad tracks. That crossing was protected with double wooden cross arms on each side of the tracks with flashing red lights and clanging bells to alert cars on Highway 101 that a train was approaching. Each wooden cross arm, the width of a lane of traffic, lowers and effectively closes that lane for cars attempting to cross the tracks. These warning signals are activated 150 yards before the crossing by the approaching train. Now, if some idiot (like you see in the movies) attempts to "beat the train across the tracks," he will hit the wooden cross arms and break them, and the train will hit the car broadside.

It was about 11:00 p.m. when we approached the scene of this tragic accident. There were flashing red lights from a Highway Patrol car reducing Highway 101 traffic to only one lane each way while the train crews worked on the signal. I pulled over to the side of the road, grabbed my camera and walked up to the patrol officer directing traffic. He said the train crew was working on the electrical system because it failed to activate the wooden cross arms and it caused a fatal accident last night. He seemed to be very upset because the railroad chose to do the repair work at night, forcing him to work overtime. It was clear to me and the officer, the only possible reason for a Railroad repair crew to be working at night was to cover up evidence that would prove the Railroad was responsible for the accident. I noticed, near the patrol car, the wooden cross arms on the ground - unbroken!

I went back to my car (everyone was asleep) and wrote down the Officer's name and the license numbers on the railroad repair crew's pickups. Then I took my Argus C-3 camera and placed it on the fender of the Highway Patrol car and started taking pictures. I couldn't use my flash for fear of being discovered by the train crew. I opened up the lens as far as it would go and prayed for decent shots in the dark. I took photos of the unbroken cross arms proving they failed to warn the driver and his wife of an approaching train. I also prayed the flashing lights and headlights of the train crew's pickups would give me just enough light for the pictures to come out (and they did!).

I returned to my sleeping family and soon we were on our way south on the 101 Highway to "Grandma's" house in San Jose and then on to Disneyland! But all the way down the highway, I couldn't help thinking how happy we were going on a family vacation and how horrible it must be for those four children who last night lost their mom and dad and were now orphans.

When we returned from vacation, I made my report enclosing the photographs and the statement of the patrol officer on the electrical breakdown of the cross arms. The case settled at a mandatory settlement conference when the railroad was forced to admit the electrical system failed at the crossing and killed a mother and father. I've often wondered what would have happened if we never went on vacation and we were not at the scene when the electrical system was being repaired. Someone must have wanted us to protect those four orphaned children or was it just Irish luck? I wonder.

A Salesman Gets A Big Surprise!

The Kirkland Hotel was built in 1872. It was a classic Victorian beauty with four floors overlooking Humboldt Bay. At street level was the Loggers' Bar with its 80-foot Redwood log bar, which was popular with the loggers who worked all week cutting down trees. The Redwood Room was a fancy restaurant of equal size but it served the upper class patrons who owned the mills and crab fishing fleets that formed the backbone of Humboldt County's economy.

The Kirkland Hotel was the only place in Eureka where the elevator operator wore a tuxedo. The elevator served all the rooms above the main floor. However, the operator would not allow anyone to get off on the Mezzanine Floor without leaving him a substantial "gratuity." The rooms on this floor were known as "comfort rooms" - the Hotel's dirty little secret that was known all over Eureka.

The Kirkland Hotel flourished until the Eureka Inn was built in the center of town. The Kirkland Hotel gradually fell into disrepair with only a few rooms rented to old-timers or travelers who were just wandering through town. The Logger's Bar however, remained a favorite watering hole for loggers and high society alike; and the elevator operator still wore a tuxedo and serviced the Mezzanine Floor with "business" as usual.

Finally, a Hollywood mogul bought the old Hotel and completely remodeled every room. He reopened the Redwood Room and hired a chef from Las Vegas and the news spread like wildfire. The Logger's Bar received a makeover but the 80-foot log bar stayed put. The elevator operator with his tuxedo remained in business, too. The old Hotel gradually came back to life with businessmen and salesman preferring the hotel rates that were much lower than the Eureka Inn. Oh, and it had other benefits as well.

I had my own Adjusting office in the Bank of America Building on Fourth Street in Eureka and one day the phone rang. It was Sam Beer, the Agent who insured the Kirkland Hotel. He said there had been a bad accident at the Hotel - someone had fallen out of a third story window and onto the roof of the Redwood Room Restaurant. I grabbed my briefcase, my camera and drove over to the Hotel. I gave the Hotel manager my card and told him I represented the insurance company who insured the Hotel through their Agent Sam Beer. The manager told me the occupant of the room was a cigarette salesman who came to the Hotel about every three months. He always insisted on renting room #231 on the second floor but this time that room was occupied so he was given the room directly above, on the third floor.

The Manager took me up to the third floor room and I could see where the salesman had opened the window and fell onto the roof of the restaurant. But after inspecting the window sill closely, I noticed two handprints on the dusty sill. This told me the salesman didn't *fall* out the window but for some unknown reason, he *climbed* out of the window and held onto the window sill with both hands. Then he fell onto the roof of the dining room, a fall of at least ten to twelve feet. The Manager told me he fractured his right leg in the fall.

Then it all started to make sense. I asked the Manager if the Mezzanine Floor "comfort rooms" were still in operation. He feigned surprise that I would ask, but sheepishly said yes they were. Now I understood why our salesman always insisted on a second floor room: he could hang out his window, a drop of only six feet and land on the roof of the dining room. Then he could enter any one of the "comfort room" windows on the Mezzanine Floor and bypass the elevator operator who always demanded a "substantial gratuity." I took several photos of the hand prints and the outside of the Hotel showing the third, second and Mezzanine Floor windows. The handprints on the windowsill confirmed the probable cause of the accident.

I decided to pay a visit on our cigarette salesman who was recovering in the hospital. It didn't take long before he reluctantly admitted he always had the same room on the second floor and would pay a "visit to a friend" on the Mezzanine Floor. But this time, he forgot he was on the third floor and now he had to explain his broken leg to his employer and...his wife!

I called Sam Beer and told him we were closing the file...no payment. It would have been a lot cheaper for the salesman to have paid the elevator operator in the tuxedo the "substantial gratuity."

Hold-up at Mike's Liquor Store

Mike's Liquor Store was only a few blocks from our home in Eureka. It was always busy because Mike not only sold liquor but he also had a small deli and cashed payroll checks. It was on a Monday morning when I received a call from Freddie Slack, who wrote the insurance on the liquor store. Mike had been robbed over the weekend and Freddie wanted me to adjust the claim under a burglary/robbery policy Mike had with The Freeman Insurance Company.

I drove out to the liquor store and found Mike standing behind the empty cash register. He was a nice-looking guy, about 40 years old with wavy brown hair and a strong build. He appeared very excited and anxious as he fidgeted with his hands and shifted his weight behind the register. This was the third robbery in the last two years at his store and I had adjusted all of his claims. When I arrived, he had his cash register receipts and records of the payroll checks all ready for me to examine. It didn't take long to verify Mike's loss. This time it came to $3,825. He signed the necessary claim forms and I sent the papers to the insurance company for payment. Unfortunately, Freddie had to cancel Mike's policy because he had three losses in the last two years and his liquor store was obviously a high-risk operation.

About a month later, I stopped at Mike's to buy some beer for a BBQ. He proudly told me he didn't need insurance anymore. He said all three robberies followed the same pattern: The same two men would come into the store in the middle of the afternoon when it was quiet. One man would stand by the front door and the other one would walk over to Mike with a gun in his right hand. This man had a tattoo of a small cross on his right arm. He would demand all the money in the cash register. He knew there was also money in the storage room so he would order Mike into the storage room, take all of his cash, and the two men would drive away in a blue Cadillac.

Now, Mike smugly showed me his idea that would replace his cancelled insurance policy. He had me walk behind him (pretending I was the robber with a gun) and as he turned left into the storeroom, he grabbed a shotgun hidden in the doorway, and then quickly turned and fired at me (it was empty thank God!).

About a year later, the same two men showed up at the liquor store. It was a quiet afternoon when the man with the tattoo ordered Mike into the back room. But this time, Mike was ready for him. He grabbed the shotgun, turned and fired into the face of the surprised gunman. Brains splattered all over the ceiling. His partner fled in the blue Cadillac and was never caught. The killing made headlines in all the newspapers and Mike became a proud, local hero.

Two years went by with no further robberies at Mike's Liquor and after the third year, even Mike had forgotten the gruesome killing. Then one afternoon Mike was alone in the store when a nicely dressed man about 60 years old, with gray hair and a deep scar across his left cheek, walked up to Mike. He got right in Mike's face and said in a smooth voice, "You don't know me Mike, I just got out of prison and learned you killed my son right here in this store. I want you to know someday, someone will come into your store and blow your head off." The man turned and calmly walked out of the store and was gone. Mike was shaken to the core.

After that encounter, Mike broke into a cold sweat every time a stranger walked into his store. I used to stop in for beer on weekends and could see a noticeable change in Mike. His hands shook when he gave you your change and he never smiled any more. Freddie Slack told me his wife divorced him and took the kids to live with her mother in Utah. Mike was terrified and alone. The last I heard, Mike sold the liquor store and had become a familiar face on "skid row" in San Francisco…a homeless and broken man. It was a very sad ending for such a nice guy who, unfortunately, took the law into his own hands.

Lesson learned? Mike's shotgun proved to be a very expensive "insurance policy."

A Lawyer Who Loved Arabian Horses

Terry McGovern was the best criminal defense attorney in Humboldt County. He was feared by the County Prosecutor's Office and idolized by young lawyers who were newly admitted to the Bar. They sat in awe when they witnessed the antics of this grey-haired legend. His signature attire always included a pair of expensive cowboy boots. They made him look taller than his actual 5'8" frame. He was only 55 years old but his long grey hair and ruddy complexion made him look at least ten years older. In addition to practicing law, Terry raised Arabian horses on a ranch that had been in his family for at least three generations. He and his father (deceased) were both lawyers but their first love was raising Arabian horses. The judges had a love/hate relationship with Terry McGovern because while he was always late for court, he was a gifted trial lawyer. When he was in trial, half the lawyers in Eureka would be seated in the courtroom watching this "wild Irishman" passionately and zealously defends his client.

In the ten years I had my Insurance Adjusting office in Eureka, I can't recall Terry McGovern ever losing a criminal case. He was that good. Finally, along came a case that almost broke Terry's winning streak. A well-known surgeon in town was out with his secretary one evening when he crossed over the centerline and hit a young couple head-on, sending them to the hospital. Terry McGovern represented the doctor on the reckless and drunk driving charges and my office handled the injury cases of the young couple in the other car. (*See, An Adjuster at a Crossroads*). This was a case Terry had to win because any publicity would ruin the doctor's marriage and his reputation in the community.

I interviewed the doctor in Terry's "office," which was a small side room in his horse barn. His desk was a huge slab of polished redwood held up with four carved piano legs. We sat on leather chairs next to an old pot-bellied stove and waited for Terry who was out tending his beloved horses. Finally, he came in, sat down and listened. The doctor told us he had gone to dinner with his secretary (his wife was out of town) and he had too much wine to drink. He was driving his new Buick Rivera when he crossed over the centerline and hit a small sports car head-on. The people in the other car were badly injured. My job was to settle the injury claims and Terry's job was to keep the doctor out of jail - this was his third arrest for drunk driving in the past two years.

At the preliminary hearing in early September, Terry pled the doctor "not guilty" and Judge Watson set the trial date for the first week in November. This gave Terry two full months to prepare for trial. But the months flew by with Terry spending most of his time attending Arabian Horse Auctions throughout the state. The day came for *People of the State of California v. Camelli* to go to trial in Judge Watson's court. However, Terry McGovern was nowhere to be found. Dr. Camelli had not heard from him in weeks. A young lawyer from his firm arrived and requested a continuance from Judge Watson, saying Mr. McGovern had to attend his brother's funeral in Kansas (no one ever knew he had a brother in Kansas). Nevertheless, the continuance was granted and trial was set for the second week in December.

Finally, that day came and there was Dr. Camelli and his attorney Terry McGovern all set for trial. Judge Watson was impressed. Terry stood up and addressed the court. "Your Honor, I must beg the Court's indulgence." He sadly looked down at his cowboy boots, shook his head and admitted to the court, he had accidentally stepped on some horse manure in his barn this morning. He asked for an hour's recess so he could return to his ranch for another pair of boots. The court reluctantly granted one hour's recess and ordered the bailiff to open all the windows of the courtroom.

Then Terry opened his briefcase and pulled out a subpoena for the repair records on the Breathalyzer unit used on his client the night he was arrested. He said it was just a formality but maybe the prosecutor could produce those records while he was changing his boots. Judge Watson agreed with Terry, and ordered the repair records to be presented to the court during the recess.

Terry ran to the payphone in the hall. He called the young attorney in his office and told him to research the county regulations on the proper care of breathalyzers used to determine the exact amount of alcohol a person has in his/her system before an arrest can be made, and also find him a clean pair of boots. On the way to his ranch, he finally formulated a possible defense, which, if he was lucky, would keep Dr. Camelli out of jail and save his marriage. He vaguely remembered, from a previous case, a clause in the county regulations that said breathalyzers had to be repaired and recalibrated every thirty days or they could give a false reading. It was a gamble and he cursed himself for not preparing the case earlier.

As he pulled into his driveway, there was the lawyer with the manual in one hand and a pair of boots in the other. He even had the exact section clearly marked that said the Breathalyzer had to be recalibrated every thirty days or the readings could be inaccurate.

Terry put on his clean boots and returned to court where Judge Watson was patiently waiting to re-convene his court. The Prosecutor stood up and presented the court clerk with the Breathalyzer records. They were marked and entered into evidence. Terry opened the file and found the unit used in the arrest of his client had never been recalibrated. Terry immediately asked for a meeting in chambers. He demanded the case against Dr. Camelli be dismissed on grounds that the failure to recalibrate the machine per regulations was overly prejudicial to his client due to the likelihood of a false or inaccurate reading. Over objection by the prosecution, Judge Watson agreed and dismissed the case.

The doctor went free and he swore he would never take another drink. Terry McGovern went back to his ranch to take care of a sick Arabian colt and I went back to my office firmly convinced even great lawyers, like Terry McGovern, sometimes just get lucky!

The Strange Case of Raymond Nelson

It's really weird how a case can burn its way into your memory and last a lifetime. My office in Eureka was very busy with five adjusters (and me) handling 100-120 cases a month, and during the eight years we spent in Eureka, we must have adjusted about 8,000-10,000 claims. Now this "Nelson" case is over 50 years old and I still remember it as though it happened yesterday...strange.

During those eight years, I found myself being more of an office manager than an Insurance Adjuster. We had four "outside" Adjusters who went out and settled the claims; and one "inside" Adjuster, taking all incoming calls. It took five secretaries just to keep up with the dictation going to the insurance companies. Our biggest account was the Zurich

Insurance Company. They insured all the California Highway Patrol Vehicles in Humboldt County and our office handled all of their accidents. Each Patrol vehicle had my office and home phone numbers in the glove compartment.

One evening about 10:30 p.m., my phone rang. It was a Highway Patrol Officer who said he had just struck a pedestrian on Highway 101 near Table Bluff (about eight miles south of Eureka). The pedestrian had been standing on the centerline of the highway when he was hit by the officer. An ambulance took the injured man to the County Hospital so I told the officer I would see him in the morning when his shift ended. At least, it would get me away from my desk at the office and that would be a blessing. I went to sleep wondering why someone would stand in the middle of the highway at night, unless he was trying to commit suicide.

The next morning, I met with the officer at the CHP office. He told me he was chasing a drunk driver south on Highway 101 with both cars going over 70 mph as they crested the hill at Table Bluff. Suddenly, the drunk swerved wildly to his right onto the dirt shoulder of the road. Then the officer saw a pedestrian right in front of him, standing on the centerline, holding something in his hand. He swerved to his left and into the north bound lane. He locked his brakes but it was too late, he hit the pedestrian with the right rear fender as he slid out of control. The pedestrian flew into some heavy brush on the right side of the road and was knocked unconscious. The officer called for an ambulance, which took the pedestrian to the hospital. He called the hospital this morning and was told the young man was alive but had a fractured left leg. I told him I would be back to pick up a copy of his report and I left for the hospital.

I stopped at the admissions desk and fully expected to be told the pedestrian (whose name I learned was Raymond Nelson) was still in intensive care because he was hit so hard by the patrol car going 70 mph, he must have been badly injured.

But I was wrong. He had been released from ICU and was now in room 420. I took the elevator to the fourth floor, went down the hall to his room and there was Raymond Nelson propped up on a pillow, his left leg in traction and his right leg dangling off the end of the bed. When he saw me he had a big smile on his face and leaned over to shake my hand. He had to be at least 6'4" and very thin - not more than 160 pounds. He told me he was 28 years old. I handed him my card and noticed he had quite a shiner on his left eye.

I asked him why he was standing in the middle of the road when it was totally dark and with cars roaring past him. His answer took me totally by surprise. He said he was a sheepherder looking for work. He was staying at the YMCA in Eureka and noticed in the newspaper, a ranch in Fortuna (about twenty miles south of Eureka) needed a sheepherder. It was about 10:00 a.m. when Raymond started walking south along Highway 101 to Fortuna. Later in the afternoon, he stopped along the Highway and "took a little nap." When he awoke it was getting dark so he decided to turn around and get a fresh start in the morning (he was definitely not the sharpest knife in the drawer). He said on his way back to Eureka, his shoelace broke and he tried to retie the laces but it was dark...very dark. So he reasoned if he stood on the centerline, the lights of the passing cars would give him the light he needed to retie his shoelace. Then along came the Highway Patrol car and the drunk driver. Now Raymond had enough light to read a newspaper! He woke up in the hospital.

What was I to do as an Insurance Adjuster? On one hand, Raymond Nelson was dead wrong for standing in the middle of the road – that's a given. But the Highway Patrol Car was speeding and going south in the northbound lane when Raymond was hit. Just then a nurse came in his room. I asked her how long Raymond would be in the hospital. She said four to five days at the most. I told Raymond I would be back to see him before he left the hospital and the insurance company would pay his hospital bill. He told me all he wanted was a Greyhound Bus ticket back to his home in Dallas, Texas so he could go home rest awhile. I agreed to meet him when he was released from the hospital and said I would buy him a bus ticket to Dallas.

It was a Friday afternoon when the head nurse at the hospital called and said they could not release him from the hospital because he had only one shoe. His other shoe must have flown into the brush when he was hit. I said I would buy him a new pair of shoes on my way to pick him up at the hospital and then take him to the Greyhound Depot. I bought him a pair of GallenKamp work boots, a one-way ticket to Dallas, Texas and gave him $250 spending money. That's how I settled the case. I had Raymond sign the release papers and I waved goodbye to him as he got on the bus. He was such a trusting, nice guy, I felt like I was saying goodbye to a close friend as the bus drove away. Certainly, the settlement was unusual, but I thought it was fair to him and the insurance company.

End of story? Well not quite.

It was a year later, almost to the day, when Evelyn my secretary, said I had a strange-looking visitor in the waiting room who wanted to see me. I walked out and there stood Raymond Nelson back from Dallas, all smiles. I asked him why he came back to Eureka. He said he came back just to thank me for his work boots! He hadn't changed a bit. He was still the tall, skinny, trusting sheepherder I had met the year before. His leg had healed and he was walking without a limp. When we shook hands, I noticed he was wearing the same blood spattered tee-shirt he wore on the night he was hit!

I must confess I miss the strange unemployed sheepherder who came into my life over fifty years ago. I only hope and pray he isn't on some lonely road at night, trying to tie his shoelace. If so, his Guardian Angel will go on strike!

A Gambling Debt Turns Fatal

Mr. Joseph Wilkins (Dr. Joe) was our family doctor who delivered the first five of our kids. We both belonged to the Eureka Rotary Club and had become close friends. After one of the noon meetings at the Eureka Inn, Dr. Joe asked me to meet him at the bar. He said he was in trouble and needed my help. We sat in a corner booth while he told me why he was so deeply troubled. Dr. Joe confessed he was a compulsive gambler. About twice a year, a private plane would pick him up at the Arcata Airport and fly him to a casino in Las Vegas. He was known at this particular casino as a "high roller," a gambler who won and lost lots of money. Only his wife knew of these secret gambling trips to Las Vegas but she refused to go with him. I knew Dr. Joe came from a wealthy family and was accustomed to always having lots of money to spend but this confession took me by surprise.

I noticed while we were talking, his hands were shaking. He said his nightmare began about three months ago when the plane picked him up and took him to Las Vegas, as usual. He had a few drinks and headed straight for the Black Jack tables. At first, he was winning and the waitress kept his cocktail glass full. Then he started to lose and lose badly. By midnight, he had lost all of his winnings and more. He ended up having to write a check to the casino for $25,000. He was drunk and left the table swearing the Black Jack Dealer was crooked. He vaguely remembered a Security Guard escorting him to his room.

The next morning, he awoke hung-over and still mad. He stormed out of the casino and caught a commercial flight to San Francisco and then onto Eureka. When he landed, he went to his bank and stopped payment on the $25,000 check he wrote to the casino.

Two months went by and he thought the matter was forgotten. Then one morning when Dr. Joe opened the front door to his office and turned off the burglar alarm, he was shocked to see an elderly man seated behind his desk in his locked office. How he got there was a complete mystery because Dr. Joe had the only key to his private office and only he knew the code to disarm the alarm. But there sat this stranger, smoking a cigar and smiling. He said he came to collect the $25,000 Dr. Joe owed the casino. Dr. Joe was outraged at seeing a total stranger seated in *his* chair in *his* office; he grabbed the old-timer by his coat collar and threw him out the front door. The man fell down the steps and onto the sidewalk. Slowly he got up, in obvious pain. He limped to his car and drove away

Now, this morning before our Rotary meeting, Dr. Joe was in his office returning phone calls when a young man about 25 years old stormed into his private office and slammed the door behind him. He yanked the phone out of Dr. Joe's hand, hung it up, and said, "You threw a friend of mine out of your office two months ago. You messed his knee up bad. Now, I'm giving you just ten days to pay the casino the $25,000 you owe them or you will be very sorry. Do you understand?" He left the office as quickly as he entered and drove away in a new Mercedes without license plates.

Dr. Joe and I walked over to his bank and he withdrew a cashier's check for $25,000 and $500 in cash for my expenses to fly to Las Vegas and make peace with the casino. This was the first case I ever took as an investigator and, for the first time, I was working for an individual and not an insurance company. What I didn't tell Dr. Joe was I had a close friend in Las Vegas (let's call him Chuck) who was a detective on the Las Vegas Police Department. We worked on a will contest case a year before and I was reasonably sure he had contacts at the casino who could easily make peace with their "collectors."

Chuck met me at the Las Vegas airport and we found the nearest coffee shop. I told him the whole story and he said there shouldn't be any problems because he knew the "head man" at the casino. I gave him the cashier's check for $25,000 plus $250 (of my $500) for his help. He promised to call me within the week.

The following week, Chuck called and said I should come back to Las Vegas. It was quite important we meet in person and not talk on the phone. I grabbed the first plane out of Arcata to San Francisco and a connecting flight to Las Vegas. We met at the coffee shop in the airport. Chuck told me the "head man" took the $25,000 cashier's check but there was a problem because a contract had already been issued on Dr. Joe's life and he doubted if the contract could be cancelled.

Chuck then explained to me how the contract on Dr. Joe worked: The old-timer who Dr. Joe threw out of his office was like a father to the angry young man who recently threatened Dr. Joe. The young man came to them and demanded a contract be issued against Dr. Joe. A hit-man was selected and a price was agreed upon with half paid now and half to be paid when the job is finished. A date was selected (usually within three years) with the understanding the "hit" would be made by that date or else the hit-man would be eliminated.

We sat for a long time in the coffee shop trying to find a way to void the contract on Dr. Joe. Finally, Chuck came up with an idea we thought just might work. Chuck knew the owners of the casino and over the years he had done many "favors" for them. After all, they owned the place and he felt certain they could go to the hit-man and demand the contract be cancelled.

I decided on my way home to Eureka not to tell Dr. Joe the bad news. All I told him was the $25,000 had been accepted. A year went by, then two years and even I was convinced Dr. Joe's nightmare was over. He never went back to Las Vegas. He spent his spare time doing what he always loved - fishing and hunting. He was a good doctor, a good husband and good father to his three sons. He was well respected in the community and we met every Friday at the Rotary Club.

In the spring of the third year, word went around town that Sturgeon was running in the Klamath River. Now, this was indeed a rare occasion and just about every fisherman in Eureka closed up their shops and grabbed their fishing poles. Dr. Joe was no exception. It was 5:00 a.m. when Dr. Joe parked his car and waded into the Klamath River near Garberville. He was alone and it was cold and windy. He was wearing a new fishing jacket and hip waders. He waded into the water at his favorite fishing hole where he and his sons had caught countless Steelhead over the years but never a Sturgeon.

Now, the Klamath River runs from Oregon south to the Sacramento Delta with a series of small dams that hold back the water from the heavy winter storms. Before a dam overflows, floodgates are opened and a wall of water goes downstream. And that is just what happened- -*someone* opened a floodgate and a wall of water, at least four feet high, raced downstream and hit Dr. Joe. His waders filled up with water and because of his heavy clothing, he was unable to swim ashore. The next afternoon Dr. Joe's body was found a half-mile down the Klamath River.

All of Eureka mourned the passing of Dr. Joe. He was a well-respected citizen and at just 39, he was too young to die. The newspaper dubbed it an "unfortunate accident." But I will always wonder, was it just an accidental drowning or was it the completion of a contract made three years ago?

An Adjuster at a Crossroads

It's strange, very strange, how one single case can change your whole life. In Eureka, I owned my own Insurance Adjusting business. We had a beautiful small "Cape Cod" office on 3rd Street near the world-famous Carson Mansion. Cathy and I bought a new Pearson Home in the suburbs to house our growing family of Jim, Tim, Mary and Margie with Therese due in three months. Life was good, we were making lots of money and we even had a summer cabin on the Van Duzen River. We planned to make Humboldt County our home and someday we would retire to our cabin on the river. But along came this case and it changed our lives forever.

It was a cold and windy Monday morning in Eureka (as usual) when my office phone rang. It was my best agent, Freddie Slack calling and he wanted to see me right away. I grabbed my coat, jumped into my Pontiac Firebird and drove the three blocks to his office. He was waiting for me at his front door.

He didn't say a word until we were in his private office and the door was closed. Then he explained his reason for needing to see me: He insured our mutual friend (let's call him Dr. Camelli) who was a well-known surgeon and a fellow Rotary Member. On Saturday night, the doctor went to dinner with his secretary, while his wife was in San Francisco visiting her mother. He had too much to drink and on his way home, he crossed over the centerline and hit a small sports car head-on. Dr. Camelli was driving his new Buick Rivera and neither he nor his secretary was injured. However, the young couple in the small Hillman Minx were both badly injured and taken by ambulance to the hospital. Dr. Camelli was arrested on suspicion of driving under the influence and taken to jail.

Freddie Slack called Attorney Terry McGovern who agreed to represent the doctor on the drunken driving charge and post his bail (*See, A Lawyer Who Loved Arabian Horses*). Freddie asked me to personally handle the case because if the newspaper got wind of the story, the doctor's reputation and his marriage would be ruined. And a lawsuit with all its publicity must be avoided at all costs. I agreed to handle the case personally.

My first stop was the Highway Patrol Office. Captain Bill Duffy was a good friend of mine. He agreed to put a "hold" on the drunken driving citation pending a confirmation of the blood-alcohol content on our doctor. So far, I was in luck.

My next stop was the *Humboldt Times* newspaper. Sag Caputo, the Editor, was not aware of the accident and he agreed not to publish anything until the blood-alcohol content was verified and the citation issued. I was in luck again!

Then I went to the hospital to visit the young couple Mike and Bobbie Sanderson. I stopped at the front desk and learned Mike had a broken right arm and was discharged yesterday. His wife, Bobbie, was out of ICU and now in room #302. I took the stairway to the third floor and there was Bobbie Sanderson all propped up with pillows and the whole right side of her face covered with a huge white bandage. Mike was seated at her bedside with his right arm in a sling. I introduced myself and gave them my card. I said I represented the insurance company and we would accept full responsibility for this unfortunate accident. I explained there would be no reason for them to hire an attorney because I would see to it the insurance company gave them a fair and reasonable settlement. Finally, I told them to maintain a complete list of all their expenses and to call me when Bobbie was released from the hospital. They appeared to understand and were relieved at not having to hire an attorney.

Two weeks went by and finally Bobbie called and told me she had been discharged from the hospital. She asked me to come to her home in Arcata around 4:00 that afternoon. I parked in front of their home. It was a beautiful old Victorian with an outstanding view of Humboldt Bay. I wondered, while I was ringing the doorbell, how a young couple could afford such an expensive home. Then a distinguished lady answered the door and introduced herself as Bobbie's mother. She explained that Bobbie and Mike lived in the small guesthouse over the garage. She invited me inside and said Bobbie was in the living room waiting for me and that Mike was expected home any moment.

While we were waiting for Mike, I learned many things about this young couple: Bobbie was 18 years old, a bright young girl who had just been accepted at Humboldt State College in the fall. Mike was 19 years old and working for the Pacific Lumber Company with a well-paying job as a lumber grader. Bobbie's mother was a registered nurse at the hospital and her dad was an executive at Pacific Lumber.

When I walked up to their home, I noticed their Hillman Minx in the driveway, all smashed up and an obvious total loss. I grabbed my camera from my briefcase and suggested I take some photos of the car. By the time I returned, Mike had come home and was in the living room. His right arm was still in a sling and I could see the cast was from his elbow to his right wrist.

I asked Bobbie's mom to do me a favor and remove the bandage from the right side of Bobbie's face so I could photograph her injury and send the photos to a well-known plastic surgeon in San Francisco for an evaluation. I had to grit my teeth as her mom removed the bandage exposing the extent of damage done to this young girl's face. The deep laceration would likely result in a scar she would wear the rest of her life. I doubted if any amount of plastic surgery would erase the scar. It started at her right eyelid and travelled down to the right corner of her upper lip. Honestly, it looked like she had been hit with an axe when her face went through the windshield. Luckily, her eye was not damaged but it was still purple and slightly swollen. Her mom told me it took 143 stitches to close the wound. I left the family with my solemn promise to get Bobbie and Mike a fair settlement without them having to hire an attorney.

I sent a full report to the insurance company, including the photos of Mike's arm and close-up photos of Bobbie's wound. I recommended the insurance company consult a plastic surgeon in San Francisco to evaluate the extent of the damage to Bobbie's face and the cost of reconstruction. I told the claims manager once we had the plastic surgeon's opinion on whether or not Bobbie's scar could be repaired, and if Mike could ever return to work as a lumber grader, then we would be in a position to evaluate the claim and make the Sandersons a fair offer in settlement.

About a month later Mike called to say the cast was off his arm and wrist. While he was cleared to go back to work, he could no longer work as a lumber grader. The double fracture to his arm and wrist caused him to lose the grip in his right hand. He was given a desk job with a 20% pay cut. Mike said the bandages were finally off Bobbie's face and they were ready to talk settlement. The Claims Manager had not given me a copy of the plastic surgeon's report or his opinion of how much the surgery would cost. I had my own general idea of the amount of money it would take to settle the Sanderson cases but after all, it was insurance company money and it was up to the claims manager to authorize the settlement offer. I called him repeatedly but he never returned my calls.

I parked my car and walked up the steps of the beautiful Victorian mansion. Bobbie's mom opened the door and ushered me into their living room. Everyone was there, Bobbie, her mom, dad and Mike. I had a gut feeling that Mike's case was worth around $10,000 - $12,000 for his fractured right arm and wrist, lost wages and inability to return to his old job as a lumber grader. The Hillman Minx had a Blue Book value of $2,300. But Bobbie's face was a different matter. She was, an 18-year-old girl who had been a beautiful young newlywed, and now she was literally scarred for life.

Over the years, I had been in probably 500 "settlement conferences" like this one and it was my job to be fair with the clients and get the insurance companies to settle the cases without the need for a lawyer. My instinct told me Bobbie's case was worth at least $25,000 if she didn't need plastic surgery and $35,000- $40,000 if she did. I had given the Sandersons my solemn promise to see they would be given a fair and reasonable settlement and that is exactly what I intended to do.

I opened my briefcase, grabbed a tablet and started my "routine" of listing all the medical bills, the car rental, Mike's lost wages as a result of his losing the grip in his right arm, and the value of the Hillman Minx. Everything was going smoothly, but then Bobbie interrupted me and said there was a widow who lived just three doors down the street, who lost her husband a few years back in a trucking accident and I handled her case. The woman told Bobbie that I was very fair and she trusted me (I had no memory of the case). Then Bobbie made a statement that almost knocked me off of my chair and rings in my ears to this very day. She said, "Mr. O'Brien, Mike and I have no idea how insurance companies work or how much our cases are worth but we trust you. We have talked it over and decided that whatever you think our cases are worth, we will accept."

Now, this was the first time anything like that had ever happened to me. For a long moment I was speechless. All I had was a gut feeling of what the cases were worth but I had no authorization to settle for any amount from the insurance company. After a few moments, I said the insurance company had not yet sent me the plastic surgeon's report with the estimated cost of future surgery. I told the Sandersons I would call the Claims Manager in the morning, get the surgeon's report and estimated cost for surgery, and then I would get the insurance company's authorization to settle. We agreed I would meet with them tomorrow afternoon and settle their cases.

All the way home, I wondered what the cases were really worth. Mike's injury case was easy. It was worth at least $10,000 but I knew he would probably settle for around $7,500. The car had a Blue Book value of $2,300 but I knew they would take around $1,800 because of the high mileage. But with Bobbie's case, I was puzzled…what was it *really* worth? If she were my daughter or my wife, who was badly scarred for life what would the case really be worth? And for the rest of Bobbie's life, because her cheek muscles had been severed, her smile would look more like a snarl.

Yet, I was an Insurance Adjuster and my job was to settle cases for the least amount possible, right? That's how I was trained and for nine long years, I suddenly realized that is exactly what I did - settled cases for the cheapest amount possible. That was my job. But I couldn't silence the one nagging question: should I settle the cases for what I thought was a fair amount for the Sandersons or for the amount the insurance company was willing to pay them? What was an Insurance Adjuster (me) to do? I found myself at a dangerous and perplexing crossroads. I had to decide what was right and what was wrong.

The next morning I called the claims manager and told him the Sandersons were ready to settle. We went over the out-of-pocket costs (medical, prescriptions, car rental, and lost wages) but before we got to the value of the Hillman Minx or Mike's loss of grip or Bobbie's awful scar, he asked me how much it would take to settle all three cases. I said in my opinion, Mike's case was worth around $10,000 and the Minx was valued by Kelly Blue Book at $2,300 but $1,800 was a fair value. Bobbie's case would depend on the plastic surgeon's report and the cost of future surgeries. However, if Bobbie elected not to have any future surgeries, in my opinion the value of her case would be around $20,000. I chose not to tell him about my conversation with Bobbie. I wanted to see if his evaluation of the cases was close to mine.

There was a long pause as he went through my report, the bills and out of pocket expenses. Finally, he got back on the phone and said, "Offer the Sandersons $12,000 and not a penny more." That was not a fair settlement and he knew it! Of course, it would make him a hero with his company but no way was it a fair settlement offer for the Sandersons. I tried to reason with him but it was useless. All he would say was, "You're a good Irishman and with a little of your Blarney you can convince them to settle." Then he hung up!

He must have been having a real bad day otherwise, how could I have been that far off in my evaluations? All I knew was there was no way I could face Mike and Bobbie and recommend they settle for $12,000. I was caught between a rock and a hard place. On one hand, the Sandersons trusted me and would probably settle for $12,000 if I recommended it. But on the other hand, if I didn't recommend the $12,000, the Sandersons would go to an attorney and sue our insured. The publicity would ruin the doctor's marriage and his professional reputation.

I had to get out of there so I told the Sandersons I had to go to a meeting in Garberville and asked if we could meet again tomorrow afternoon. My head was spinning as I got back to my office and told Evelyn, my secretary, I had to go home and see Cathy on a personal matter. As I was driving home it dawned on me, if I refused to offer the $12,000 settlement to the Sandersons and recommend they see an attorney, I would certainly lose the Freddie Slack account if not all the insurance companies I represented once the news got out that I was referring clients to attorneys. I would be out of business and I had five hungry mouths to feed. If I didn't have a conscience, the choice would be easy - just turn on the "Irish Charm" and settle the case for $12,000. But my conscience wouldn't shut up. It was screaming, "You can't settle the case, it's not fair to the Sandersons! It's not fair - Mike and Bobbie trust you and you gave your solemn promise."

As I drove into my driveway, I knew I had to talk to Cathy and maybe she could shed some light on what I should do. Now, Cathy is a smart girl...very smart (that's why I married her!) We sat in the living room and, because of my demeanor Cathy was convinced someone had died. Then I told her the whole story and the dilemma I was facing. This was the very first time I had ever asked her opinion on a case I was handling. In fact, I wasn't exactly sure she even knew what an Adjuster did for a living. She was too busy running a household (and changing diapers!). She sat for a full minute mulling over my problem. Then she asked me three questions:

(1) Are you a lawyer representing the Sandersons?
(2) Are you a doctor qualified to evaluate the injuries to Mike and Bobbie?
(3) Are you a judge or a juror charged with determining the value of the Sandersons' cases?

The answer to all three questions was a resounding "No." I told her I was an Insurance Adjuster. It was my job to settle cases as cheaply as possible and follow the orders of the insurance company. She just shook her head in disbelief and said, "Who are you, or the insurance company for that matter, to evaluate the Sandersons' injuries? It's just not fair." Our daughter Margie started crying so Cathy got up off the couch and walked away. The meeting was over.

All night long, I lay awake listening to Cathy's words of wisdom. Finally at about 4:30 a.m., I knew what I had to do and it would be very painful. After breakfast, I called Mike and Bobbie and told them to meet me at my office around 2:00 p.m. They agreed and showed up on time. I sat them down in my office and closed the door. I told them the offer of the insurance company was totally unreasonable (I never told them the exact amount) and I could not, in good conscience recommend they settle their claims. They needed the help of an attorney.

My entire future hung in the balance but I just had to advise them to meet with attorney Gerald Hill, the leading plaintiff lawyer in Humboldt County. The Sandersons agreed. I placed a call to Gerald and he said to come right over. I drove them to Gerald's office and waited for them at a Denny's coffee shop.

For the next hour and a half, I sat in agony as I tried to justify what I had just done. I had just given two personal injury cases and one property damage case to a plaintiff lawyer! It was professional suicide! And when the news spread on what I had done, I was going to be out of business with no income and no way to pay the mortgage on our home or feed the kids. But at least that annoying conscience of mine would finally shut up!

A chapter in our lives was coming to a close and another exciting chapter was about to open. Believe it or not, suddenly, good things started to happen. An Adjuster from Ukiah walked into my office one morning and said he wanted to buy my business and office building! Then within weeks our home sold (at a whopping profit!) and a young lawyer from Fontana bought our cabin on the Van Duzen River! Cathy and I were absolutely convinced someone upstairs was looking over our shoulder. Finally, we had enough money to return to our hometown - San Jose.

Oh, and by the way, Gerald Hill took the Sanderson case. The first thing he did was order independent medical examinations for Mike because of his severe loss of grip and for Bobbie because he wanted to know the extent of muscle damage and permanent scarring. When those reports came in, the injuries to this young couple proved to be far more serious and permanent than even I imagined. Gerald Hill provided the claims manager's boss (a vice-president of the Company) with copies of the doctors' reports and then Gerald demanded a Mandatory Settlement Conference before Judge William Rusinko. The Vice-President personally attended the Settlement Conference and the case settled for a whopping $229,800!

Our doctor was able to save his marriage and his professional reputation because there was no publicity in the newspaper thanks to Attorney Terry McGovern who successfully defended the doctor on his drunken driving charge and kept him out of jail.

And what happened to the claims manager? He was fired!

And what happened to the O'Brien family? We moved back to our hometown of San Jose!

My Adventures in San Jose

Meet Walter Ward

My dad once told me if you make five good friends in a lifetime, you would be a very lucky man. Walter Ward was "Number Five" on my list, so I guess I'm one of the lucky ones. We had just moved from Eureka to San Jose and I was out of a job. A friend of mine from high school, Larry Doyle, was now a lawyer in the City Attorney's Office in San Jose. One morning, I met him for coffee and told him I wanted to be an investigator. I asked if he could introduce me to any investigators. Without hesitation, he said the *best* investigator in town was a man by the name of Walter Ward. When Larry got back to his office, he called Walter who agreed to meet us later that morning at the cafeteria in the courthouse.

We went over to the cafeteria and took a seat in a corner booth. Just then, in walked a man wearing a suit and tie, with glasses, about sixty years old. He was not tall, only about 5'7" and weighed no more than 145 lbs. soaking wet. This was Walter Ward – the best investigator in town? You bet.

Larry introduced me and we ordered coffee. Larry had to leave for a court appearance so Walter and I sat and got to know each other. I told him how I decided to move back to San Jose and wanted to become an investigator, as I was tired of being an insurance adjuster who was constantly pushed to settle cases as cheaply as possible.

Walter had a gift for being a great listener. An instant friendship formed between us and I knew this was the mentor I had been seeking who would teach me to become a great investigator. Over the next three hours, I learned we were almost *total* opposites. Walter was a Mason. I was Catholic. Walter was married to Grace but they had no children. I was married to Cathy and we had five children. Walter was loaded with money and I was almost broke, without a job. But as time went on, I think we both realized we were cut from the same block of wood and we shared a central priority: we both had an overwhelming desire to help people who were injured, primarily by helping them fight the insurance companies – those big businesses that set their own values on cases without regard to the persons who were badly injured.

Over the years that followed, I saw Walter three to four times a week, usually for breakfast. Walter was semi-retired but I am sure he was the one who recommended me to the best lawyers in town because within just a few weeks after arriving in San Jose, my briefcase was full.

Our friendship grew, much like a father/son relationship. You will notice Walter Ward is referred to in many of the stories you are about to read. And now, 50 years later, I am sure it was Walter Ward, who in his own quiet way, gave me the "Magic Key" that opened so many impossible cases for me. I can explain it no other way. He taught me over the years to never give up on a case and if you work hard enough, *every* case can be won. When he first told me this, I was sure he was off his rocker. But now, a half a century later, I'm sure he was right. So, read on and just maybe it will help you in your own search for your own "Magic Key."

To tell the honest truth, I never even thought about the "Magic Key" analogy until I started writing this book (four years ago). I just figured it was simple "Irish Luck" when I started to win case after case. Deep down though, I knew I was no great investigator like Walter Ward. I was just "lucky." But now, a half century later, no other explanation is possible. Walter Ward died many years ago and yet, when I come across a "case that can't be won," it's almost as if I can still see him, placing the Magic Key in my hand.

A Bowling Alley Blows Up

Cathy and I returned to our hometown of San Jose with a brood of children. To be exact, we had Jim, Tim, Mary, Margie, Therese; and Sharon was soon to be our first born in San Jose. We had moved into a beautiful home in Los Gatos that my Dad had built for my Mom before she died. He sold it but we bought it out of foreclosure and there we were in a great home, in a great neighborhood but with one big problem: I had no job. Then I met Walter Ward. (*See, Meet Walter Ward*). I told him I wanted to be an investigator and fight insurance companies and suddenly, a whole world of opportunity opened before me. I was getting a briefcase full of good cases and I can't help but believe they came on Walter's recommendations.

One morning, I was reading an article in the *Mercury Herald* about the Saratoga Bowling Alley blowing up. All forty-eight alleys, with a restaurant and a poolroom, all gone. Just then, my phone rang. It was Nick Bebek, the owner of the bowling alley. He said Walter Ward gave him my phone number because of my years of experience as an Insurance Adjuster and he needed my help in preparing his claim to present to his insurance company.

I agreed to meet Nick at what was left of the bowling alley, within the hour. When I arrived, I found the parking lot full of debris and there was a yellow police tape around the huge concrete foundation. Firemen were all over the place, putting out small fires while an Arson Squad was trying to determine the cause of the explosion. Nick and I sat in his Cadillac while he filled me in on the details of the previous evening: He said he closed the bowling alley at 8:00 p.m. so his crew could come in and sand the forty-eight alleys and then apply a fresh coat of shellac. The crew turned off all the pilot lights in the building prior to their sanding the floors because they knew of the extreme danger of explosion should the shellac be exposed to an open flame.

The job was finished around 2:00 a.m. Nick took the whole crew to an all-night Denny's Restaurant just down the street from the bowling alley. Soon after they were all seated, they heard a terrific explosion. The whole restaurant shook as Nick and his crew's worst nightmare was realized - the bowling alley had blown up. They raced back to the bowling alley and found the building completely leveled. Huge pieces of 6' x 12' rafters from the ceiling were sticking into the roof of the apartment building next door. Fortunately, the bowling alley was empty and there were no injuries reported in the apartment house.

Nick wanted me to make a complete list of all the items damaged and/or lost in the explosion and present his claim to the insurance company for payment. I shot a roll of film showing all the damage and emergency personnel including the PG&E trucks and crews making sure all the gas lines were shut off. Fortunately, Nick's accountant had most of the receipts, purchase orders and even a set of building plans from 1951. Nick had a $2 million insurance policy on the bowling alley, which seemed sufficient to cover the building and its contents. It would be a big job but Nick had agreed to pay me $65.00 per hour and the job was right up my alley (pardon the pun).

I called Walter Ward and thanked him for the referral. He warned me that insurance adjusters would be all over the place looking for something that would allow them to deny the claim. He suggested part of my job as an investigator, would be to determine for myself, the exact cause of the explosion as well as itemizing the loss. Walter said with any fire claim over a million dollars, you can count on the insurance company denying the claim and alleging arson. He suggested we meet for breakfast as the case progressed.

I'll never know why, but the next morning I woke up at 5:30 and told Cathy I had to go down to the bowling alley to look around. The sun was just coming up as I parked my car in the lot and turned off my lights. I was sitting there wondering why I was up so early. Then I saw two PG&E trucks parked near the center of the concrete foundation of the bowling alley. Two men were swinging sledgehammers and cutting a hole in the center of the concrete slab foundation. Two other men were hauling away the chips of concrete into one of their pickup trucks. I grabbed my camera, opened the lens and started taking pictures. They seemed to be in a hurry and didn't even notice my car over in the parking lot. Finally, they had made a hole in the concrete about 3'x 4' wide. Then one of the men took a shovel and started digging into the dirt below the foundation. I could see he was taking soil samples at one, two, and three feet deep. Then without turning on their lights they hurriedly drove away.

When one of Nick's foremen drove up, I mentioned the strange behavior of the PG&E men. I told him to wait there while I went to a 7-Eleven Store and bought some Mason Canning Jars. I returned a short while later and told the foreman to get one of his men and take soil samples from the same hole at one, two and three feet deep. We put the soil samples in the jars and placed them in the trunk of my car. Then I drove down to the coffee shop on First Street to meet Walter for breakfast.

Walter reasoned the only explanation for the PG &E crew to take the risk of breaking a hole in the bowling alley concrete slab, was to find out if there was an underground break in the main gas line that traveled down the center of Saratoga Road. If there were a break then the gas, under high pressure, would go underground following the bowling alley gas line until it reached the concrete foundation of the bowling alley. A concrete slab of that size would likely have numerous cracks that would allow the gas (under terrific pressure) to seep into the bowling alley and cause the explosion. Walter was probably right and this could prove to be the cause of the explosion. I promised to keep the soil samples in my basement until such time as a soil test could be made.

But right now, I had a job to do that required my full attention: I had to prepare a complete itemization of the entire loss and present it to the insurance company for payment. It took a full week and a half before I had what the Insurance Adjusters call a "Proof of Loss" which totaled $1,689,000. We presented the claim and the next day, Nick received a telegram of only two words: "Payment Refused." Nick took my file and the telegram to Tony Cable, his attorney who just happened to be an old baseball buddy of mine from Bellarmine Prep. A lawsuit was filed and in due course a Settlement Conference was set up in Judge Foley's Chambers. Nick and I both attended this most important conference and we were seated in the rear of the courtroom as four attorneys showed up representing the insurance company. A court reporter sat between Tony Cable and opposing counsel. Suddenly, the lead counsel for the insurance company stood up and proudly announced, "Gentlemen, we believe the plaintiff is guilty of arson. Our investigation proves Nick Bebek paid to have his own bowling alley blown up therefore, we have no intention of paying this claim. We have turned our entire file over to the DA's office and we fully expect the plaintiff will be arrested for felony arson." With that, he motioned for his team of lawyers to leave the courtroom before Tony even had a chance to object.

The weeks and months flew by and poor Nick lived on borrowed money but he paid me weekly (thank God). We found an expert in Los Angeles who had the soil samples tested and found gas in the samples. He was prepared to say there was a major leak in the main line and the gas traveled under the grass of the neighboring apartment house (I had photos of the dead grass.). Then the gas went underneath the bowling alley foundation under high pressure, and found its way to an open pilot light and caused the explosion.

After depositions and discovery, the civil case was set for Mandatory Settlement Conference on the issue of the insurance company's bad faith and refusal to pay a valid claim. The defense showed no interest in trying to settle the claim and continued to argue that our client had committed arson. The defense argued it was a *criminal* matter that was being investigated by the DA and it was not a *civil* matter. But, Walter Ward had a friend in the DA's office who said no felony charges would be filed for lack of conclusive evidence of any wrongdoing. Meanwhile, the soil samples remained in my basement and were never examined by the defense team.

Finally, the civil case came up for trial in Judge Foley's court. After a jury was seated, Tony Cable stood up and made his opening statement. He told the jury the insurance company failed to pay an honest and just claim and therefore was responsible for insurance bad faith. Additionally he said punitive damages should be assessed for their willful failure to pay the claim. Defendant's breach of the insurance contract had forced his client to near bankruptcy. The trial went forward on the sole issue of insurance bad faith.

Then it was time for the opening statement by defense counsel. He stood up, slammed his notebook on the desk and in a voice that could be heard in the hallway, he bellowed: "The plaintiff, who sits here before you, hired an arsonist to blow up his bowling alley in order to collect money from his insurance company." He said it was "Peter Green" who caused the bowling alley to explode and he is a known arsonist who works for the Las Vegas Mafia. He would now be in jail for these crimes had he not died in a car accident last winter. Before he sat down, he said, "Ladies and gentlemen of the jury, we do not owe this plaintiff, one single dime."

It was time for lunch and Judge Foley recessed the jury until 2:00 p.m. This gave us time to evaluate this bombshell witness presented by the defense. We asked Nick if he had ever heard of a Peter Green. He said the name was vaguely familiar but he would make a phone call to a friend of his in Las Vegas who also owned a bowling alley and he would ask him if he had heard of a Peter Green. Nick's friend would be a good position to know if Peter Green was alive or dead and whether or not he was in the Mafia.

While Nick called his friend, Tony and I went to lunch across the street from the courthouse. Before we were even served, Nick came in all smiles. He sat down and told us Peter Green was alive and that he was the salesman who sold him tableware for his dining room when the bowling alley was being built ten years ago. However, "Peter Green" was also the name of an arsonist in a popular non-fiction book *The Green Felt Jungle*. Nick handed me a note with salesman Peter Green's address in North Hollywood. Nick's Vegas friend said he had worked with Peter Green for years and as far as he knew, that Peter had no connection with the Mafia. His friend agreed to contact Peter on Nick's behalf and ask him to fly to San Jose and testify.

At 2:00 p.m., before the jury was seated Tony Cable asked Judge Foley for a recess until tomorrow morning to confer with his client on this newly discovered evidence. His request was granted. I grabbed my briefcase, a clean shirt and was on my way to find Peter Green in North Hollywood. I caught the next flight to Los Angeles and arrived around 4:30 p.m. I rented a car and drove over an hour in heavy afternoon traffic from LAX to the North Hollywood address.

As I parked my car at the address, there was Peter Green waiting for me on the porch of a run-down apartment house.

He was all packed and ready to leave for San Jose. He was a friendly, nervous little guy who said he was able to find his United Air Line tickets and hotel receipts proving he was in Detroit when the bowling alley blew up. He claimed he was a tableware salesman and not a member of the Mafia. He said he was currently suing the author and publisher of *The Green Felt Jungle* for libel! We caught the next flight back to San Jose. Peter wanted to be paid for his testimony and I told him Nick would handle all of his expenses. I checked him into a motel near the courthouse, under an assumed name and I agreed to meet him for breakfast in the morning.

At 10:00 a.m., Tony Cable stood up and called his first witness: Peter Green. Suddenly the courtroom became deathly silent as Peter Green stood up and walked to the witness chair. He was not dead but alive! There was absolute silence from the gallery as Peter Green, dressed in his expensive suit, walked to the witness stand, raised his right hand and swore to tell the truth. He made an excellent witness as he offered into evidence the hotel and airline tickets proving he was in Detroit, not California, when the bowling alley blew up. He spoke with great credibility when he denied the references made in the *Green Felt Jungle* about him being an arsonist for the mafia. In fact, he testified he had a lawsuit pending against the author of *The Green Felt Jungle* for libel as there was no disclaimer in the book about coincidental references to real people.

Defense counsel was obviously dazed by this "dead man's" testimony. When Tony was finished questioning Peter, defense counsel cleared his throat and said, "No questions, your Honor." Then he requested a short recess to confer with his team and call his insurance company. When they returned, Judge Foley had all lawyers meet with him in chambers. Walter and I sat with Nick and Peter in the courthouse cafeteria and waited. About an hour later, Judge Foley called in the jury and announced the case had been settled. He thanked the jury for their attention and dismissed them. Tony Cable met with us across the street at the Barrister's Bar and told us the case was settled for $1,689,000 in damages plus $1,200 per day for loss of income from the date of the insurance company's denial until today! It was a great win for Nick who now had the money needed to rebuild his bowling alley.

By the way, Tony Cable did turn over the soil samples to the insurance company so they could sue PG&E as the responsible party causing the explosion. But that case, as far as I know, never went to trial.

The "Wonder Worker" Takes a Bow

There was a lawyer in Los Gatos, California who gained the reputation of being a "Wonder Worker" because he would take cases no other lawyer would handle and he would turn an obvious "loser" into a "winner." He had only one requirement: there had to be substantial injury before he would exert his "wondrous powers." I decided to work a case with him just to see what made him earn such an illustrious reputation.

He called me into his office one day and asked me to review a file for him. Six weeks prior, a grandfather was carrying his grandson on his shoulders and walking down a two-lane street to his son's home. The police diagram showed the grandfather walking in the street because there were no sidewalks. He was walking east in the westbound lane of traffic. Suddenly, a Corvette with a drunk driver crossed over to the wrong side of the road and hit the grandfather from behind. The child flew into the bushes of a neighbor's yard and sustained only minor injuries, but his grandfather landed on the pavement twenty feet from the point of impact.

The grandfather was badly injured with two broken legs and severe brain damage. He had been in a coma since the accident. The Corvette driver tried to leave the scene but was stopped by neighbors who saw the accident. He was arrested for hit and run drunk driving, driving without a license and in violation of his parole and he was sent back to prison. He was without automobile insurance and the grandfather's medical bills were in excess of $100,000.

Inside the file were six letters from attorneys who had "reviewed" the police report and denied the case because the defendant was without insurance and was now in prison. Plus the fact, the grandfather was walking east in the westbound lane when he was hit. That would be enough for any attorney to deny the case…right? But for the "Wonder Worker," it was a challenge worthy of his magical talents. I agreed to "take a look" at this impossible case and see if there was any possibility of finding a way to help this family because the client was still in a coma and the family was facing financial ruin with over $100,000 in medical bills. The outlook was bleak but I went to the scene and rang a few doorbells.

I talked to the four witnesses listed on the police report. They were the ones who stopped the Corvette driver when he attempted the leave the scene. I also introduced myself to the client's family and told them it was a very difficult case because although the Corvette driver was totally at fault, he was in prison and without insurance. However, I said I would do all I could to help them. The Vehicle Code requires pedestrians to walk against traffic. Therefore, in this situation, the plaintiffs were not at fault for walking eastbound facing the westbound traffic.

While I was at the scene, I diagrammed it and shot a roll of film showing the plaintiff's home, their son's home, the point of impact, and the point of rest of the plaintiff's body. This was a post-World War II neighborhood in Los Gatos that consisted of four blocks of homes near a public golf course. The homes were on small lots with most of them in need of paint and landscaping. There were no sidewalks, only street mailboxes, power poles and telephone lines where the sidewalk should have been.

I ran a check on the ownership of the Corvette. If the car was owned by someone other than the driver then maybe that someone might have insurance to cover this accident. The report came back in the driver's name only…no help.

I went back to my office convinced that the entire responsibility for this accident was the Corvette driver who had no insurance and was now in prison. And yet, I had the feeling I was missing something, but what could it be? I sat in my office and re-read the police report. The investigating officer cited the Corvette driver as the sole cause of the accident. It seemed to be an open and shut case but I decided to visit the scene one more time before I dictated my closing report to the Wonder Worker.

It was about 3:00 p.m. when I parked my car at the scene. It was a one-block street with a golf course entrance at the west end and a dairy farm at the east end. I parked facing the golf course in the approximate area where the client's body landed. I opened my briefcase and pulled out the police report (again). The officer had noted the accident occurred at 3:20 p.m. I rolled down my windows and started going through my notes and photographs.

Then all of a sudden, I looked up and saw a school bus unloading thirty elementary school children (I counted them). They were all walking toward me blocking both east and westbound lanes of traffic because the children had no sidewalks to walk upon. *No sidewalks* and suddenly the lights started to flash in my thick head. If our client had a sidewalk to walk on, this accident would not have happened. Because there were no sidewalks, he had to walk in the street! But who was responsible for allowing the power poles, mailboxes and telephone poles to be placed in the exact area where the sidewalk should have been? It had to be the responsibility of the City of Los Gatos for failing to build the sidewalks and placing pedestrians in danger.

I went back and talked to the four witnesses and they told me the contractor who built the homes agreed with the Building Department of the City Los Gatos to dedicate a park within the subdivision if the city would agree to construct the curbs and sidewalks for the subdivision. The contractor went broke and the City never built the curbs and sidewalks. In fact, two of the neighbors told me they complained at several council meetings about the dangerous condition created by having no sidewalks, but the City said they were without funds to build them.

The next morning, I walked into the City Library and asked the librarian to let me read the City Council minutes because they were public records and open to anyone for review. The librarian refused to allow me to examine the files without a subpoena. So I went back and took written statements from the witnesses who made the complaints to the city council about the serious need for sidewalks and the admission that sidewalks were needed but the city said they did not have the money to build them.

I wrote up my report and submitted my bill for services. The Wonder Worker was most complimentary and said he was demanding $3.5 million from the city. The ball was in his court now and he had to work the case and take depositions, do his discovery, and file a claim against the city.

My bill went unpaid after ninety days and the Wonder Worker failed to return my phone calls. His secretary told me he was busy giving speeches to service clubs and legal associations as he basked in the glory of being a master of impossible cases. The months flew by and finally my bill was paid.

I learned the client had died and the case settled for a confidential amount but if it had gone to trial, it had a reasonable value in the millions. I remembered a very valuable lesson Walter Ward taught me many years ago: There really is no such thing as a "Wonder Worker" lawyer. Some lawyers get lucky and settle a multimillion-dollar case and the one-third fee sets them up for life. But most successful lawyers do their homework. They take their depositions and do their discovery. They care about their clients and hire an investigator on all of their major cases. Over the years I have learned it is very easy for an investigator to second-guess a lawyer who settles a case for 10% of its real worth. In this particular case our lawyer did get his case filed and it certainly wasn't his fault when his client died. Life goes on and good cases come and go. The only thing I have learned is you must work as hard as you can for your client and not just work a case for the money you can make.

Occasionally, a lawyer comes along who gets a big multimillion-dollar verdict and a huge fee, but the newfound wealth can take away his/her discipline and in time, their reputation becomes nothing more than a distant memory. In this case, our "Wonder Worker" retained his reputation and was able to shake his fist at the six lawyers who turned the case down. He was able to place the blame on the City of Los Gatos. And in case you are wondering, it is always the lawyer who takes the bow for winning a case. The investigator just stands on the sidelines and nods in agreement.

Boom-Boom Gets Wet!

Football season brings out the die-hard fans at college campuses across our nation. In 1968 Stanford University guaranteed to draw a crowd from all over California for two reasons: Their quarterback was an All-American and their All-Conference Defensive End was Walter Hayward, who struck terror in the opposition line. He would sack the quarterback and the crowd would erupt with a deafening "BOOM-BOOM" as he hit the poor lad who would usually fumble the ball. He was loved by the crowd and the newspapers crowned him with the moniker, "Boom-Boom." Unfortunately, in his senior year he blew out his left knee and there went Boom-Boom's dream of becoming a pro-football player.

He graduated (barely) and began the grueling hunt for a "regular" job. He was very big at 6'8" and 248 pounds. But he struck the same fear in prospective employers as he did opposing linemen. The only thing Boom-Boom knew well was football and he was lost when he was out of uniform. However, he desperately needed a job. He was becoming despondent and worried about his future now that his glory days at Stanford were sadly over and soon forgotten.

One day an old friend from Stanford who had become a lawyer, called Boom-Boom and offered him a job serving divorce papers and taking pictures of unsuspecting spouses in compromising positions. They met for lunch and suddenly, Boom-Boom had a job. The photographs would be used to prove the spouse's infidelity, which, at the time, was required in order for the divorce to be granted. (In 1970, California became a "no-fault" state. Proof of infidelity is no longer required to grant a divorce.) Boom-Boom proved to be an excellent fit for the job – he was both fearless and intimidating, which enabled him to get in and out of awkward situations with relative ease. He went out and bought a new camera with the last bit of money he had in the cookie jar.

His first job was to follow a banker who was suspected of having an affair with his secretary. Photos were needed to prove the banker's infidelity. The banker's wife offered to pay Boom-Boom a $1,000 bonus if he was successful in getting the photos. Boom-Boom took his camera and followed the unsuspecting couple to a motel in San Jose. Their motel door was locked but Boom-Boom hadn't lost his signature move from his days at Stanford. When he needed to sack the quarterback, he simply lowered his shoulder and BOOM! He employed the same strategy here and BOOM! - the door shattered and he burst in on the couple who must have thought it was an explosion! He took the pictures and ran to his car.

The next morning, he gave the photos to his boss and received his $1,000 bonus from the wife. Boom-Boom gladly paid for the broken door and even gave the motel owner a $100 dollar bill for the inconvenience. Before long Boom-Boom's reputation grew among family law attorneys who needed his wild and unconventional talents. Boom-Boom's fame was growing in Santa Clara county and so was his bank account. Always one to be somewhat eccentric, Boom-Boom went out and bought himself a pink Cadillac.

Shortly after, he was given the assignment of following a man by the name of Nick Bebek, whose wife suspected him of having an affair with a waitress at his newly rebuilt bowling alley/restaurant. More than a year before, Nick's bowling alley and restaurant had blown up, the result of an underground gas leak (*See, A Bowling Alley Blows Up*). It took almost a year for him to collect the insurance proceeds that would enable him to begin construction on the new alley and restaurant. As soon as construction was completed, Nick picked right up where he left off, staffing the restaurant with employees, and filling the building with bowling and restaurant equipment.

Nick's wife Helen was insanely jealous and often made life miserable for him. Even though he never gave her reason to be suspicious, she would walk in on him, always unannounced, just to check in and make sure he was "behaving." One morning, Nick was in his office interviewing an applicant for a waitress position. Suddenly, Helen walked in just as the young woman was leaning over Nick's desk to sign her employment contract. Helen went ballistic. In a blind rage, she stormed out of the office shouting that she was going to see her attorney and file for divorce. Helen did just that, and the firm she used happened to be where Boom-Boom worked as a process server. Helen offered Boom-Boom $1,500 if he could take the photographs required to support her divorce petition.

Nick had been married to Helen for over thirty years. He had never seen her fly off the handle like this before, and he could only hope she would eventually calm down and listen to reason. Unfortunately, he could tell this time, she was serious and had every intention of following through on her threat. Nick tried calling Helen at home all afternoon, and when she still didn't answer, he became more and more convinced she was resolved to make good on her threat.

Helen gave Nick the silent treatment for the next week. On a hunch, Nick called their bank and learned Helen had written a $1,500 check to a law firm in Santa Clara. Nick was familiar with the law firm as he had read several stories in the paper about their now "famous" process server, a big guy called "Boom-Boom." He had read with amusement the stories of this giant who drove a pink Cadillac and would burst through unsuspecting couples' doors and leave just as quickly with all the evidence needed to support a divorce decree. Nick decided it was time to teach his jealous wife and Boom-Boom a lesson they would never forget.

That afternoon, Nick took the shotgun he kept in his office and drove to the Caravan Motel. He rented a room on the 2nd floor and put the gun in the closet. Then he returned to the bowling alley where the new waitress that Helen saw in his office was just finishing her afternoon shift. Nick asked her if she would do him a big favor and have dinner with him that night at the Caravan Motel. She was taken aback by this odd request and at first, declined the offer. Nick knew his request put her in an awkward position so he explained the situation to her. Then he offered her $100 plus cab fare home if she would help him. When she was finally convinced nothing illegal, creepy or dangerous was afoot, she agreed.

It was getting dark when Nick and the waitress left the bowling alley and drove to the Caravan Motel. He noticed Boom-Boom's pink Cadillac following them as soon as they left the bowling alley parking lot. At the Motel, Nick parked his car and took the waitress into the restaurant for dinner. The pink Cadillac was parked at the far north end of the parking lot, with a clear view of the restaurant and motel. An hour-an-a-half later, Nick and the waitress left the restaurant and headed toward the motel. Their room on the balcony level had a wrought iron railing that overlooked the swimming pool. Nick and the waitress walked into their room and quickly turned off the lights. Nick thanked her and they shook hands as he led her out the side door of the suite to an exit down the back stairwell. Nick returned and grabbed the shotgun from the closet. Then he sat in a chair in the center of the room, directly opposite the front door and waited for Boom-Boom to make his entrance.

It was about 10:00 p.m. when Nick heard heavy footsteps coming down the breezeway toward his room. Suddenly, the door burst open and there stood Boom-Boom in the doorway poised ready to take pictures. At that exact moment however,

Nick pulled the trigger of his shotgun and fired into the ceiling. The sound was so deafening, it sounded like a bomb went off! Boom-Boom thought for sure he was hit. He grabbed his stomach and fell backwards against the wrought iron railing on the balcony. The railing couldn't withstand the force of his huge body and it collapsed causing Boom- Boom to fall from the balcony into the swimming pool below.

Boom-Boom wasn't injured but he screamed, "Help! I can't swim! Someone help me!" Lights came on all from all over the motel and people rushed to drag him out of the pool, in nightgowns or less. When the excitement died down, Nick calmly walked down the back stairway with his shotgun wrapped in a blanket. He got into his car. Mission accomplished, or so he thought.

When Nick got into his car he almost jumped through the roof when he looked over at the passenger seat and saw Helen. She was crying hysterically, repeating over and over how she never wanted a divorce but when she saw him with that "pretty, young girl" in his office, her temper got the better of her and she lost control of herself. Then she sobbed and said, "I heard the shotgun blasts…now you've killed my lawyer's process server! Our lives are ruined! You'll go to prison!"

For the first time in thirty-one years, Nick understood his wife was not some crazy, jealous woman. Nick finally realized she acted the way she did because she loved him but was also terribly insecure and lonely. He realized he had never included her in the day-to-day operations of the bowling alley, even though their three sons were now grown and out of the house. Nick decided it was time for him to shift his focus from himself and his work, to his wife and their marriage. He decided to make her his "personnel director" responsible for all the hiring and firing at the business. Nick and Helen were going to run their business and their marriage as a team from now on.

The next day, Nick stopped by the Caravan Motel and paid for the bullet holes in the ceiling. Boom-Boom had to pay for the broken door, the wrought iron railing and he had to buy a new camera to replace the one that followed him into the pool. After this experience, Boom-Boom raised his fee to $2,500 because of the "inherent risks involved" in taking such pictures!

The Black Panthers Strike Terror

In the 1960's, the very name "Black Panther" struck terror in people all over California. They were an angry group of African Americans who hated the white man who, they believed, was trying to lower their people to the status of a slave. Now 50 years later, it is doubtful if anyone in this new generation of baby boomers would even recognize the name. But in the 60's in Santa Clara County, the Black Panthers were terrorizing a newly opened shopping mall called Valley Faire, which was in a predominantly white community. It consisted of over 100 stores, a huge supermarket and a 15-acre parking lot.

Business was booming and the parking lot was always full...that is, until the Black Panthers came to town. The gang members would walk up to a customer carrying bags of merchandise to his/her car and slit the bags with a knife, allowing the goods to fall onto the pavement. Then, they would point the knife at the customer's throat and threaten if they ever returned to the mall, they would die. The news spread quickly that the Black Panthers had knives and would intimidate people who patronized the Valley Faire Mall. It didn't take long before business at the Mall came to a complete standstill and the parking lots were empty.

Now, that is where I came into the story and almost got myself killed. At the time, I had several big cases pending in Superior Court but no real money was coming in. Walter Ward had warned me about what he called "dry spells" and suggested for some fast income, I could do some process serving. The pay was not great but it was paid when the papers were served, and for several weeks it kept the "wolf" from our door.

One morning a local attorney, John Steelman, called and said he wanted to see me. It was very important. I went over to his office on the 5th floor of the Bank of America Building in San Jose. He said he represented the owners of the Valley Faire Mall Corporation and for the last three weeks the Black Panthers had been terrorizing their customers. John had the Presiding Judge sign a restraining order prohibiting the Black Panthers from loitering at the Mall but it had to be served on the head of the Black Panthers at their office in San Francisco. He said none of his regular process servers would take the job because it was too risky.

John wanted me to accept the job. I turned it down thinking there was no way was I going to serve a Black Panther for $10 (the going rate for service). But when I learned there were eleven papers to be served and when John said for me to name my price, I thought of our mortgage that had to be paid and I named a price: $100 per paper. I never dreamed he would accept the high price but he surprised me when he picked up the phone and called his clients. They agreed to pay me $1,100 to get the job done. Now the ball was in my court!

I borrowed Walter Ward's new Lincoln Continental because my Plymouth was getting a new set of tires and it was a full hour's drive to San Francisco. John had given me the Black Panther's address on Mission Street. The address turned out to be an old abandoned church, badly in need of paint with rickety old wooden stairs leading up to heavy double doors. I grabbed the restraining orders and went up the stairs. I walked inside and was surprised to see the church was empty with no pews and no altar. It had about four or five card tables on each sidewall of the church with Black Panthers seated and talking. When I entered, it was as though the air had suddenly been sucked out of the room. Then I heard someone whisper, *"There's a white man in here."*

I guessed there were at least thirty men staring at me but none of them moved or said a word. They just sat there as I walked down the aisle to where the altar used to be and there sat a large black man seated in a high-backed leather chair behind a long library table. This had to be the "Head Man." John had given me his name (but I can't remember it now). I shoved the papers into his hands, turned around and walked back to the front doors, my heart pounding in my ears.

I cursed my new Florsheim shoes with the leather heels because they made a loud "clack-clack" noise on the old wooden floors. When I was about halfway to the front doors, I could hear a roomful of angry Black Panthers shove aside their chairs and come running after me. I broke into a run to the doors, swearing the whole way at the noise those darned shoes were making. I raced down the stairs and into Walter Ward's Lincoln. As I peeled away from the curb, one of the Panthers pounded on my window and I could see seven or eight Black Panthers running to their cars. I was in big trouble. It was 5:00 p.m. and traffic was going to be heavy on my drive home. Probably, that $1,100 fee would have to be used for my funeral!

I had to get onto the freeway and away from these angry men. I blessed Walter's Lincoln for its horsepower as I swerved from lane to lane but I couldn't shake them. In fact, they were gaining on me. Traffic was even heavier because as I passed Candlestick Park, a Giants afternoon game was just getting out. Then, I got lucky. I saw a Highway Patrolman giving a driver a ticket and both cars were parked on the right shoulder of the road. I slammed on my brakes and skidded to a stop right behind the patrol car. I got out of my car and told the officer my problem. He came up with a solution that saved my life.

We could see three cars of Black Panthers stopped about 100 yards behind us, pretending they had a flat tire. The officer told me to pull into the slow lane of traffic and he would follow right behind me. When we got to the next off-ramp, I was to suddenly turn into the exit lane. As I did this, the officer swerved his patrol car across the lane and blocked all cars behind him from trying to exit the off ramp. I went up several side streets just to be sure they were not following me. Then I returned to Los Gatos on old Highway #1 rather than returning to the #101 Freeway.

End of story? Well, not quite.

The next day was a Saturday and I returned Walter Ward's Lincoln to him in Palo Alto. I filled up his gas tank and thanked him for the use of his car. I never told him of my adventure with the Black Panthers. On Monday morning, as usual, Walter and I had breakfast at a coffee shop next to his office on First Street. He told me he was puzzled when a group of black men began walking toward him as he was getting into his Lincoln this morning. They took a long look at him, shook their heads and drove away. It was clear to me the Black Panthers had run Walter's license plate in Sacramento and learned of the Palo Alto address. But when they saw Walter who was twenty years older than me, they knew they had the wrong man. I never told him the real story. I only replied, "Strange, Walter...very strange."

What's An Heir Chaser?

W e have all heard the term "Ambulance Chaser." It was a name conferred on lawyers by insurance companies to vilify lawyers who chase ambulances and sign up injured parties while they are in the hospital. And yet, Insurance Adjusters are allowed to roam the halls of hospitals and have injured people sign releases for a fraction of their true value.

However, there exists in our country a select breed of investigators who make their living as "Heir Chasers" and it is all perfectly legal and ethical. Usually, they work in the larger cities where 25 or more wills are probated every day. Walter Ward was an "Heir Chaser" when he worked in San Francisco as a young investigator but now he was in semi-retirement and he only checked the probate calendar in Santa Clara County occasionally.

So what *is* an Heir Chaser, you ask? Every courthouse has a probate department where a person's will is filed and the decedent's property is distributed by order of the court. Most wills are routine where the decedent leaves everything to a spouse or family members. All wills are public record and every once in a while, a will comes along which names a "stranger" as the primary beneficiary of the will. Now, the "stranger" is someone usually unknown to the family of the decedent and yet he/she is the primary beneficiary in the will. If the will is substantial (over $250,000), then an "Heir Chaser" will try to find the "stranger" and tell him/her of their good fortune. For a percentage (usually 10%) of the amount gifted to the "stranger," the Heir Chaser will tell the stranger where the will is being probated and assist them in collecting the money gifted to them.

It's all perfectly legal because the other beneficiaries are told by the court that if the "stranger" cannot be found within a reasonable length of time then the bequest to the stranger will revert to them. The heirs therefore, have no incentive to find the stranger. Walter Ward knew we had moved to Claremont (about 50 miles east of Los Angeles) and that I had joined the Wortel Law Firm. One morning Walter called and said he was working an Heir Chaser case and needed my help. He told me quite a story about two brothers Dan and Don Bledsoe, who owned a 500-acre apricot orchard in Sunnyvale, California. This was before it became known to the whole world as the Silicon Valley. Dan was married and had two sons; Don never married and lived on the ranch. In the evenings, Don would often drive into San Jose and stop at Tony's Drive-In Restaurant. He would order a hamburger and milkshake from a beautiful carhop waitress named Dorothy Morandi. For Don, it was "love at first sight" but while Dorothy recognized him, she didn't even know his name.

Then one day, there were headlines in the *Mercury News* that Dorothy Morandi had been 'discovered" by a talent scout who was passing through San Jose. She was signed to a contract with Warner Brothers Studio and landed a small part in Humphrey Bogart's movie, "The African Queen." She left San Jose and moved to Hollywood to pursue a career in acting.

Four years passed when one morning, while Don Bledsoe was working in his apricot orchard, a branch from a tree fell and hit him in the head, knocking him unconscious. A ranch-hand found him and called an ambulance to take him to the hospital but sadly, he died en route from a brain aneurysm. Don was only 39 years old when he died. He left a will giving $50,000 to each of Dan's two sons; and the rest of his estate, he left to "Dorothy Morandi, formerly of Warner Brothers Studios in Hollywood, California."

Walter Ward wanted me to find Dorothy Morandi, if she was still alive. I agreed to try and find her if she was here in Southern California. Walter cautioned me that if I was successful in finding her, I should simply call on her and tell her she had been named in a will but do not, under any circumstances, tell her where the will had been filed or how much was left to her.

Now, in our Wortel Law Firm, we had a worker's compensation lawyer whose brother, also a lawyer, worked for the Screen Actors Guild. In less than half an hour, I had Dorothy Morandi's address in North Hollywood. On my way home, I decided to drive by the address and introduce myself. Before I left my office, I called Walter and told him I had found Dorothy Morandi. He cautioned me again to only tell her she had been named in a will and possibly, we could help her.

The address was in the old part of North Hollywood with 40 year-old apartment houses all crammed together. It was 6:00 p.m. when I walked up the stairs and rang the bell to her apartment. When she opened the door, I introduced myself and told her she had been named in a will. She asked me to come in and have a seat in her living room. She was a tall and slender lady; maybe 55 years old but the lines in her face told me of the many years she had lived the fast life in Hollywood. Yet, I could also see the underlying beauty that Don Bledsoe and the talent scout saw in her years ago.

She offered me a martini (she had one in her hand) but I politely declined. Then she called her dad who was fixing dinner in the kitchen. He was a distinguished gentleman who entered the room with a scowl on his face, obviously wondering who I was and why I was calling on his daughter at dinnertime. She told him she had been named in a will. Her dad had only two questions for me: (1) Where was this will filed? (2) How much money was involved? I tried to skirt the questions by telling him we could help her find the will but our standard fee was 10% of any money left to Dorothy. I could tell by the smug look on his face that he assumed the will was filed in Los Angeles County thus there was no need to hire me to find out how much money was coming to his daughter. He thanked me for stopping by and ushered me to the door. I gave him my card with my home phone number and left. He said he would call me if they needed any help.

I called Walter when I got home and he said not to worry - when he finds out the will was not filed in Los Angeles County, he will call you and admit he needs your help. Four days later, my phone rang and sure enough, it was Mr. Morandi. He was not the angry, officious and protective father I met a few days ago, now he was friendly and courteous. He said he wanted to see me right away but I had a problem: I had never handled an Heir Chaser case before and I needed time to talk with Walter and learn how to proceed. I told Mr. Morandi I had to be in San Diego but agreed to meet with him tomorrow afternoon.

I called Walter and, as usual, he had the solution. He dictated a contract for me to have Dorothy Morandi sign calling for a 10% fee of all amounts recovered in "a will naming Dorothy Morandi as a beneficiary." Neither Don Bledsoe's name nor the court's location was mentioned. At first, Mr. Morandi refused to allow his daughter to sign the contract. But finally, when she started to cry because she had no money of her own, he relented and passed her the pen and she signed. A next-door neighbor witnessed the signature because I was sure Mr. Morandi would try to find a way to void the contract. I called Walter from their apartment and read him the contract. Then I passed the phone to Mr. Morandi and Walter told him he would meet both of them at the San Francisco Airport the next day, which was a Saturday. I put the contract in the mail to Walter that evening.

Walter didn't trust Dorothy's father either and that is why he didn't suggest they meet at the San Jose Airport or on a weekday when Mr. Morandi could check the local probate courts and try to find Dorothy's name on someone's will. I made a reservation for Dorothy and her dad for the weekend at a San Francisco motel near Fisherman's Wharf and Walter said he would meet them at the motel at 8:00 a.m. Monday and take them to the proper probate department where the will was filed. What he didn't tell them was on Monday at 10:00 a.m. the Bledsoe will was to be probated in San Jose.

I received an interesting phone call on Saturday morning. An attorney who introduced himself as James Ritto said he represented Dan Bledsoe and his two sons and that Walter Ward had given him my home number. Mr. Ritto said it was very important I meet him at the Los Angeles Airport that afternoon. His flight was arriving at 1:00 p.m. at LAX. I reluctantly agreed to meet him but I wanted to talk to Walter first so I called Walter but there was no answer. I had to handle Mr. Ritto on my own.

Mr. Ritto said he would be wearing a dark blue suit and carrying a tan briefcase. I jumped into the shower and headed for the airport. The flight was on time and before long, I saw Mr. James Ritto in his blue suit carrying an expensive leather briefcase. I vaguely recognized him as an attorney I met in court several years before when I had my office in San Jose. I didn't like him then but I couldn't remember why. We walked to the nearest coffee shop and sat down.

He placed his briefcase on the table and said Walter Ward told him I was trying to find Dorothy Morandi. Walter obviously didn't tell him I had found her. I just listened and let him talk. He said the Bledsoe will was being probated on Monday morning and he wanted me to sign an affidavit saying I had searched for Dorothy Morandi but she couldn't be found. He wanted to present the affidavit to the court on Monday morning. He smiled as he opened his briefcase and there was $10,000 in cash! He said it was for me if I would sign the affidavit. I was reminded of what Walter had told me: if a stranger to a will could not be found, then the stranger's gift would revert to the heirs. In this case, Dan Bledsoe would inherit the remainder of Don's estate. I stood up, slammed the briefcase shut and walked away. I now remembered why I never liked the guy!

I called Walter Ward and told him of Ritto's attempted bribery. He just laughed and said James Ritto was in for a big surprise on Monday morning when he attended the probate hearing because there would be Dorothy Morandi all ready to testify in court.

At 10:00 a.m., Walter Ward, Dorothy Morandi and her father were seated in the front row of the courtroom when Dan Bledsoe and his two sons entered with their attorney, James Ritto. Walter told me I should have seen Ritto's face when he saw Dorothy Morandi seated there in court. The hearing lasted only a few minutes with the court recognizing Dorothy Morandi as the primary beneficiary.

After the hearing, James Ritto made Dorothy a substantial cash offer for her interest in the estate, which consisted of the apricot ranch. Dorothy accepted the offer because they had absolutely no interest in running an apricot ranch, and the price, which was more than one million dollars, was acceptable to Dorothy and her father. Walter took Dorothy, her Dad, Mr. Ritto and Dan Bledsoe down to the Bank of America branch in San Jose and had them issue two cashier's checks: one to Dorothy Morandi for her interest in the farm and one to Walter for our 10% interest. Then everyone went home happy. I took my cut and made a down payment on an apartment building in Pomona! Now you know what it's like to be an Heir Chaser!

How Many Have You Killed?

One of the saddest days in American history was the day John F. Kennedy was killed. All America was at a standstill as the tragic news spread nationwide. It was 10:30 a.m., November 22, 1963 and Dick Kiely and I were on our way from San Jose to Santa Cruz to start a medical malpractice trial when we heard the news on the radio that President Kennedy had been shot and was not expected to live.

We had three doctors ready to testify that the defendant doctor committed malpractice when our client died as the result of a massive overdose of insulin. We met our doctors who were waiting for us on the courthouse steps and we went directly to Judge Peterson's courtroom. Then Tom Kelly, the defense lawyer, and Dick Kiely went into the judge's chambers to discuss a continuance. There was no way the trial could begin in the face of such tragic news. A settlement was out of the question so Dick suggested a continuance of at least two weeks and all agreed. The three doctors and I were waiting on a bench in the hallway while the lawyers finalized details of the continuance. Then we all agreed it was time for an early lunch (with Dick Kiely paying of course).

One of our doctors had just returned from a vacation in Japan and he suggested we have lunch at a popular Japanese restaurant in Aptos. We needed to do something to ease the sadness we were all feeling in light of the news. It was an authentic Japanese restaurant all right! It was the first time I ever had to take my shoes off and sit on the floor to eat! The doctor who had just returned from Japan suggested we all have a cup of Sake before lunch. It came in a small shot glass and looked like just water but I quickly learned it had the kick of an angry mule. The thought flashed in my mind that I should never drink while working and I could still see the angry little man seated behind that massive desk shaking his finger at me for having martinis at lunch *(See, Even One Drink is Too Many)*. But what the heck, our case had been continued and our President had just been killed. So I was "off duty," and it was such a little glass…We sat and relaxed as we told stories of our beloved President. The hours flew by and the Sake kept flowing. Finally, around 2:30 p.m., we ordered lunch!

I honestly can't remember what I had for lunch, but I do remember our conversation with the doctors. It started out with the three of them going over their testimony concerning the defendant doctor who administered the fatal dose of insulin to a diabetic patient with a severe heart condition. The defendant was an alcoholic, working on a suspended medical license. It was clearly malpractice and all three doctors agreed.

Then the doctor who had just returned from Japan mentioned how easy it was though, when you are over-worked and tired, to make a mistake and overdose someone. He suddenly turned to the two doctors beside him and asked with a straight face, *"How many have you killed?"* But before they could answer, he said, *"I've killed five."* Then the younger one said, *"Three"* and the one with the bald head said *"Six."* Obviously, that darned Sake had loosened their tongues enough for them to confess weighty secrets that had been locked away in their consciences.

Finally, lunch was over and we headed to our cars for the long drive home. I was glad Dick was driving and not me. I just sat in the car and fell asleep. I remember Dick driving into his parking space next to his office. My car was parked beneath a shady oak tree. There was a cool breeze so I went to my car, rolled down the windows and fell back asleep. Dick went inside his office and fell asleep on the leather couch in his library. The next morning, Dick told me that after lunch yesterday, our three doctors returned to their offices and saw patients for the rest of the afternoon!

P.S. For a long time, I wondered how our "expert" doctors were able to return to their offices and see patients, while Dick and I (loaded with Sake) were sound asleep. I think I have it all figured out: Someday, a hotshot scholar will announce that Sake has been found to affect legal minds as a sedative and medical minds as a stimulant!

A Summons & Complaint - A Secret Weapon

M ost lawyers use process servers to serve their Summons and Complaints. It's a simple chore, all you have to do is ask the person (defendant) his/her name and if it corresponds with the name on the Summons and Complaint you simply give him/her the Summons and Complaint and they are served. They don't have to take it from you and even if they throw it on the ground, once you've confirmed their identity and put the papers before them, your job is complete. A good process server can make a decent living working for several law firms serving their legal papers.

Over the years, Walter Ward taught me that on occasion the serving of a Summons and Complaint can be very exciting (*See, The Black Panthers Strike Terror*); and for personal injury lawyers it can be a secret weapon.

The process server can usually determine the following three things about the defendant:

(1) Does the defendant have insurance?
(2) What kind of home and neighborhood does the defendant live in?
(3) (Most importantly) What kind of witness will the defendant make at trial?

At the very least, all these things can be learned by an investigator who is familiar with the facts of the case when he serves an unsuspecting defendant with a Summons and Complaint. Obviously, a trained investigator (at $65-$90 per hour) can't be used as a process server in every case, but on the major cases with serious injury, it always proves to be money well spent.

A classic case comes to mind that proves this point. Years ago, I was working for the Mercer & Ryan Law Firm in San Jose. One morning while we were having coffee in the office, Tony Mercer's wife called. She was very keyed up as she told Tony her sister had been in an accident and her new Ford was heavily damaged. Her sister had a broken wrist and was taken to the hospital where her wrist was put in a cast and she was released. The San Jose Police investigated the accident and no citation was issued at the scene. Tony hung up the phone and told me to get the police report and give the case my special attention because it was his sister-in-law and everyone in the family (most importantly, his wife) would be interested in the outcome of his sister-in-law's case.

I grabbed my briefcase and headed to the police department. I knew the report would not be ready for at least a week, but with a little luck, I could talk to the investigating officer and learn how the accident happened. The girl at the front desk said the officer investigating the case was off duty now and would return tomorrow.

The *Mercury Herald* had a short write-up on the accident. I bought the paper and read the article. It gave the name of both drivers and said the accident occurred at the intersection of Saratoga Road and Meridian Road. The article went on to say Tony's sister-in-law was westbound on Saratoga Road and at the intersection of Meridian Road she turned left in front of a Cadillac travelling eastbound. The article concluded by noting the accident was under investigation by the San Jose Police Department.

I decided to drive by the scene and take some photographs. I knew the area well and traffic is heavy all day long with four lanes going each direction. You would take your life in your hands trying to get photographs but you could drive by the scene and see if there was any skid at the intersection. I went west on Saratoga Road and when I approached the Meridian Road intersection, I drove into the left turn lane and could see impending skid from the eastbound Cadillac as it hit the right side of Tony's the sister-in-law's car. But this was a 45-mile-per-hour zone and the skid of the Cadillac did not appear to be enough to prove excessive speed.

From what I saw, it looked like Tony's sister-in-law was at fault for turning directly in front of the Cadillac and violating its right-of-way.

On the way back to my office, I stopped by the tow yard and found both cars and took photos of them. The new Ford was likely a total loss with heavy damage to the entire right side; the Cadillac showed some light damage to the front end. However, inside the Cadillac there was a lot of broken glass on the right front seat . . . strange.

The next morning, I got to the police station in time to see the investigating officer as he was getting ready for his morning shift. He was a real nice guy. He was writing up his report on the accident when I came into the squad room. He was recommending a violation of right of way citation against Tony's sister-in-law. I had to agree with him but I asked him, as a personal favor, to hold up the report for just a few days while I completed my investigation. He agreed, but said he could only hold it for a week at the most.

I called Tony and told him the police officer was about to issue a citation to his sister-in-law for violation of right of way. She would get the citation in the mail in a few days. Poor Tony was caught between an angry wife who felt her sister could do no wrong and her family who never liked lawyers anyway; and now he couldn't protect his "innocent" sister- in law who had been injured. To make matters worse, I was telling him it looked like his sister-in-law was responsible for the accident. And if he filed suit and claimed the lady in the Cadillac was at fault, when the police report clearly claimed he sister-in-law caused the accident, he could be in trouble with both the lady in the Cadillac and the State Bar for filing a frivolous lawsuit.

Sam Ryan and I sat in the law library and pondered the problem. It was a no-win situation. If Tony refused to handle his sister-in-law's case because there was no liability, his wife and her whole family would go ballistic. Tony would forever have to endure the anger of his relatives. On the other hand, if they pressured him to proceed with the lawsuit, he could easily be found guilty of filing a frivolous action and he would be disciplined by the State Bar.

Then I remembered Walter Ward telling me about the "secret weapon" lawyers sometimes used on a difficult case (and this was certainly a difficult case). I suggested Tony file a standard civil lawsuit against the Cadillac driver alleging simple negligence. He could file it that same day and I would serve it on the defendant. I hoped by some miracle I could find a valid reason for the lawsuit. If not, Tony could dismiss the suit for valid reasons when I submitted my investigation report saying the sister-in-law was negligent. Tony agreed and filed the lawsuit.

I picked up the Summons and Complaint and drove to the defendant's home. I rang the doorbell. She answered and I introduced myself as" an investigator "on the accident (I didn't say who I represented). She said she was glad to see me and asked me to come into her living room. She was a distinguished-looking lady, well dressed, about 55 years old. She told me she was widowed and owned an antique shop in downtown San Jose.

Her home was expensive and furnished with a collection of very fine antiques from all over the world. There was a beautiful Waterford crystal vase on her fireplace mantle that had to be worth a fortune! She said was she on her way to her store when the accident happened.

She had a collection of very fine china packed in a box on her right front seat and when she saw the Ford making the left turn in front of her, she had to make a difficult decision: There was plenty of time for her to apply her brakes and avoid the collision, but she feared if she hit the brakes hard, the box of China would slide off the seat and be ruined. So she decided to wrap her right arm around the box of china and slide into the Ford. She told me she felt responsible for causing the accident and had called her insurance agent admitting it was all her fault. And by the way, the force of the impact ruined her box of expensive china.

Then she went into her den and returned with her insurance policy. It showed her coverage was $ 100,000-$300,000. She signed a short statement saying she was completely at fault for causing the accident. I served her with the Summons and Complaint and I told her to tell her agent exactly what she told me. She agreed and I was on my way home.

The very next morning, I placed the statement on Tony's desk and Sam and I went into the library for a cup of coffee.

Soon after, in came Tony with the statement in his hand. He was one happy guy. He now had a valid lawsuit after all and he was certain to be a hero with his wife and her whole family! And once again, the lawyer's "Secret Weapon" worked!

By the way, I gave a copy of her statement to the police officer and he decided to withhold the right-of-way citation based on "newly discovered evidence!"

Burned Beyond Recognition

One morning about 6:30 a.m., my phone rang at our home in Los Gatos. It was Roger Millhaus, my old roommate from Notre Dame. He was all apologies for calling me so early but he was calling from his office in Milwaukee, Wisconsin, where it was already 8:30 a.m.

After graduation, Roger went to law school, passed the bar and joined American Mutual Life Insurance Company's legal department. Roger was a brilliant lawyer and in ten years he rose to Department Head with twelve lawyers working under him. Over the years, we remained close friends. He knew we had moved recently from Eureka to Los Gatos and I was making a living as an investigator. He said he needed my help on a very important case. I sat down in the den with a pen and paper and started taking notes.

Roger said American Mutual insured Thomas Rhodes, age 27, with a $300,000 life insurance policy. The policy had a double indemnity clause that said, in the event Thomas Rhodes met his death by accident, the beneficiary (his wife Maxine) would be paid $600,000. The policy went into effect on January 1, 1964. On September 9th, 1964 Mr. Rhodes died in a fiery automobile accident in central California. His body was burned beyond recognition. Roger wanted me to contact his widow, Mrs. Maxine Rhodes, who happened to live in Los Gatos, and explain to her that all double indemnity cases must be investigated before any payment can be made. Roger said American Mutual prided itself on prompt payment of claims and he asked me to give this case my immediate attention. I cancelled several appointments and drove to the home of Maxine Rhodes in Los Gatos.

The Rhodes' home was in the old part of Los Gatos and I noticed as I parked my car, a "For Sale" sign on the front lawn. I rang the bell…no answer. I rang it again and I heard a woman's voice call out, "Just a minute, I'm on the phone." I looked at my watch; it was only 8:15 a.m. I guess I should have called before I came over but then I remembered something Walter Ward had told me years ago: Never make appointments with clients or witnesses. It's too easy for them to get prepared for the interview or just say, "No." You will always get better results by just dropping in on them. The element of surprise will usually result in facts that will surprise you.

Finally, the door opened and there stood Maxine Rhodes, in pin-curlers and a bathrobe. I gave her my card and apologized for calling on her so early in the morning. She said her Insurance Agent, David Stein told her to expect me. She excused herself to change and told me I could wait in the living room. I sat down on the couch and noticed a *Cattleman's* magazine sitting on the coffee table with a picture of a Black Angus Steer on the cover. The byline said it was an elite new breed of cattle from Brazil. She returned a short while later, her hair and makeup tended to, wearing a light colored dress and holding a thermos of steaming hot coffee. Her eyes never left mine as she removed the magazine from the table and casually dropped it behind her chair.

Maxine was about 24-25 years old, a bit overweight but nice-looking with light brown hair. She said she and Tom Rhodes were married four years ago and they had one son, Thomas Jr., who was sound asleep in his bedroom. I asked her about the "For Sale" sign on her front lawn. She said she was planning on moving to Capistrano Beach and living with her mother now that her husband was gone. She was holding a handkerchief in her hand but during the entire time I was there, she never shed a tear or showed any real emotion one way or another. I thought that was strange, very strange.

She said Tom was a wholesale optical salesman whose territory was the entire west coast of California. He had to attend an optical seminar in Los Angeles and he left home around 6:30 a.m. on the day he died. He planned to stop at his Uncle Jim Rhodes' cattle ranch near San Luis Obispo for lunch. From there, he planned to drive on into Los Angeles in the evening when it cooled off and he was to call her from a hotel. The next thing she knew her phone rang at around 9:30 p.m. It was Uncle Jim calling to tell her Tom had been killed in a car accident. Her hand was shaking as she poured herself a second cup of coffee, but she never cried…strange. She told me that Tom's body was taken to Monahan's Funeral Parlor in Los Gatos for cremation.

I told Maxine I was on my way to San Luis Obispo to get Tom's death certificate, the coroner's report and the Highway Patrol report confirming the circumstances surrounding Tom's death. Hopefully, within a week the investigation would be complete and the insurance claim would be paid.

My next stop was Monahan's Funeral Parlor. It was a century-old Victorian masterpiece of a home, freshly painted and now used for a more somber purpose. The owner, Richard Monahan was an old friend of my dad's. He greeted me at the front door and ushered me into his office. I told him I was investigating the Thomas Rhodes death in San Luis Obispo. He said his son, Stanley picked up what was left of the body from the Coroner's office. It was so badly burned, the remains were loaded into a body bag and he drove back to the funeral home to prepare it for cremation. I asked Mr. Monahan if there were any personal belongings of Tom Rhodes found in the body bag, like maybe a watch or a wedding ring or even teeth. He just shook his head. He did remember something odd, however: Maxine never cried nor did she appear to be too shaken up at the funeral service. She wasn't wearing black and when friends and neighbors stopped by to pay their respects, she appeared to be almost *happy*.

It was 10:30 a.m. when I stopped at a payphone to call Cathy and tell her I was heading to San Luis Obispo to pick up the death certificate, a highway patrol report and the Coroner's report. It was about a three-hour drive each way but if I was lucky, I'd be home late in the evening and not have to stay in a crummy motel. These reports should be enough to prove it was Thomas Rhodes who burned to death in the accident.

I parked my car at the San Luis Obispo City Hall and walked over to a building with the somber sign, "Coroner's Office." I asked the young woman at the front desk if I could obtain a copy of the Death Certificate and Coroner's Report on Thomas Rhodes. She said the entire file had been taken to the District Attorney's office "for review." She suggested I talk to Attorney Tim Drury who was handling the case and let me use the phone to call his office.

Fortunately, he was available so I walked down to his office. I told the secretary at the front desk I was there to meet with Tim Drury. She called him on the intercom then walked me down to his office. There, behind a stack of files, sat Tim Drury. He waved me to a chair as he tried to conclude a telephone conversation with an angry Jury Commissioner.

I learned he was married and had two young boys in little league and was a member of the Rotary Club; he was a golfer and a graduate of Loyola Law School class of 1960. All this I learned from looking at all the photographs on his office wall and the confusion on his desk told me he was a young lawyer who had the minor cases that needed "review" dumped on his desk. When he ended his call, I introduced myself and asked to see the "Thomas Rhodes" file. He stood up and started searching through the stacks of files on his desk. Finally, Tim found the file. He remembered it was assigned to him for "review" because the body was burned beyond recognition and the Coroner could not positively identify it as that of Thomas Rhodes.

To further complicate matters, the only witness to the death of Thomas Rhodes was a parolee named Clint Fowler who had just been released after spending the last ten years in prison for attempted murder. I told Tim all I needed was a Death Certificate and a Coroner's report that would prove it was Tom Rhodes who died in the accident. Tim said he would review the file and return it to the Coroner's Office within the week.

My next stop was the California Highway Patrol office. I was told Officer Chuck Ringold did the investigation and was just coming off duty. We sat in the "duty room" and had a cup of coffee. He was a young officer who had joined the patrol two years ago. He said he arrived at the scene about twenty minutes after the accident. He recalled several fire trucks parked on the road with at least a dozen firemen trying to control the blaze that threatened to involve a number of expensive homes on the other side of Deep Creek Road.

Officer Ringold said he checked the license plate with Sacramento's DMV and learned the car was registered to Thomas Rhodes. Then he took a statement from the only eyewitness, Clint Fowler, who said he was ranch foreman for the Lazy R ranch, just up the road. Fowler told Ringold he was taking delivery of some Black Angus cattle at the front gate and he waved to Tom Rhodes as Tom left the ranch. According to Clint, Tom was alone. Then within a minute Fowler said he heard a crash and saw smoke coming from the bottom of Deep Creek. He ran to the scene and saw Tom's Firebird fully engulfed in flames. Clint said he tried to get near the car to rescue Tom but the flames were too hot. He ran to the ranch and called the Highway Patrol. Officer Ringold said he based his identification of the body on the information given him by the DMV and the statement of Clint Fowler. He said his full report would be available in three to four days.

My next stop was the scene of the accident on Deep Creek Road. Officer Ringold told me it was about ¼ mile west of the entrance to the Lazy R Ranch. I pulled my car over when I saw the badly burned creek bed, grabbed my camera and shot a roll of film. I found the area where the Firebird came to rest at the bottom of Deep Creek, but when I got up on the road I could not find any prior skid left by the car before it went down into the creek bed. For some reason the driver failed to apply his brakes as evidenced by the absence of skid marks. Did his brakes fail? Or possibly Tom suffered a heart attack?

I saw the Lazy R Ranch sign in the distance on the left side of the road. It was 5:00 p.m. and the old wooden gate at the entrance to the ranch was open. I drove down the dirt road to the ranch house and noticed a herd of beautiful black cattle standing around under the shade of a huge oak tree. They looked just like the Black Angus cattle I saw on the cover of the magazine on Maxine's coffee table. Interesting…

As I drove into the circular driveway in front of the ranch house, I saw an old man in a straw hat holding a glass of iced tea. He was seated in a rocking chair on the front porch. This had to be Jim Rhodes, Tim's uncle because he matched the picture I saw on Maxine's fireplace mantle this morning. He waved to me and stood to shake my hand as I walked up the old wooden steps. I handed him my card and said I was from the life insurance company. He was a distinguished-looking older gentleman about 70 years old and thin with snow white hair, his skin darkened by years of working in the sun. Jim Rhodes said he was expecting me; Maxine had called him this morning. I started to apologize for coming so late in the afternoon and hoped I wasn't interrupting their dinner. Jim said it was too hot to eat anyway.

As he poured me a tall glass of iced tea, a big ranch hand in a dirty tee-shirt with tattoos covering both arms and an angry scar on his left cheek, walked up the stairs. Jim introduced me to Clint Fowler, his ranch foreman. He was just the man I wanted to see. He was a big man, maybe 6'4" and not an ounce of fat on his 250-pound frame. We shook hands (it hurt) and we all sat down on the porch. I asked Clint how the accident happened. Clint told me what he had told Officer Ringold: He waved to Tom Rhodes as he left the front gate of the ranch and Tom was alone in his car. Then Clint heard the crash and saw the fire. Suddenly, Clint got up, muttering something about me cross-examining him and stomped back toward the barn swearing. Jim Rhodes and I just sat there. Jim said, "Don't be bothered with Clint, it happens all the time. Clint has an uncontrollable temper as you might have guessed by the scar on his face. He got it in a prison fight." Jim said despite his temper, he was a very hard worker and was respected by the hired hands.

I asked Jim if Clint was the last person to see Tom Rhodes leave the ranch. At first, he said yes and then he remembered the driver who unloaded the Black Angus cattle at the front gate. *He* must have been the last person to see Tom Rhodes alive. Jim rushed over to his desk in the living room and found the receipts for the delivery. It named the "Reardon Cattle Company" of Grapeville, Texas and their driver was a "Jason Miller." I shoved the receipts into my briefcase and promised to make copies and return them to Jim. I thanked him and said goodbye. It was getting late and I had a long drive home.

On my way to the freeway, I drove through Willow Creek, a quaint little town with a Bank of America building on one corner and a restaurant next door. I was starving, so I parked my car, walked in and grabbed a stool at the counter. It was a clean place with a sign on the door, "Willow Creek Grille." A gray-haired waitress took my order and hollered to the cook (probably her husband) "cheeseburger and fries, Joe."

She smiled at me as she brought me an iced tea and said "you must be from out of town stranger, because you aren't wearing cowboy boots or a straw hat and you smell good." I laughed and told her I was an investigator on the death of a young man on Deep Creek Road near the Lazy R Ranch. I asked her if she knew of anybody who may have seen the accident. Just then, I noticed a Mexican woman coming out from the kitchen. She was wiping her hands on a dishtowel wrapped around her waist and listening intently to our conversation. In broken English, she told me her son, Juan Garcia, worked at the Lazy R Ranch for the last year-and- a-half. She said he used to come into the Grille every night for dinner and then he would help her with the dishes. He was saving his money for college. But, she said, "the day of the accident, he no come here to see me anymore." The waitress interrupted her and said, "Rita, Juan probably went back to Mexico to see his girlfriend." Rita shrugged and returned to the kitchen shaking her head.

I made a mental note of the strange coincidence of Juan's disappearance on the same day as the accident but it probably had no connection with my investigation. My job was to prove or disprove it was Thomas Rhodes in the Firebird when it crashed. I paid my bill for a great hamburger and headed home.

It was after midnight before I crawled into bed. On Friday morning, I called Roger Millhaus and told him the Death Certificate, the Coroner's report and the Highway Patrol Report would all be ready by Wednesday of next week. But I had a problem, more of a hunch, really. I told Roger I felt Clint Fowler was not telling me the truth and actually, he was not the last person to see Tom Rhodes alive. There was a truck driver named Jason Miller who was unloading a shipment of Black Angus cattle to the ranch the day of the accident. He could have been the last person to see Tom alive and his office was in Grapeville, Texas. This is a $600,000 case and I felt it was worth it to see Jason Miller. Roger agreed but said the agent, David Stein, was demanding immediate payment based on his conversation with Officer Ringold who said his report would show Tom Rhodes was the driver of the Pontiac Firebird.

I caught a flight on Delta Airlines and we touched down in Dallas, Texas at 1:21 p.m. I rented a car and headed to Grapeville, about 80 miles west of Dallas. I stopped at a service station in Grapeville and asked directions to the Reardon Cattle Company. The store clerk's answer was a classic. He said, "It's about three miles down the road and when you smell it, you're there."

I parked in the parking lot at the Reardon Cattle Company and thanked God the wind was blowing in the opposite direction. I went to the front office and was told Jason Miller was just parking his truck after a long-haul trip to Phoenix, Arizona. I waited for Jason in the coffee lounge. He came in and literally fell into the booth. He was around 35 years old, sporting a three-day growth of beard and a baseball hat turned backwards as he motioned to the waitress for a beer. I told him I was the investigator on the accident at the Lazy R Ranch near San Luis Obispo in California. He said he remembered the incident quite well because the driver of the Pontiac Firebird "almost killed" him. He cursed the big guy with tattoos down his left arm that was driving the Firebird.

"I got a good look at the jerk. He was in a big hurry and cut in front of me. I had to slam on my brakes and almost jackknifed my truck. He had his arm out the window...his arm was all covered with tattoos. Oh, and there was a passenger in the front seat who looked like he was asleep." After he finished unloading the cattle, Jason said he drove away in his truck and saw the Pontiac on fire at the bottom of Dry Creek. He said he didn't stop because he was still furious with the driver for cutting him off. Suddenly, those tattoos became very significant.

I took a short statement from Jason, covering the driver of the Firebird and the passenger who was asleep in the front seat. I headed back to the airport and home to California. The statement conflicted with what Clint had told Officer Ringold and I learned there was a passenger asleep in the right front seat. Could the driver have been Clint Fowler? Who was the passenger? But there was only one body found in the car. What did all of this have to do with proving or disproving Thomas Rhodes was dead or alive?

I called Tim Drury from the airport and told his secretary I would see him with some very interesting news. It was too late to call Roger Millhaus but I left a message with his answering service saying I would call him in the morning. Bright and early on Monday, I was knocking on Tim Drury's door with a copy of Jason Miller's statement. He read it carefully but said it only showed that Miller's statement conflicted with what Fowler told Officer Ringold (that Tom Rhodes was the driver and alone in the Firebird); and it raised a question of the identity of the "sleeping" passenger. Tim said he did not have enough evidence for Clint Fowler's arrest for lying to Officer Ringold but he definitely became a "person of interest" if Tom Rhodes' body was the "sleeping passenger" in the Firebird.

I called Roger and told him Jason Miller identified Clint Fowler as the driver of the Firebird when it left the ranch and he had a "sleeping passenger" with him who could have been Tom Rhodes. Roger reminded me we still had to prove whether Tom Rhodes was dead or alive. My investigation was at a standstill

I had a cup of coffee and wondered what Walter Ward would do. Over my third cup, his answer came to me: Walter would go back and check the Firebird. Just maybe there was some evidence in the car that the Coroner's investigators had missed. Tim Drury had given me authorization to inspect the car and the impound lot was only three blocks away.

The inside of the car was mostly ashes so I stopped at a 7-Eleven Store and bought a strainer to sift through the ashes. It was hot, very hot when I got to the tow yard and started rummaging through the wreckage. After three long hours, all I had was a ruined pair of slacks and lungs full of ash! But then, I got lucky. Tom's Firebird was a two-door car with a small rear seat behind the driver and passenger. I reached behind the driver's seat and over in the corner underneath what was left of the back seat was a charred metal bracelet! It was badly burned but with a little rubbing (spit), I was able to read the name plate: *JUAN GARCIA*. This had to be the son of Rita Garcia, the dishwasher I talked to at the Grille. Juan was the passenger Jason Miller saw who appeared to be asleep in the Firebird but he was not asleep – he was dead - and Clint Fowler was the driver! But all this didn't explain where Tom Rhodes was…nor did it answer the burning question: Was he alive or dead?

Finally, all the pieces started falling into place in my thick head. Was it possible that Clint Fowler and Tom Rhoades planned to fake Tom's death and put Juan Garcia's in the Firebird and set it afire? If true, Maxine could collect the $600,000 insurance policy money. There was no question now, after finding the bracelet, that Juan Garcia was the dead body recovered from the Firebird. And the driver with all the tattoos *had* to be Clint Fowler. I raced over to the courthouse and caught Tim Drury during a recess and gave him the bracelet. He agreed the DA's office now had enough evidence to at least call Clint Fowler in for questioning as a "person of interest" in the death of Juan Garcia. But if all this was true...where was Tom Rhodes?

It was almost 3:00 p.m. I was starving, having eaten only a lousy breakfast that day. I stopped at the Grille in Willow Creek and had one of their great hamburgers. I told Rita Garcia that Juan's name had come up in the DA's investigation and possibly someone would be questioning her in a day or so about his disappearance. I didn't have the heart to tell her I had found Juan's bracelet in the wreckage.

After lunch I drove out to the ranch, parked my car and walked up the front steps. Uncle Jim Rhodes met me at the screen door and I told him I wanted to talk to Clint Fowler. I said it was no big deal; I just wanted to ask him if he recalled seeing a passenger with Tom Rhodes when he waved to him as he left the ranch. Jim called Clint who was in the barn. Clint came in and we all sat down in the living room. I told them I had just returned from Grapeville, Texas and the truck driver told me he saw a passenger in the Firebird. I said I just wanted to clarify this while I was waiting for the Coroner's Report and the Death Certificate. But when I mentioned Grapeville, Texas, Clint Fowler sat bolt upright on the couch and shouted, "there was no one in the car with Tom Rhodes. That trucker is lying...*no one*! And what are you trying to pull, O'Brien? Are you trying to find a way not to pay Maxine the money?" Then he lunged at me swearing he was going to kill me.

I knew I was in BIG trouble. I had to get out of here and into my car--fast! Uncle Jim grabbed Clint by the waist and they both fell to the floor. I made a mad dash for the screen door and out to my car. Clint must have realized the trucker saw him driving away in Tom's car with Juan's body in the passenger seat...dead. Now he wanted to silence me...forever!

It was just starting to get dark as I raced to the front gate. I could see in my rear view mirror, Clint running to his pickup with a shotgun strapped to his rear window. Because of the dusty dirt road, it was hard to tell if he was gaining on me. I pushed the accelerator to the floorboard and raced to the front gate. As I made the right turn onto Deep Creek road, (thank God the gate was open), I could see the lights of Clint's pickup about a hundred yards behind me.

I headed into Willow Creek but I knew Clint could catch me downtown, so I made a sudden left turn onto a side street that ran parallel to Main Street in Willow Creek. It was in the old part of town with homes built long before World War II. There were no street lights and most of the homes were dark. I noticed one home with a "For Sale" sign. I hoped it was empty when I turned into the driveway and turned off my lights. A few seconds later, I saw Clint's pickup race past me and continue on to Main Street. He probably thought he had a good chance of catching me in downtown Willow Creek, before I made it to the freeway onramp. I prayed I was safe, at least for now. I sat and waited with my lights out and doors locked and said a quiet prayer.

In the darkness and silence, I couldn't help but feel Clint Fowler sneaking up to my car, smashing the windows and firing his shotgun. Finally, I could stand it no longer. I backed down the drive way and turned on my lights. I didn't go through downtown Willow Creek to the 101 freeway because I was afraid Clint would be waiting for me and the madman had a shotgun. Instead, I turned south and headed home on old Highway #1. It was a little longer but a whole lot safer! Three hours later, I was parking my car at home, dead tired but at least I was alive!

Early the next morning, Tim Drury called me from the DA's office in San Luis Obispo. He was excited. He said last night, Clint Fowler was racing down Main Street in Willow Creek (after me!) when he hit a car pulling out of a McDonald's restaurant. He left the scene but was arrested by the Highway

Patrol as he entered the #101freeway. He was jailed on a hit-and-run charge.

I told Tim my adventure with Fowler and now that he was in jail, Tim brought him in for questioning on the death of Juan Garcia. Clint stumbled through one lie after another during three hours of questioning. Tim showed him Juan Garcia's bracelet and read him the statement I had taken from Jason Miller.

Finally, Clint admitted he and Tom Rhodes had conspired to kill Juan Garcia and put him in the driver's seat of the Firebird. Clint would then drive the car off the edge of the road, set it afire and jump out, leaving the car to careen into the creek bed and explode. He confessed to telling Officer Ringold it was Tom Rhodes in the car, not Juan Garcia whom he said he killed with a shovel in the barn. The plan was for Maxine to collect the $600,000 insurance and the three of them would disappear to some place in South America and raise Black Angus cattle. When Tom Rhodes saw Clint kill Juan, he panicked and ran from the barn, never to be seen again.

Clint was placed on $1million bail. He later pled guilty and was sentenced to life in prison. A warrant for the arrest of Thomas Rhodes as an accomplice to murder was filed. An all-points bulletin was sent out for his arrest but he has never been found. The DA's office decided not to file charges against Maxine and Uncle Jim Rhodes, for lack of sufficient evidence.

The mystery appeared to be dying down but American Mutual had a big problem. Their agent, David Stein, obtained a copy of Chuck Ringold's Highway Patrol report. It listed Tom Rhodes as the dead body found in the Firebird and the Coroner's office said the body was not identifiable so they relied on the Highway Patrol's identification of the body as that of Tom Rhodes. David Stein obtained a copy of the highway patrol report and insisted American Mutual (which put Tom Rhodes behind the wheel of the Firebird) pay the $600,000 to Maxine.

Roger Millhaus said we had strong evidence Tom Rhodes was not in the Firebird and a murder had been committed but my investigation still failed to prove whether Tom Rhodes was alive or dead.

Roger was ordered to settle the claim. He told me to stop my investigation and submit my bill for services. Then, unbeknownst to me, Roger and the CEO of American Mutual flew from Milwaukee to San Jose and drove to Los Gatos to discuss settlement with Maxine Rhodes. Roger called me a week later and said the case had been settled for $80,000 based primarily on the evidence we had that proved Tom Rhodes was not in the Firebird when it caught fire. Maxine sold her house and told her neighbors she was moving to San Juan Capistrano to be near her mother.

End of story? Well not quite.

I must tell you the remainder of this story as it actually happened. But I confess I was tempted to put an interesting "twist" on the ending. However, I am no Conan Doyle or Agatha Christie or John Grisham. I'm just an old, retired investigator who is determined to tell the truth in this book. So here is how this story actually ended:

Clint Fowler was sentenced to life without the possibility of parole for the murder of Juan Garcia. Three years later, he was killed in a prison riot.

Jim Rhodes was never arrested but he lost his cattle ranch in foreclosure and was last known to live in a trailer park in Carmel, CA.

Tim Drury, who was able to get the confession from Clint Fowler, got a lot of favorable publicity. He ran for DA and won.

Chuck Ringold, the Highway Patrol Officer, refused to alter his report.

Rita Garcia, Juan's mother, learned from the DA's office that her son was buried in Tom Rhodes' grave in Los Gatos.

Now, every Christmas and Easter Sunday she places a bouquet of flowers on his grave and says a prayer.

Maxine Rhodes finally sold her house in Los Gatos and changed her mailing address to San Juan Capistrano but she never bought a home there. She stayed in a motel with her son and for three months she picked up her mail every afternoon at the San Juan Capistrano post office. Then one day, she moved and left no forwarding address.

Tom Rhodes was never seen or heard from after he ran from the barn when he saw Juan Garcia murdered. The warrant for his arrest is still pending but probably long forgotten.

And me…Roger told me to stop my investigation and submit my bill for services because the agent David Stein and American Life Insurance had decided to settle the case for a nominal amount rather than risk a lawsuit.

I felt I failed Roger Millhaus because I never found Tom Rhodes. For my own peace of mind, I had to know if he was dead or alive. Suddenly one day, I had an idea while I was waiting for the bank to open in Los Gatos: I knew Maxine's home had been sold, and she had to use an Escrow Company to process the sale. And the equity she and Tom had in their home had to be mailed to them with a settlement check…Right? Now, where did that check go? Was it cashed and if so, who signed it? Where was it cashed? All these questions raced through my mind and I had to have answers even if no one was paying me. I simply had to know.

Now, Los Gatos is a very small town with only one Escrow Company and I had a "friend" who owed me a small favor. I asked him to open the closed Escrow file of Tom and Maxine Rhodes. He pulled it out of storage. It showed a closing check of $126,200 payable to *Thomas and Maxine Rhodes* and sent to a post office box in San Juan Capistrano. The cashed escrow check was not in the file but in the accountant's office at the Bank of America building. My "friend" made a phone call to the accountant in charge and said I needed to have a copy of the front and back of the check.

A few days later, I returned to the bank and the cancelled check was on the manager's desk waiting for me. The check was made payable to "Thomas and Maxine Rhodes" because they were both on the Deed of Trust. On the reverse side of the check it showed the check was not cashed in a San Juan Capistrano bank but it was cashed at Banco Del Sol in Sao Paulo, Brazil and the back of the check showed both Thomas and Maxine Rhodes had signed the check.

I ordered certified copies of the check (both sides) and mailed them to Roger's home. He called me and said he had contacted the FBI and they told him they were "handling the matter." That's the last Roger and I ever heard of Tom and Maxine Rhodes...for all we know they are still down in Brazil somewhere raising Black Angus Cattle!

Murder at the Monte Carlo Hotel

It was going to be a perfect Saturday morning. I planned to stay home and watch the Notre Dame vs. USC football game on TV. The National Championship was hanging in the balance. But instead of watching the game in my favorite leather chair with a cold beer, I was driving to Irvington to see a witness on a pedestrian death case. I could think of a thousand reasons why I should stay home but with eight hungry mouths to feed, I had no choice. Anyway, with a little luck, I would be home before halftime.

Yesterday afternoon, Attorney Ted Cowan called me into his office. He handed me a police report and said he represented a mother and daughter. The mother was in ICU but was expected to survive. However, her four-year-old daughter had been killed. The San Jose police report indicated the mother and daughter were crossing San Carlos Street on the green "walk" sign, when a Corvette going eastbound ran the stop sign and hit them. There was a witness to the accident, but for some unknown reason, the officer didn't include her statement in his report. The Corvette driver insisted the light was green for him and the mother and daughter walked into the side of his car on a "don't walk" signal. It didn't look like a very promising case but everything depended on what this witness saw and with a daughter killed and a mother badly injured, I wanted to see the witness before any insurance adjuster contacted her. The witness, Mrs. Margaret Catto, gave her address to the police officer as "The Monte Carlo Hotel, Irvington, California."

Years ago, Irvington was a sleepy little farming community with acres and acres of prune, apricot and pear orchards. This was before it became known to the whole world as part of the Silicon Valley. The Monte Carlo Hotel was its only real historic landmark. It was built in 1886 and stage coach drivers stopped at the hotel to rest their passengers and change horses before going on into San Francisco. In the 1930's, the Monte Carlo Hotel was one of the few places where a thirsty rancher could get a drink of good bootleg whiskey. During World War II, it was rumored there was a brothel on the mezzanine floor. (*See, A Salesman Gets a Big Surprise*). As the years passed, the old Hotel fell on hard times. Several owners tried to revive the beautiful old Victorian mansion but failed. The only part of the hotel that managed to survive was the Italian restaurant, located in the dining room.

About six years ago, Tony Silva, a retired "businessman" from Chicago, purchased the Hotel at a foreclosure sale. It got the attention of the locals when they learned he paid cash for the old place. He closed the five-story Hotel except for a dozen rooms on the second floor, which he reserved for retired war veterans. He kept the dining room open because it was known as the best Italian restaurant between San Jose and San Francisco. It was rumored Tony Silva had connections with the Mafia in Chicago but no one knew for sure. He ran the bar with the help of his wife, Caroline.

I parked my car and walked up the old front steps of the Hotel. In the lobby was the guest registry and to my left was the dining room with a sign on the door, which read "Open – 6:00 p.m." The bar was to my right. The lights were on and an old juke box was playing softly. I walked through the swinging doors and I felt like I was in a John Wayne western movie. There was a thirty-foot redwood log bar complete with a brass rail and bar stools, but no spittoons. A huge mirror hung on the back wall behind the bar with shelves on both sides filled with all varieties of liquor. The side walls were covered with photographs and autographs of celebrities who had stayed at the Hotel years ago. Behind the bar on the right, was a circular staircase going up to the owner's apartment.

At the left corner of the bar sat two "old timers" drinking beer and talking to the owner, Tony Silva. He was tall and lanky, at least 6'3" with balding gray hair and he weighed a sickly 175- 180 pounds. He was around 60 years old, rough-looking with dark circles under his eyes. His hands were huge, like a pair of meat hooks. From his appearance, he was obviously not well. When he saw me with my briefcase, he probably thought I was a bill collector. He walked to the center of the bar and growled, "Can I help you, stranger?" I asked him if a Margaret Catto was staying at the Hotel. He nodded and pointed to a group of six little cottages that formed a semicircle around the back of the Hotel. He said, "Margaret is in Garden

Cottage #4." He gave me a cold stare and walked back to the old timers at the end of the bar.

It sounded fancy, "Garden Cottage #4," but it wasn't. The "Garden" was overgrown with weeds three-feet-tall and the "Cottage #4" was in dire need of a fresh coat of paint. The front screen door was ragged, with a big hole in it. After the third ring of the doorbell, the door squeaked opened a crack and I heard a brusque female with a New York accent say, "Who are ya? And whaddaya want?"

I took a step back and answered, "My name is Eldon O'Brien, Mrs. Catto; I am an investigator…" Suddenly, the door flew open as she made way for me to enter. "C'mon in! I've been expecting you." That sure caught me by surprise. I didn't call her for an appointment and yet she was expecting me? Weird, but investigators meet a lot of weird people. I walked inside. It was a tidy little cottage. Neat as a pin, Mrs. Catto looked as prim and proper as a school librarian. She wore a pink apron around her waist and the house smelled a fresh batch of cookies in the oven. She was around fifty years old with a clear olive complexion and dark brown hair pulled back in a bun. It was plain to see in her day, she had been a very beautiful woman. But today, a bandage covered her left eyebrow and her left eye was blackened and bruised.

"Have a seat on the couch, Mr. O'Brien. Would you like a cup of coffee?" she asked as she touched the bandage, suddenly conscious of her appearance. "Yes, please." I sat down and started to open my briefcase. She seemed to be a nice, quiet lady and that gruff voice I heard on the porch had disappeared. I only hoped that her version of the pedestrian accident would help us and not the Corvette driver. And, with a little luck, I could return home and watch the rest of the Notre Dame game.

When she returned with the coffee, I started to read the police report to her. She stopped me and said, "Oh, my goodness, I thought you were a Homicide Investigator on the murder I witnessed last Thursday evening. I've been calling the police every day but they haven't called back."

"No, Mrs. Catto, I am an investigator on the pedestrian accident you witnessed Thursday afternoon in San Jose. Your name was on the police report. I represent the mother and her little girl. I was hoping you could help me."

"Oh yes, I remember. I gave my name and address to the police officer just as I was getting on the bus to Irvington. I told the officer I had seen the accident but I had to go because the bus driver was getting impatient and wouldn't wait for me. By the way, how are the mother and little girl?"

"The mother is in intensive care but she is expected to live. Her daughter died on the way to the hospital."

Mrs. Catto gasped and put her hand over her mouth. She looked up at me with tears in her eyes. She said in a subdued voice, "Is there anything I can do to help that poor mother? I know the pain of losing a child. It's horrible."

"Just tell me what you saw Mrs. Catto, and if you don't mind I'll take a few notes to show my boss." I tried not to sound insensitive but this could go on all day. She agreed and I started writing. After about thirty minutes, Mrs. Catto read and signed her statement: It read:

"My name is Margaret Catto. I live at the Monte Carlo Hotel, Garden Cottage #4, Irvington, California. On Thursday, November 6, I was waiting on San Carlos Street in San Jose for the 4:30 p.m. bus to Irvington. Suddenly, I saw a red Corvette run the red light at the San Carlos Street and Second Street intersection, and hit a mother and her daughter who were walking in the crosswalk on the green "WALK" signal. The mother was hit a glancing blow but the little girl rolled up on the windshield of the Corvette. She flew through the air and hit her head on the cement curb. The driver of the Corvette tried to leave the scene but a crowd of people stopped him. I gave my name to the police officer but I had to leave because the bus driver wouldn't wait for me. Signed: *Margaret Catto*"

I thought to myself, bingo! Here is a perfect witness who will help prove our case against the Corvette driver and his insurance company. She will make a great witness if the case ever goes to trial. And with a little luck, Ted Cowan might be able to settle the case on the strength of Margaret Catto's statement alone.

When she finished reading the statement, she signed her name. But when I asked her if she had a permanent address or a close relative or friend who would always know where she could be located, she shook her head. She explained she traveled a great deal since her husband died and she really had no permanent address. Finally, she said that if I really needed her to testify for the mother, the Hotel would always be able to get word to her. I placed the statement in my briefcase and started to leave.

"Now, wait a minute, Mr. O'Brien. I need to tell you about the murder I saw last Thursday evening. You are an investigator and maybe you can help me." I thought about that football game I was missing and reluctantly, I set my briefcase down and listened. Mrs. Cato said, "It was about 5:30 p.m. last Thursday when I got off the bus and walked into the Monte Carlo Hotel Bar. There were about fifteen people having cocktails and waiting for the dining room to open. Tony Silva, the owner, was behind the bar with Caroline, his wife who was also serving the customers. I told Caroline about the awful accident I had just witnessed in San Jose. She poured me a double Scotch on the rocks and the drink helped settle my nerves…a little."

Mrs. Cato went on: "I usually sit at the bar in the evenings and Caroline and I talk. But Thursday evening was different. I noticed Caroline's eyes were red and she had been crying. I asked her if something was wrong and she just glared at Tony at the other end of the bar. It had not been a very successful marriage. Tony was fifty-seven years old when he married Caroline and she was only thirty-one. She was a beautiful girl and Tony was insanely jealous. Then, Tony caught Caroline's glare and came down to our end of the bar in a blind rage swearing, "You rotten whore!" He accused Caroline of sleeping with some life insurance salesman. Tony had been drinking, as usual. Then Caroline threw an empty beer bottle at him and ran up the circular stairway to their apartment. She was crying and said "I am through with you Tony! I want a divorce." The uneasy customers waiting for the dining room to open, left their drinks at the bar and walked out into the lobby...all except the two old timers seated at the far end of the bar."

"Well you're not getting a divorce," Tony screamed as she ran up the circular stairway. He grabbed the shotgun he kept hidden behind the stairs. He took the stairs two at a time as he raced up to their apartment. Within seconds, Mrs. Cato said, she heard two shotgun blasts. Tony slowly came down the stairs, the shotgun still in his hand.

"I was seated at the bar in front of the stairway," continued Mrs. Cato. The two men were still over at the far end of the bar. "Tony looked at me with an icy stare and said, "Caroline has just committed suicide. You had better keep your mouth shut or I'll shut it for you...permanently!"

"You rotten liar! You bastard! You just killed Caroline!" Mrs. Cato was beginning to tremble as she recounted her story. "I started to climb over the bar to get at him when he hit me with the butt of his shotgun. That's how I got this black eye and six stitches on my forehead. I remember screaming for someone to call the police then I guess I blacked out. I came to when the paramedics were carrying Caroline's body down the staircase but then I must have passed out again. The next thing I remember was waking up in the hospital emergency room. A detective from Homicide introduced himself. He said he would interview me in the morning, but he didn't show up on Friday and he hasn't returned my calls today. And that rotten Tony, he is still pouring drinks like nothing ever happened! I just can't understand why the Homicide detective has not contacted me or why Tony hasn't been arrested. I really want to see Tony *die* for killing Caroline!"

As Margaret Catto was telling me this disturbing tale, I noticed an eerie change come over her. No longer was she sweet, calm and polite. She slowly changed into a vengeful, angry person. Her eyes were evil and her voice lowered to a growl as she clenched her teeth and snarled, "I want to be there when Tony Silva gets the electric chair." It sent chills down my spine.

She must have noticed my apprehension because suddenly she regained her composure and returned to the sweet, nice lady I thought I knew. She said, "I would appreciate it if you could help me, Mr. O'Brien." I told her I knew several detectives in Homicide and promised to call her on Monday. I thanked her for the coffee, grabbed my briefcase and ran to my car, turned on the radio and listened to the Notre Dame game. I got home just in time to watch Notre Dame kick the winning field goal. It turned out to be a great day after all! A great witness, a great statement and a great win for Notre Dame!

By 9:30 a.m. on Monday, I had dropped off Mrs. Catto's statement with Ted Cowan's secretary. He was in court, but I knew the statement would make his whole day. Then I was on my way to meet with my old friend, Walter Ward at the courthouse cafeteria. I had learned long ago that more law was practiced over a cup of coffee in the courthouse cafeteria than in all the courtrooms combined. The place was packed. Walter was waiting in his corner booth reading the morning paper.

I told him about Margaret Catto and the "murder" at the Monte Carlo Hotel. Walter listened intently then said, "If there were two shots fired, it wasn't a suicide. But Mrs. Catto didn't actually witness the killing, did she? She just heard the two shotgun blasts...correct? And let's not forget the two "old-timers" at the far end of the bar. Did they hear the gunshots? What did they do?" Walter said there must be a good reason why the homicide detective to not contact Mrs. Catto. He said he would pay a call on his old friend Pat Cassidy, the head of the Homicide Division in Santa Clara County. He said he would see me tomorrow for breakfast and he would hopefully have some answers.

I called Margaret Catto at her Cottage and told her I talked with my friend and would have some answers for her tomorrow morning. She wasn't at all happy with my message. I thought I heard the evil voice that scared me on Saturday, but it was probably just my imagination. Anyway, she was in a hurry getting dressed to go to Caroline's funeral and said she was sorry for being so curt with me on Saturday. It seemed clear to me she had a valid reason to be upset. Nevertheless, I had a strange feeling Mrs. Catto was a woman to be feared. She was intent on sending Tony Silva to death row for killing Caroline.

The next day, I walked into the cafeteria and there was Walter sitting in his corner booth, reading the paper as usual. He handed me the morning paper and pointed to a small headline in the second section that read:

"HOTEL OWNER'S WIFE DIES:
APPARENT SUICIDE"

"On Thursday evening, Caroline Silva, the 34-year-old wife of Tony Silva, owner of the historic Monte Carlo Hotel in Irvington, apparently committed suicide in their apartment at the Hotel. Silva told police that his wife had been suffering from severe depression for several months and was under a doctor's care. The funeral was held yesterday at Calvary Cemetery in San Jose."

Walter said, "I had a long talk with Pat Cassidy yesterday. All I am at liberty to tell you Eldon is to *stay away* from the Monte Carlo Hotel and Margaret Catto. Do you understand? Do nothing further on this case." It didn't make any sense to me. It seemed like the wheels of justice had just come to a complete stop and the killer, Tony Silva was as free as a bird. I guessed I would have to trust Walter on this one, but it still made me mad. We finished our coffee. Walter went upstairs to check on a trial and I left to see the investigating officer on Ted Cowan's pedestrian/death case.

On the way out of the Cafeteria, I ran into my old friend, Johnny Blocker. He was a retired Naval Intelligence Officer and was now Chief Investigator of the Narcotics Division in Santa Clara County. He was sharp and it was apparent he wanted to talk to me. We sat down and I ordered a second cup of coffee. I almost spilled my coffee when he began the conversation with, "Eldon, I understand you are working on a murder at the Monte Carlo Hotel." I remembered what Walter Ward had told me about keeping my mouth shut. I just told him I was working a pedestrian death case and a witness lived at the Hotel. I said I had read something in the newspaper about the suicide at the Hotel and we let the matter drop.

As he was leaving he said, "Just be very careful, Eldon. Do me a favor - stay away from the Monte Carlo for the next week or so." Now it was becoming clear to me, Caroline's death had something to do with the Narcotics Division and I was getting in the way of their investigation. Just then, I remembered I promised Margaret I would call her this morning with an update. However, since Walter Ward and now Johnny Blocker had warned me to stay away, I didn't call her. I knew she would be mad and my gut told me she was not someone I would *not* want to see mad.

The following day, I met Walter at the courthouse cafeteria again. As usual, he was seated in his corner booth, but this time he was not alone. Pat Cassidy, Chief of the Homicide Division, was with him. They were deep in conversation and they only nodded as I sat down. No introductions were needed. I had followed Pat's career as a star quarterback at Stanford University and after his graduation he joined the Homicide Division in Santa Clara County. He became one of their top investigators and two years ago took over the Division. Pat had the reputation of being a very hard worker and true to his word. I waited. Finally, Pat turned to me and said, "I had a meeting with Judge James yesterday afternoon and he wanted me to tell you what all this secrecy is about, because you have a right to know. So here goes:

"On the night Caroline Silva was murdered, your star witness, Margaret Catto, was seated at the bar drinking a double scotch on the rocks. We received this information from two of my men, Terry Wilson and Sal Russo. They two 'old timers" who were seated at the far end of the bar and they heard the two gunshots also. They saw Tony Silva come down the stairs and hit Mrs. Catto with the shotgun. Mrs. Catto was taken by ambulance to the hospital." Pat continued, "On a hunch, Terry Wilson picked up Mrs. Catto's highball glass and had her fingerprints run. When the results came back we learned your star witness Margaret Catto was, in fact, a wanted killer named Margo Santinni. She is without a doubt the most feared 'contract killer' in the mafia organization. She works strictly for the Godfather in Chicago. She is a master of disguise – only a handful of men in the mafia can identify her. She speaks five different languages and plans her murders with absolute precision. She has been the prime suspect in at least seven high-profile killings in the last five years. To date, she has never been convicted of any of these murders.

"Somehow, the mafia learned we were setting up a sting operation to shut down the laundry of drug money Tony Silva was running from the bar at the Monte Carlo Hotel. They must have known Tony was cooperating and allowing us to install cameras and microphones in the bar to catch the 'runners' who brought the mafia money to him for 'laundering.' It would explain why Margo Santinni was there. She must have had a contract on Silva's life and for the first time, we had a chance to catch her in the act of a contract killing. This is why we cautioned you to stay away from her and the Hotel. Not only would you be in extreme danger but our whole sting operation could have been compromised."

Chief Cassidy went on, "We spent all last month setting it up the sting. We installed cameras and tape recorders in the bar and so far we have identified sixteen 'runners' for the mafia who have delivered money to Tony Silva. With the murder of Caroline and the identification of Margo Santinni, we put together a team to watch Margo 24/7. This Saturday, our men will arrest all the mafia members operating the laundry, and simultaneously we'll arrest Tony for the murder of Caroline."

"Now let me bring you up to date on what we are doing right now," continued Pat. "As we speak, two of my men, Frank Rossi and Terry Wilson, are at the Hotel Bar. They pose as regulars; they play cards, read newspapers and argue with Tony Silva. Their real job is to identify the 'runners' who come into the bar. In addition, I have a man in Cottage #3 watching every move Margo Santinni makes."

Just then a waitress came over and told Pat he had a phone call. He excused himself and when he returned he said, "Frank Rossi has been shot and Tony Silva has been killed. You guys want to come along for a ride to the Hotel?" Walter and I agreed but said we would follow in my car.

As we drove up to the Hotel, there was a crowd of people gathering and police cars were all over the place. Two paramedics were loading Frank Rossi into an ambulance. Terry Wilson, visibly shaken, came up to us and said, "Frank has lost a lot of blood. He's unconscious. I hope he makes it." We watched as the ambulance drove away. Pat Cassidy introduced Terry Wilson to us and we sat down at a booth in the empty dining room. "Now, Terry, tell us exactly what happened."

Terry's hands were shaking. Finally, he looked at Pat and said, "Well, Boss, I was a little late coming to work this morning. My car had a dead battery and I had to call a tow truck. It was about 9:20 a.m. when I finally drove into the parking lot. I walked up the front stairs. The bar was empty. I figured Frank was in the back room setting up the cameras and Tony was in the storeroom getting some booze for the bar. I hollered for Frank but there was no answer. I looked over to the end of the bar where we always sit and saw Frank lying on the floor in a pool of blood. I was sure he was dead. Then I looked behind the bar near the cash register and saw Tony on the floor, dead. The whole back of his head was gone. His skull was blown clear off."

Pat asked Terry if there was anyone else in the bar. He shook his head, "No sir, the lights were all on, but the place was empty. Oh, there was a cleaning lady leaving the bar just as I came in. She was pushing one of those cleaning carts through the swinging doors when she bumped into me. I remember, she looked at me and said, 'Sorry Mister, the bar is closed,' and she left. I didn't recognize her. She must have been a new hire because Frank and I know most of the workers here by name."

Pat asked, "Do you think you would recognize this cleaning lady if you saw her again? Sure, she must be around here somewhere."

"She was about 5'1" and had a red bandana covering her forehead," answered Terry. "She wasn't young, maybe in her early fifties. She was wearing the usual blue maid's uniform and pushing a cleaning cart." Pat ordered one of his men to bring in all of the cleaning staff for questioning.

While we were waiting, it dawned on Walter Ward that maybe Frank Rossi had already turned on the cameras before he was shot. He may have captured the whole murder scene on film. Terry grabbed the cameras from the back bar and we found a blank wall in the dining room to serve as a screen to view the films. He set the cameras up and we turned out the lights. In silent anticipation, we waited for the film to hopefully answer the questions: Who killed Tony Silva? Who Shot Frank Rossi? Who was this mysterious cleaning lady?

Camera #1 showed Frank Rossi reading the newspaper and we could see the back of Tony Silva's head as he was stocking whiskey on the back bar. The second camera caught the cleaning lady as she pushed her cart through the swinging doors. She pushed her cart up to the bar where Tony was working. The tape recording was not clear but it sounded like Tony said, "You're late!" Then, without warning, the cleaning lady reached into a large handbag on her cart. She pulled out a gun and fired at Tony who was hit in the shoulder. As he fell, she reached over the bar and fired again. That bullet hit him in the back of the head. We then saw Frank reaching for his gun but it was too late. The cleaning lady turned and fired, hitting Frank in the chest. She calmly placed the pistol back in her handbag and slowly pushed the cart out the swinging doors. It was then that she bumped into Terry as he was entering the bar. Suddenly, it was all over. Tony was dead. Frank was shot in the chest and the mysterious cleaning lady was gone.

Pat said, "OK, we now know our murderer was the cleaning lady. But who is she? She is obviously a pro. Did you see how she turned and fired at Frank and calmly left the bar?" We all wondered who she was. We played the tape back a second time but it was of no help. Suddenly, it dawned on me. I saw something on the film that rang a bell. I told Terry to run the film back to where the cleaning lady was reaching over the bar and fired her second shot. Pat and Walter both looked at me, confused. Terry rolled the film back anyway. "There it is!" I shouted. "Stop the film! Look at that bandage over the cleaning lady's left eye. If you look closely you will see that her left eye is black. I'll bet you a hundred bucks our mysterious cleaning lady is my star witness, Margaret Catto, also known as your infamous Margo Santinni! She must have known Tony Silva would be alone in the bar but she didn't count on Frank Rossi witnessing the murder."

We entered Cottage # 3 and asked the undercover officer if Margo Santinni was still in her apartment. "Yes, only a cleaning lady has entered and left the cottage. It was about a half-hour ago." We raced out the back door and over to Cottage #4. The front door was open. On the floor, half naked, lay the real cleaning lady. Her hands were tied behind her. She had a rag stuffed in her mouth and appeared to have been hit with a heavy object and was unconscious. Pat called for an ambulance and ordered his fingerprint team to come down to Margo's cottage and confirm it was actually Margo Santinni aka Margaret Catto who occupied Garden Cottage #4. If so, this would prove she also acted as the cleaning woman who murdered Tony Silva.

It didn't take a rocket scientist to figure out our mysterious cleaning lady was my prize witness, Mrs. Margaret Catto, aka "Margo Santinni." An APB was sent out and the Highway Patrol was alerted to stop all cars with anyone fitting her description. Time was of the essence, and with a little luck, we would apprehend her before she could make a clean getaway.

Pat was totally involved with his men, so Walter and I excused ourselves and headed back to town. I dropped Walter at his office and then I remembered I had a lunch date with Ted Cowan to discuss the pedestrian case. I decided not to tell Ted about Margaret Catto, being investigated for murder. Why ruin his whole day?

When I entered his office, Ted was on the phone with the Claims Manager for the insurance company on our pedestrian case. He was bragging about his eyewitness who clearly placed all the blame on their Corvette driver. He read Mrs. Catto's statement to him over the phone and agreed to mail him a copy. I sat there praying the statement would satisfy the Claims Manager and he would not send an adjuster out to the Hotel and discover all the chaos unfolding there. Ted hung up the phone. He rubbed his hands together and said he thought the case was settled. The check and releases would be in the mail within a week.

Ted laid the Catto statement on his desk and asked me why Mrs. Catto had not given me a permanent address. If the settlement negations fell through, we would need to know how to contact her to testify at trial. I told Ted that Mrs. Catto said the Monte Carlo Hotel would always know how to contact her.

Suddenly, bells started ringing in my thick head. Somewhere in the Hotel's records must be an address or a phone number or something that would lead us to our mysterious cleaning lady, Mrs. Margaret Catto, aka Margo Santinni. I lied when I told Ted I had to rush to a lunch date. Instead, I raced to the elevator and grabbed a payphone. I called Pat Cassidy and told him to have one of his men look in all the phone records at the Hotel and in Caroline's apartment. There had to be an address or phone number for Margaret Catto/Margo Santinni because she told me the Hotel would always have a way to contact her. Pat agreed to get on it right away. It was a long shot but one worth taking.

Thursday, I met Walter for breakfast. He was seated at his booth at the rear of the restaurant. As usual, he was reading the morning paper. Suddenly, the front door opened and there stood Pat Cassidy with a big Irish grin on his face. He said, "Gentlemen, I have some amazing news for you and it's not *just* that I'm buying breakfast!" He took a seat, leaned back in his chair and said, "First of all, let me tell you my fingerprint team picked up several good prints of Margo Santinni in the cottage, on the cleaning cart and they were identical to the ones found on the cocktail glass and on the bar. This is the first time Margo

Santinni has ever left her fingerprints at the scene of a crime, she always wears gloves. She's either getting sloppy or for some reason, this was a very emotional killing for her and she got careless."

Pat said, "Remember when Terry stopped the film as the cleaning lady was leaning over the bar and shot Tony Silva the second time? We had the film enlarged and we could see Margo was left-handed and she left a perfect right hand print on the bar. That print will clearly prove Margo Santinni was actually the cleaning lady who killed Tony Silva."

Pat took a long sip of his coffee and continued. "There's more. One of my men was looking through an old card file in Caroline's apartment. He found a registration card for 'Margie.' On the back of the card was a series of numbers. At first, it looked like a Social Security Number: 5632065387, but there were too many numbers. Then it dawned on us it could possibly be a phone number. The 563 is the area code for Davenport, Iowa and the 206-5387 could be the phone number for "Margie" Catto (aka) Margo Santinni. I called the Chief of Police in Davenport, Iowa and warned him Margo Santinni could be in his neighborhood. He knew of Margo Santinni's reputation and her possible connection with the mafia. He promised his full cooperation. I told him she could be recognized by a bandage and cut over her left eyebrow, and a black left eye. He called the telephone company and learned the phone number 206-5387 belonged to a Mrs. Dorothy Grant who lived at 5668 North Wilmington Road in Davenport. I told the Chief it was possible Margo Santinni/Margaret Catto could be at that address possibly visiting her daughter or a close friend, over the Thanksgiving Holidays.

"The Chief and I hatched a little scheme. He had one of his best detectives dress as a United Parcel deliveryman. He borrowed a company truck and drove out to the 5668 North Wilmington address with a large package to deliver. He rang the doorbell and waited. The door opened and a refined lady about fifty years old with a slight New York accent said, "Is that package for me young man?"

"Are you Mrs. Dorothy Grant?

The nice lady with the New York accent said, "No, but I'm her mother and I can accept the package for her."

When she leaned over to sign the delivery sheet, the officer noticed a bandage over her left eye and her left eye was black. That did it. He radioed for a squad car to pick them up. She was arrested and booked for the murder of Tony Silva and held without bail. She said her name was Margaret Catto; however her fingerprints matched those of Margo Santinni. She is being extradited from Davenport, Iowa to Santa Clara and will be held for the murder of Tony Silva.

End of story? Well…not quite.

At Margo Santinni's murder trial the criminal teams were assigned to Judge Colla's courtroom. He was known to be a liberal judge and would allow almost all evidence to go to the jury. However, he drew the line when it came to admitting any evidence of Margo Santinni's possible connection with the mafia. He ruled it was prejudicial and without proper foundation because Margo Santinni had no criminal convictions. Even though she was a prime suspect in seven prior murders, all of them resulted in defense verdicts.

The prosecution offered the film of the cleaning woman with a bandage over her left eye when she shot and killed Tony Silva. The Santinni fingerprints found on the cleaning cart in the cottage matched her right hand print on the bar when she leaned over and shot Tony Silva.

Frank Rossi survived the gunshot to his chest and testified he saw the cleaning woman kill Tony Silva. When the defense attorney took Frank on cross-examination, Frank had to admit he could not positively identify the prim, well-dressed woman with the New York accent seated at the defendant's table, as the cleaning lady he saw kill Tony Silva. Terry Wilson had the same problem. The defendant seated in the courtroom appeared to be much older than the fifty-three year-old Margo Santinni. Also, this defendant walked with a limp and had grey hair.

The maid's clothing was found at a Greyhound Bus Depot near the San Francisco Airport, thus proving, hopefully, that Margo had taken a Greyhound bus to the airport and changed clothes before boarding a plane under an assumed name, to Iowa. The maid from the hotel was never called as a witness because she suffered a fractured skull and had no memory of the incident at all.

Walter and I thought the prosecution had more than enough evidence to convict Margo Santinni of the murder of Tony Silva. The most convincing evidence was the handprint Margo left on the bar as she fired the fatal shot. Walter Ward and I sat through the entire trial and when the prosecution rested its case, we thought it was a "slam dunk" conviction. At last, we believed, the infamous Margo Santinni would be behind bars for the rest of her life.

Sal Romero, the defense lawyer, called as his first witness, defendant Margo Santinni (AKA) Margaret Catto. She looked like everyone's grandmother. Throughout the trial, she sat quietly with her hands folded in her lap and an innocent look on her face. She walked with a slight limp and she appeared to be at least seventy years old. Her hair was grey and she wore glasses. During the recess, she would sit out in the hall quietly knitting a shawl. She wore the same plain gingham dress every day. The scab over her left eye was carefully covered with makeup. Her answers were sincere and she steadfastly maintained that her name was Margaret Catto. She admitted her maiden name was Margaret Santinni and some of her friends did call her Margo. But her married name was Margaret Catto. She denied any connection with the mafia or organized crime. She cried as she told how Tony Silva hit her with the shotgun and she had to be taken to the hospital for stitches. She said she was at the bar when she heard the shotgun blasts. She was so emotionally upset, she attended Caroline's funeral and then decided to visit her daughter, Dorothy Grant in Davenport, Iowa.

However, on the day Tony Silva was murdered, she was not in the Monte Carlo Hotel. She testified she was terrified of flying and hated trains. She bought a Greyhound bus ticket that proved she left the Monte Carlo Hotel right after the funeral on Monday afternoon and arrived in Davenport, Iowa on Tuesday evening. Her arrival in Davenport two days before the murder was confirmed by her daughter, Dorothy Grant, who testified she picked her up at the bus terminal on Tuesday evening.

A fingerprint expert testified for the defense that the fingerprints on the bar could have been old prints left by Margo who admitted she sat at the bar almost every evening talking to Caroline Silva.

In his closing argument, the prosecutor was between a rock and a hard place. In those days, Greyhound Bus tickets could be purchased by anyone and a person could travel anywhere in the United States without providing any identification. The prosecution was unable to prove Margo Santinni aka Margaret Catto only purchased the bus ticket as an alibi. The fingerprints on the bar did not lie. But the tape clearly showed Margo Santinni/ Margaret Catto leaning over the bar and killing Tony Silva. Additionally, the time stamp on the Greyhound bus ticket was just a clever alibi used to cover up the heartless murder.

In the defense closing, Sal Romero said the time stamp on the bus ticket proved without question that his client was in Davenport, Iowa when the killing occurred and it was only by coincidence that both the cleaning lady and his client had bandages over their left eyes.

It all depended on who the jury believed: the prosecution argued the film proved it was Margo Santinni, leaning over the bar and leaving her right hand print, then killing Tony Silva; or the jury could believe the defense whose fingerprint expert testified it was an old print of Margo's and the Greyhound bus ticket was valid. Despite the conflicting evidence, how could the jury convict this kind, refined, seventy year-old woman of a murder, committed by a much younger cleaning lady, when she was in Davenport, Iowa visiting her daughter?

After three weeks of trial and four days in jury deliberation, the verdict came in for the defense: NOT GUILTY. After the verdict was read, Walter and I cornered several of the jurors as they were leaving the courtroom. Their answer was simple: "Margaret Catto was such a nice and sincere person. There is no way she could have killed Tony Silva. She was in Davenport, Iowa when the murder was committed. The cleaning lady on the film was someone else, much younger. The true killer was probably an assassin hired by the mafia to kill Tony Silva. The fingerprints were probably old prints left by Margo when she talked to her daughter Caroline every evening." Reasonable doubt at its finest.

I was standing in the courthouse hallway with Walter Ward when Margo Santinni walked past us. The courtroom was empty. I shall never forget the look on her face when she recognized me. Her eyes narrowed, she gritted her teeth and never took her eyes off of me. She didn't smile or say a word. It was an evil all-knowing look that will haunt me for the rest of my life. I was speechless. As she walked past us, she slowed, leaned in to shake my hand and whispered, "Eldon, Caroline was my daughter."

As she continued down the hallway to the elevator, I noticed her limp was gone. In fact, she had a spring in her step and I watched as she tossed her gray-haired wig and her half-knitted shawl into a trash can. She smiled at me as she entered the elevator and waved as the door closed…

Walter watched the whole scene. We walked to Nick's Bar across the street from the courthouse in silence and ordered a beer. Finally, Walter looked at me and said, "Eldon, I think you just shook hands with Satan."

The Case that Refused to Die
(Part One…San Jose)

It was in the spring of 1965, when an old friend of the family, Pat Concannon called me at home with a problem. He was one of my Dad's best friends and he had just been promoted to Senior Vice President of Almaden Vineyards. His foreman, Conrad Snyder, had a son Stephen, who had been in a terrible accident and was paralyzed from the neck down. Pat said the insurance company admitted their insured ran a stop sign and hit the Snyder boy. They sent a "Release of All Claims" form and a check for $15,000 to the Snyders, claiming that was their policy limits. Pat wanted me to determine if the true policy limit was $15,000 per person and to do an asset check on the owners of the car that hit Stephen Snyder. I agreed to take the case and report my findings to Almaden Vineyard's lawyer, Ted Rankin who would review my Investigation and be in a position to determine if the "Release of All Claims" should be signed and the check cashed.

My first stop was the California Highway Patrol Office where I purchased a copy of the report on this accident. The investigating officer cited the driver of the other car, Ralph Carlson, age 16, with a drunken driving violation. The report listed his father Richard Carlson as the registered owner of the 1963 Chevrolet Impala. Three passengers in the Impala were listed as witnesses on the report. It appeared to be a simple financial investigation to determine if the Carlson's had any other assets beyond the $15,000 insurance policy. The amount had to be verified because the medical bills for Stephen were already over $75,000.

The facts of the accident were fairly simple, Pat told me Stephen had gone to a movie with his girlfriend and he was returning home in his father's 1961 Volkswagen Beetle. He was southbound on the Old Almaden Road. The Carlson boy and his three high school passengers had been drinking at a graduation party. Ralph Carlson was driving westbound on Third Street in Campbell when he failed to stop at the stop sign at Almaden Road. His Impala hit the Volkswagen broadside and Stephen Snyder was thrown out the right front door of the car. Stephen and Ralph were taken to the Santa Clara County Hospital by the Campbell Ambulance Company. Ralph had a broken left arm and Stephen was unconscious.

My second stop was to drive by the Carlson home in Campbell. It was a rundown old house in a bad part of town. A model "A" Ford was parked on the front yard grass. I learned from a neighbor that the Carlson's rented the home and Richard Carlson was a mechanic at the Raines Chevrolet Dealership in Sunnyvale. Then I took a gamble that only works about 10% of the time. I rang the Carlson doorbell. I didn't say I was from their insurance company when Mrs. Carlson opened the door. I simply told her I had to check her automobile policy because there may have been an error in the policy number. It was a wild story but it worked. She went into the den and came back with her auto policy. The policy limit was $15,000. I wrote down the policy number, thanked her and left before she had a chance to ask my name or whom I represented.

The patrol report showed the Impala had been taken to a tow yard in Campbell. I decided to physically inspect the car for bad brakes as it would explain why Ralph Carlson was unable to stop at the stop sign. This could be important because there were no skid marks mentioned in the patrol report prior to impact. I checked the brake pedal - it worked properly and the car had plenty of brake fluid. Therefore, no service station or car dealership could be held responsible for causing this accident.

Back at my office, I called a "friend" of mine at the Credit Bureau and learned the Carlson's were overdue on payments at several department stores and their MasterCard and Visa Cards had been cancelled. I stopped by the County Assessor's office to see if the Carlson's owned any real property but they owned nothing. It was becoming quite clear the Carlson's had no assets beyond the $15,000 insurance policy.

The next morning, I met Walter Ward for breakfast. He suggested we drive out to the scene of the accident to see if maybe the stop sign had been knocked down in a prior accident or possibly obscured by tree branches or even bad street lighting. Then the City of Campbell could be held responsible for this accident. On the way to the scene Walter said sometimes the owner of the property on the corner will allow plants, hedges and even trees to grow and make it impossible to see the stop sign or approaching vehicles at the intersection. Then it is called a "blind intersection" with the property owner and the City responsible for causing the dangerous condition to exist. Walter and I checked the scene for any possible reason for this accident occurring and came to one conclusion: Ralph Carlson was a drunk driver who failed to stop at the stop sign and he was the only one responsible for causing this accident.

The next morning, I took my report to Ted Rankin and recommended the Release of All Claims be signed and the $15,000 check cashed. Ted agreed and the matter was closed (and my bill was paid). The Snyders signed the Release of All Claims and were given the $15,000 check. Case closed.

End of story? Well, not quite, but I must confess, I have a hard time believing what happened but the following facts are absolutely true. So, here goes...

It was on my birthday, November 13, 1965 and we had our family and friends over for a birthday party. We went to bed about 11:30 p.m. Now, for no explicable reason (other than I had to go to the bathroom), I awoke at 4:30 a.m. and I couldn't get back to sleep. All I could think of was the Stephen Snyder case and it had been closed for over five months! But there was a nagging voice inside me saying, "You idiot, you closed the Snyder file without ever looking into what caused Stephen's injury. Was it caused by the automobile accident or was it caused by something or someone after the accident? Maybe the spinal cord was injured in the ambulance or at the hospital. You dummy, you closed the file without ever even talking to Stephen or his parents!" I sat bolt upright in bed and woke Cathy. I told her I had to take a shower and go into the office and reopen the Snyder file. She thought I was crazy and went back to sleep.

It was 6:00 a.m. when I opened my office and found the Snyder file. On the cover of the file I made notes of the investigation to help me answer all the questions swirling around in my head. I was painfully aware no one was going to pay me for this investigation...I simply owed it to Stephen. On the file, I wrote what had to be done:

(1) *Talk to the paramedics at Campbell Ambulance Company who took Stephen to the County Hospital. Was Stephen quadriplegic when they picked him up at the scene of the accident or did something occur on the way to the hospital or at the hospital?*

(2) *Talk to the Emergency Room doctor and nurses at the hospital to see if Stephen was quadriplegic when he was admitted to the emergency room or did something happen after Stephen was in the emergency room?*

    (3) Why was Stephen not admitted to the County Hospital but transferred to San Jose Community Hospital?

    (4) See Walter Ward and get his opinion on what I had found, if anything, and how to proceed.

    My first stop was the Campbell Ambulance Company. I told the girl at the front desk I wanted to see if their bill had been paid; and I needed to talk to the paramedics who took Stephen to the hospital. She gave me a copy of their unpaid bill and I promised to send it to the Snyders' insurance company for payment. When I asked her about the paramedics, she said Ray Adams and Johnny Peal had both been fired right after the Snyder pickup and delivery to the hospital. I asked her why. She looked around the empty office and then whispered to me, "Because they picked up this Snyder kid, who had an obvious neck injury and they failed to "sand bag" both sides of his neck as required by emergency medical response rules. The boss got real mad and fired both of them." All of a sudden we had a valid defendant who failed to "sand bag" Stephen's neck, likely resulting in the damage to his spinal cord.

    My next stop was the Emergency Room of the Santa Clara County Hospital. Walter Ward had told me that if you need information at a hospital, anyone can look like a doctor provided you wear a white coat and hold a clipboard! It was busy when I arrived so it was not hard for me to poke around unnoticed and find the men's locker room. I took off my coat, found an empty clipboard and a white coat. Then I walked up to the nurse behind the admitting desk in the emergency room. She presumed I was a doctor because when I asked for the Stephen Snyder medical records, she opened the file drawer and handed me the file. Just as I opened the file, the Head Nurse came up behind me and asked who I was and why was I reading a confidential file? I gave her the same answer I gave the girl at the Ambulance Company - that I was checking to see if the bill had been paid - but it didn't work. The hospital bill had been paid. She grabbed the file and showed me the door.

Out in the hospital corridor, I wrote down the two names I saw on the admitting sheet. The doctor's name was Richard Thompson and the other name was Patricia Walker. Just then, I noticed a nurse getting a drink of water at the drinking fountain. I casually asked her if she knew if Patricia Walker was on duty. She said, "Pat doesn't work in Emergency any more. She is on maternity leave but she lives right down Race Street just a few blocks from here." I thanked the nurse and walked down the hall to a payphone where I called my "friend" at the Credit Bureau. He found a Patricia Walker at 221 Race Street. This was turning out to be my lucky day!

I rang the doorbell and Patricia Walker answered the door. She was a pretty red-haired young woman about 24-25 years old and almost six feet tall. She appeared to be at least eight months pregnant, if not more. She smiled when I gave her my card and said I represented Stephen Snyder, a young boy who was brought into Emergency with a severe cervical injury about five months ago. To my great surprise, she said she remembered the young boy with the spinal cord injury and said she hoped someone would be contacting her about this accident. She invited me into her living room and offered me a cup of coffee. Patricia Walker was married with two small girls both in grade school. Her husband worked for the Gas Company and he was being transferred to the Redding office at the end of the month. Patricia said she and her husband were both born and raised in Redding and the move would be just like going home. It went through my mind, as I was listening to her, that she would make a perfect witness. She was intelligent, pleasant, articulate and confident, and she answered my questions with precision.

Patricia Walker told me Dr. Richard Thompson was the Intern on duty in the Emergency Room when the paramedics came in with Stephen Snyder. He was conscious and appeared

144 In The Shoes of an Investigator: The True Life Adventures of a Private Eye

to have a serious spinal cord injury. She remarked to one of the paramedics, Stephen was brought into the emergency room on a stretcher but without sand bags to protect his head from rolling from side to side. The paramedic said Stephen was able to move his arms and legs when he was placed on the stretcher so there was no need to sand bag him. The paramedics signed the delivery sheet and left.

Patricia said Dr. Thompson ordered X-Rays to confirm the spinal cord injury and then placed Crutchfield Tongs ("surgical ice picks") in Stephen's skull to immobilize the fracture and protect the spinal cord from any further damage. Then he called Dr. Phillip Palmer, the Neurosurgeon on call, to report the injury and need for immediate surgery. He was able to locate Dr. Palmer at the San Jose Country Club where he was attending a wedding reception. It was close to midnight and it was obvious he had been drinking heavily. Dr. Palmer told Dr. Thompson to find out if Stephen' had any insurance to cover the medical bills. Dr. Thompson found a Hartford Insurance card in Stephen's wallet. Then, Dr. Palmer ordered Dr. Thompson to have an ambulance pick Stephen up at 5:00 a.m. and transfer him to San Jose Community Hospital for surgery. Dr. Thompson slammed down the phone and grumbled Dr. Palmer was in no condition to operate. He also said that by transferring Stephen to San Jose Community Hospital, Dr. Palmer could bill Hartford for the surgery whereas if he operated at the County Hospital he could only collect his monthly retainer.

At about 2:00 a.m., Stephen took a turn for the worse. His breathing was labored and his pulse rate was 135 and climbing. Nurse Walker found a phone number in Stephen's wallet and she called his parents and told them to come to the Emergency Room immediately. She also called the resident Catholic priest who would give Stephen Last Rites. Conrad and his wife, Mary, arrived when the priest was at Stephen's bedside. Patricia, who was also Catholic, remembered Stephen awoke when the priest was praying over him. Stephen smiled and made the sign of the cross with his right hand and Patricia noticed his toes wiggle under the sheet. To Dr. Thompson and Nurse Walker, the fact that Stephen could move his arms and toes gave a strong indication the Crutchfield Tongs were holding the fracture in place and the spinal cord was not severed.

At 5:00 a.m., the ambulance arrived to take Stephen to San Jose Community Hospital. They moved him from the hospital bed onto their ambulance gurney (Crutchfield Tongs and all) and the paramedics started down the long hallway to the awaiting ambulance. Nurse Walker, Dr. Thompson and Stephen's parents followed. When the gurney was about halfway down the hallway, Stephen slipped off the gurney, the Crutchfield Tongs came out and he fell onto the concrete floor. He went limp and lost consciousness when his head hit the floor. Mary cried, Conrad swore and Dr. Thompson knelt at Stephen's side holding Stephen's head and shoulders in his arms. Patricia said she noticed the ambulance attendants had failed to strap Stephen onto their gurney. Stephen was loaded (again) onto the gurney and wheeled to the ambulance for the trip to the San Jose Hospital.

Dr. Thompson went directly to his office and typed up a report of the entire incident exactly as it happened. He included in his report that Campbell Ambulance delivered Stephen Snyder to the emergency room without sand bags to stabilize his head and they failed to properly strap Stephen onto their gurney. He included in his report Dr. Palmer's intoxication and refusal to treat Stephen at the County Hospital when the hospital had three operating rooms available for immediate surgery. Dr. Thompson and Patricia Walker both signed the report. Dr. Thompson sent the original to the hospital Administrator and wisely kept a copy for himself and he gave a copy to Patricia Walker.

Suddenly, we had at least four defendants (Dr. Palmer, Campbell Ambulance, San Jose Ambulance and Santa Clara County Hospital) who were possibly responsible for Stephen's quadriplegia. The Snyders had to be informed of this because by now their medical bills were over $150,000. I called Ted Rankin and told him how the case had exploded into a major malpractice/ negligence case with four potential defendants. Ted was in a bind though, and told me his firm could not handle the case because the Santa Clara Country Hospital was one of their clients.

Then it dawned on my thick head: Here I had found the Magic Key to the bank for the Snyder family but they had no attorney to represent them and no one to pay me for my investigation. I met Walter Ward for breakfast and told him my problem. He recommended an attorney named Martin Wortel as the best man in the entire state for this malpractice case. Martin had written several books on the handling of medical malpractice cases and he had his offices in Los Angeles. Walter was a close friend of Martin so Walter called him and he said he would fly to San Jose and meet with the Snyders, provided the Snyders called him and asked for his help.

My Adventures in Los Angeles

The Case That Refused to Die

(Part Two...Los Angeles)

Martin Wortel met with the Snyder family and agreed to take their case. My job was to find and interview Dr. Richard Thompson who had finished his Internship and, according to Patricia Walker, was practicing medicine "somewhere" in Arizona with his father. A phone call to the Arizona Medical Board gave me an address in a small suburb of Phoenix called Anderson, Arizona.

A second phone call and I had Dr. Thompson on the line. I asked him if he remembered the Snyder boy who came into the Santa Clara Emergency Room about a year ago. His answer was almost the same as Nurse Walker's: "I've been waiting for someone to contact me." He confirmed everything Walker told me and said he would be glad to talk to us anytime.

John Dale, Martin's partner, and I flew to Phoenix in the company plane on a Friday afternoon. We had a late lunch with Dr. Thompson while he told us how concerned he was for Stephen who, at only 19 years old, was a complete quadriplegic. He made us a copy of the report he had given to the Hospital Administrator. He also told us of the conversation he had with the Administrator who demanded he tear up the report because, "it could be damaging to the hospital." We flew home that evening with all the evidence we needed to support a huge verdict for Stephen Snyder.

After we filed suit in Santa Clara County, we made a discovery motion to obtain the report Dr. Thompson made to the hospital but the hospital denied it ever existed. The Campbell Ambulance Company claimed Steven was properly sand-bagged but what they didn't know was I had a statement from Ralph Carlson (the driver of the Impala) who rode in the ambulance with Steven to the hospital. He would testify no sand bags were ever used.

The two paramedics from the San Jose Ambulance Company claimed Stephen was properly belted onto the gurney and "he just slipped through the binding" but we had the depositions of Dr. Thompson and Nurse Walker who would testify Stephen was not belted to the gurney. The months flew by and soon we were set for trial on November 2, 1967.

But first I must tell you the defendants objected to the suit being filed on grounds that it was not filed within 100-day statute of limitations as required by law. But Martin argued that the 100 days should not start running until the malpractice was discovered, not when the injury occurred. My deposition was taken on the discovery of the malpractice.

The Appellate Court sustained Martin's position and allowed the case to go to trial. We had Dr. Thompson and Patricia Walker standing by and ready to testify. The defense team never took either of their depositions. When they demanded we provide addresses for Thompson and Walker, we gave the hospital address for Dr. Thompson and the Race Street address for Nurse Walker and evidently they didn't find them. I wonder if they even tried. They were relying on the paramedics and the Hospital Administrator for their defense.

On November 1, 1967, John and I flew up to San Jose and checked into a motel. We met with Stephen and his parents at their home. When John and I entered the home there was Stephen sitting in his wheelchair with an adding machine placed on a sheet of plywood across his lap. He was holding a pencil in his clenched teeth and poking the numerals on the adding machine! He said he graduated with his class at Campbell High School and was enrolled in an Accounting class at San Jose

State. He said he was getting good grades and planned to be an accountant.

John told the Snyders he would try the case because Martin was in a Federal Court trial, and actually John had taken the majority of the depositions in this case. John said it would not be necessary for Stephen to be present tomorrow because the day would be taken up with a Settlement Conference and jury selection.

The next day we were assigned to Judge James' courtroom on the third floor. His Clerk once told me, "God may be in Heaven but Judge James is in Department Three." He was tough but fair. John asked for a conference with the Judge in chambers. It was granted and John explained the "cover up" by the hospital on the accident report, Dr. Palmer's apparent intoxication and the denials by the ambulance companies. As a result, Judge James allowed John to raise his "Prayer for Damages" from one to two million dollars! The defense attorney Charlie Perry refused to entertain any settlement offers and demanded the case go to trial. The rest of the day was spent picking a jury.

That evening we went to the Snyder home to explain the day's events and make sure everyone was ready for trial. Stephen was a fine-looking boy but this particular night he looked pale and nervous when he tried to smile. John and I simply wrote it off as "trial anxiety." We promised to call them once the jury was seated, and we went back to our rooms at the motel.

It was 3:10 a.m. when the phone rang in my room. A shaken Conrad Snyder told me he had some bad news. Stephen was dead. He died of a severe kidney infection moments ago. Conrad said he just didn't feel right all day but around 9:00 p.m. he fainted. They called their doctor and he was taken to the hospital. His condition grew worse and by 2:30 a.m. it was all over...Stephen was dead. I could hear Mary Snyder crying in the background. I promised to pray for Stephen and I hung up.

I woke John and told him the shocking news. Our giant $2,000,000 lawsuit had been reduced to a wrongful death claim and all we could collect for the Snyders was their medical and out-of-pocket expenses plus a nominal sum for loss of companionship. But the saddest part was the loss of a fine young lad who was injured in the prime of his life. Everyone who knew Stephen Snyder loved him. But now he was dead and so was our case.

The next morning we advised Judge James and defense counsel Perry of Stephen's death. All parties met in chambers and the case settled for $343,000. Judge James (bless his heart) demanded defense counsel add $100,000 to the $243,000 expenses for the 24-hour care provided Stephen by his mother. Charlie Perry knew better than to cross Judge James after he learned of all the evidence we had against the defendants. They gladly agreed to pay the $343,000 and waived their right to appeal.

John and I checked out of the motel, called a cab and flew home. We hardly talked all the way home. Stephen was dead and all our hard work went down the drain. But over the years, I learned a very valuable lesson from "This case that refused to die." Walter was right when he said if the injuries are severe enough and you honestly feel for the client (and not just how much money you can make), no matter how impossible the case may seem, keep working and someway, some how, you will find the Key to unlock the case.

A Baby Found in a Towyard

W hen I opened my office Monday morning in Century City, it was early, about 7:00, and there was Martin Wortel in his office on the phone with the State Senator from Fresno. He motioned for me to come in and sit down. When he hung up he said the Senator was a close friend whose sister and family were involved in a tragic accident. His sister and four of her five children had been killed at a railroad crossing just south of Fresno. Martin promised the Senator I would leave immediately and meet him at his office. I had to cancel several appointments, and then I jumped into my new Pontiac Firebird and I was on my way.

I met with the Senator and he told me last Friday night his sister, Maria and her five children were on their way to a drive-in movie in their Ford station wagon. Her 16-month-old daughter Rose was in the car seat next to her and her four brothers were in the rear seats. Her husband worked nights at the cannery. Maria was driving on a country road that ran parallel to the railroad tracks and she was preparing to turn right across the tracks to enter the drive-in movie lot when her car was broadsided by a southbound train. It took the train almost a half-mile to come to a stop, leaving bodies and demolished car strewn over the tracks.

I had learned long ago that all railroad crossings have lighted wooden cross arms that block traffic from going over the tracks when a train is coming. (*See, "A Railroad Crossing…Death Awaits."*) They also have a siren and blinking red lights to warn the motorist of the approaching train. The Senator handed me a copy of the newspaper with the story on the front page. The

Engineer told the California Highway Patrol Officer the cross arms were properly working and the station wagon had tried to "beat" the train to the crossing. I promised the Senator a complete investigation but I had to admit (to myself), if the Engineer's statement to the patrol officer was true and the cross arms were wrecked (showing she tried to drive through them), the case did not look promising.

My first stop was the Highway Patrol Office. The officer was off duty but his report was just being typed up. It included the Engineer's statement and the police officer's conclusion was that Maria was at fault for trying to "beat" the train to the crossing. The officer took 46 photos at the accident scene. On a hunch, I ordered all of them (at $5.00 apiece) because I wanted to see if the cross arms were actually broken. The secretary at the CHP office said the photos would be developed and ready the next day.

Next, I stopped at the tow yard so I could photograph the station wagon. The car was barely recognizable as a car - not a single panel on the station wagon was undamaged. As I was taking the pictures, the tow truck driver walked over and was obviously still upset by what he had seen at the railroad crossing. He said body parts were strewn all over the tracks and the station wagon was dragged by the engine almost a half-mile down the tracks.

Then the truck driver told me a story I shall never forget. He said he loaded what was left of the station wagon onto his tow truck and drove to the storage yard. He opened the lot with his key and as he was getting back into his truck, he thought he heard a baby cry. He was sure it was just his imagination playing tricks on him. He got back into his truck and parked next to his office. Then he heard the cry again. It was coming from somewhere inside the station wagon and sounded like it was coming from under the right front seat. But that was impossible because the head rest was touching the floorboard. He heard it again. This time, he had to check and when he lifted up the front seat there was a little baby girl still strapped in her infant carrier and she appeared to be uninjured! It had to be Rose who somehow by some miracle survived the crash and was still alive!

He unstrapped the little girl and held her in his arms. He opened up his office and called the highway patrol. He was told to wait with the baby until an officer and the baby's father (who had just been told of the terrible accident) could come to the tow yard. It brought tears to the truck driver's eyes when he described how Rose's father tenderly held her in his arms…the rest of his family gone.

I finished taking photos of the station wagon and grabbed a quick dinner, found a motel and fought to keep the images of the scene from my head.

The next morning, I had breakfast, and called the Senator. He said he could meet me around 1:30 p.m. I told him I was going to interview the patrol officer and pick up the photographs he took at the scene. I spent the rest of the morning trying to find and photograph the train's engine but it was nowhere to be found.

At 11:30 a.m. I drove to the CHP Office and asked to see the patrol officer. I was told he came on duty at noon but she said the 46 photos had been developed. She handed them to me and I sat down and started to go through the gruesome pictures. Then I came across one picture that turned a questionable case into a winner! Right there in front of me was a 3" x 5" photo of the cross arms and they were fully intact! This proved the engineer was lying when he said Maria was trying to beat the train to the crossing. It clearly proved the signal malfunctioned and failed to lower the cross arms or the train was going at a speed far greater that the 35 mph speed limit shown on the railroad tracks and it took the train over a half-mile to stop. This one photograph proved we had a solid case and a very good one!

Just then, the officer walked in and I showed him the picture. The officer agreed and changed his conclusion, now placing the blame on the railroad for causing the accident.

Armed with a enlarged photo showing the unbroken cross arms and a certified copy of the "speed tape" (all trains must have a tape showing the train's true speed), we were able to prove the train was going 72 mph at impact. Martin was able to settle the case at the Mandatory Settlement Conference and while the actual amount of the settlement was confidential, it did set a record for the largest settlement ever recorded in Kern County. And what happened to little Rose? She was guaranteed a college education at a school of her choice but her life was forever changed with the loss of her mother and her four brothers.

P.S. I forgot to tell you how we found the "speed tape." The tapes are enclosed in the engine compartment and can't be removed without a court order (similar to the voice recorder in airplane accidents). We had the engine number from the CHP report and the photos of the scene. When we demanded (with a court order) to inspect the speed tape, the railroad said the engine could not be found! We had a "friend" who was able to locate the engine in Redding. I caught a flight to Redding and learned the engine was not there but a young brakeman told me (over a steak dinner and some wine) the train had been moved to the Twentieth Century film lot, which was within a block of our Century City offices! We served the court order on the Railroad and finally we got the tape showing the engines speed at impact was 72 mph!

Colonel Sanders Gets the Shock of his Life

Catalina Island is just off the California Coast near Long Beach. A well-kept secret among the locals is that Catalina Island is a hideaway for many Hollywood celebrities. Ferries to Catalina leave several times a day from Long Beach and Newport Beach or if you are in a hurry, you can catch the Catalina Express. It is a smaller version of the Navy PBY "Flying Boat" and carries up to eighteen passengers from Long Beach to the island and back.

One afternoon the Catalina Express left Long Beach headed for Catalina. The Express Company was very proud of its 27-year accident-free record. Unfortunately, this flight was different. As the plane began its approach for a landing at Catalina harbor one of the Pratt-Whitney engines failed. The plane lost power and took a nose- dive into the sea.

On the shore was Harland David "Colonel" Sanders (September 9, 1890 – December 16, 1980) the fast food businessman who founded the Kentucky Fried Chicken Restaurants. Colonel Sanders was waiting for his wife who was returning from a shopping trip on the mainland with friends. He witnessed the terrible crash and was certain his wife Helen was on the flight. He watched as the rescue crews fought to save as many passengers as possible. Suddenly, he felt a stabbing pain in his chest. He collapsed and was taken to the small hospital on the island and air-lifted to St. John's Hospital in Long Beach. A week after open-heart surgery he was released. While the crash was an awful tragedy, killing eight passengers, Colonel Sanders' wife had fortunately missed the flight and was not on board when it went down.

About a week later, Colonel Sanders called our office and asked for John Dale. I was in his office at the time. The Colonel wanted to know if he could sue the Catalina Express for allegedly causing his heart attack. John explained to the Colonel that if his wife had been on the plane and died or was injured, then he might have a case but without more, his heart attack would not create a valid claim against the airline. The Colonel thanked us for our time and returned to Catalina, only this time he and his wife took the ferry!

Death Plays Baseball

Our Century City Office in Los Angeles represented many of the employees of the Railroad Companies. When they were injured they were taken to hospitals and treated by Railroad Company doctors and nurses. The Unions would call us in on the serious cases. Somehow, the Wortel Office learned I was a pre-med student at Notre Dame so I was elected to screen all the medical malpractice cases coming into our office. Martin Wortel was known as one of the best malpractice attorneys in California. He knew more about medical procedures than most doctors and as a result, his reputation as a medical malpractice attorney was known and feared by all the insurance companies.

One morning, Martin handed me his notes on the death of a Railroad Engineer who died during gallbladder surgery. I drove to the hospital and asked for a copy of the operation report. I was handed a one-page report which simply stated: *Patient died during gallbladder operation.* It did give me the name of the surgeon and his operating nurse but I knew it would be a waste of time to try to interview them because they were both still employed by the Railroad. This was a major case considering the 42-year-old decedent left behind a widow and three teenage sons.

On the way back to the office, I remembered something Walter Ward had told me long ago: hospitals are notorious for holding back vital information on operation reports when there is a possibility they may be at fault. Also, the nurses and sometimes the doctors involved in the procedure would often move to a job with better pay or to another hospital, usually within six months of the suspicious activity.

I told Martin about my reason for holding up any investigation for about six months and he agreed. I put a note in the file and waited. Then one day I called the Nurses' Registry and sure enough, the operating nurse was now working at a different hospital but I was able to obtain her home address in North Hollywood. I drove by her home that evening hoping she was off-duty.

It was a nice apartment in the old part of town. I rang the doorbell and I was in luck, she answered the door. I told her I represented a widow and her three teenage sons whose husband/dad died during a gallbladder operation. Her name was listed as the assisting nurse during the operation. When she heard this, she opened the door wide and asked me to sit down in her living room. It was a warm evening, and she offered me a cup of iced tea. She told me it was because of this operation she decided to leave the hospital and move to Sinai Hospital as a surgical nurse.

She recalled that about halfway through the operation, she noticed the patient's blood pressure was dropping. She motioned to the surgeon who asked the anesthesiologist, "Is everything okay?" The anesthesiologist nodded a "yes" and the operation continued. Minutes later, she noticed the "flat line" on the monitor and poked the surgeon in the ribs and said, "Doctor, your patient is dead!!!"

He threw off his mask and shouted to the anesthesiologist, "What the hell happened?" What he saw told him the answer: There was the anesthesiologist with headphones on and he was listening to Vin Scully announcing a Dodger baseball game!

The case never went to trial, it settled at a mandatory settlement conference for a whole wheelbarrow full of money. Oh, and by the way, the anesthesiologist was fired!

Serving a Summons is Easy?

It was about 6:00 on a hot, August evening. I was just leaving my office in Century City and heading home when one of our attorneys said he had a summons and complaint that had to be served in La Verne. He knew I lived in Claremont, only a few miles from La Verne, and asked if I could serve it on the defendant on my way home. I said sure. No problem! Boy was I wrong. It almost got me killed.

I drove up to the address on Bonita Avenue in La Verne and got out of my car. The screen door to the home was closed but the front door was open so I could see into the kitchen. There was a heavy-set man, in a dirty tee-shirt seated at the kitchen table drinking a bottle of beer. I rang the bell. He hollered, "C'mon in," so I did. That was my first mistake. Walter Ward told me to never, ever, walk into the home of a defendant when you are serving him with any kind of legal paper. But this guy sounded friendly so in I went. I asked him his name and when he answered, I could tell he was very drunk. I handed him the summons and complaint and told him he could contact his insurance company with any questions.

I turned to leave, saying the papers were just a formality and he was to give the papers to his insurance company. He raised his arm and said "Wait!" He was reading the complaint and when he got to the "prayer" (which is the amount we felt the case was worth) he called for his wife who was in a room down the hall. She walked into the kitchen and stood by her husband, facing me. She was also very drunk. He told her, "This guy here wants $175,000 for that stupid accident we had last month. She was standing right in front of me in shorts and a cotton blouse. She looked me straight in the eye, tore open her blouse and screamed, "Call the police, this guy is trying to rape me!"

With that, the drunk stood up and I saw he was built like a fireplug. He was only about 5'8" but he weighed at least 240 pounds with broad shoulders and forearms thick as tree trunks. I was standing with my back to the kitchen wall. He grabbed me by my shirt and with one hand he lifted me off the floor. He said he was going to break every bone in my body. That did it! I was so mad it even surprised me when I said, "Go ahead! Break every bone in my body, but when I get out of the hospital, I'm going to come back here and kill you!" He slowly lowered me and let go of my shirt.

I turned and walked to the screen door. He was close behind me and cursing all the way. I was getting into my car when he threw the papers back at me, but I knew he had been properly served so I jumped into my Mustang and headed home. In my rear view mirror I could see both of them shaking their fists and swearing at me.

When I got home my wife asked me how my day went. I said, "Oh, just another day at the office!"

A Case of Mistaken Identity

It was a cold and rainy Monday morning in February when Martin Wortel called me into his office in Century City. I had planned to dictate reports all day and stay in my nice warm office. I walked down the long hallway to his corner office where he handed me a notepad and offered me a seat. Martin said Judge Matt Rader, a close friend, had just referred a case to him where Judge Rader's son-in law, Douglas Peterson, was badly injured in a truck accident and was now in intensive care at Cedars-Sinai Hospital. I started taking notes because I knew this case would take top priority - which meant my plan of spending a full day in my nice warm office just went out the window.

Martin told me Douglas Peterson was 33 years old, married to Matt Rader's daughter Jenny. They lived in Encino and had three young sons. Douglas was the owner and part-time driver for Peterson Sand &Gravel Company. Judge Rader said Douglas was driving his new truck loaded with sand down the Sepulveda Grade when his brakes failed and he lost control of his truck. He hit a tree on his way down the grade and as a result of the accident, he was now severely brain damaged and had lost the use of his left arm and leg.

I went back to my (warm) office, grabbed my briefcase and went to the parking garage. My first stop was Cedars-Sinai Hospital in hopes I would meet some of the family members and learn more about how the accident happened. I caught the elevator to the third floor intensive care unit, but the nurse in charge told me Douglas had been released from ICU and was now in room #436 and he was recovering better than anticipated. I went to room #436 and there was Douglas, much to my surprise, propped up on pillows watching television. Jenny was at his bedside.

Jenny told me Douglas suffered a severe concussion and his entire left side was paralyzed. However, with proper rehabilitation, there was a good chance his condition would improve. Douglas turned off the television and reached out to shake my hand. I was astounded at how quickly he was recovering. He said he felt fine except for a splitting headache and that his left arm and left leg "didn't work too well."

I asked him how the accident happened. He said he was driving down the Sepulveda Grade with a full load of gravel. Suddenly, he lost his air brakes. He was in a low gear but his truck was gradually gaining speed. He said he knew every turn on the steep downgrade but he had a decision to make and make it in a hurry: If he tried to cross over the center line to stop his truck, he would have crashed against the rock cliff, but he would have hit other cars coming up the hill and risked hitting them head-on. If he continued on the right side of the road down, he was picking up speed and if he made it all the way down the grade, he might have been OK but he knew there was an elementary school and a McDonald's at the bottom of the hill. Many people, including children, could be injured or killed before his truck would come to a complete stop.

But he did have a third alternative: on the right side of the road down around the next curve, was a huge oak tree. Douglas thought the tree just might stop his truck and he would be the only one injured. He took a chance. As he rounded the curve, he aimed his truck at the oak tree but that was the last thing Douglas remembered until he awoke in the hospital. He was getting tired so I gave him my card and said I would see him after he was discharged from the hospital.

My next stop was the Peterson Sand & Gravel truck yard where the Kenworth truck was being stored after the accident. The yard foreman showed me the truck with its entire front end totally damaged beyond repair. He asked me how Douglas was doing. I said he was doing fine despite the paralysis to his left side but without a doubt, the seatbelt saved his life. I asked him if he knew why the air brakes had failed. He said he couldn't understand it, because the Kenworth truck was only a few months old and he drove it himself to the Kenworth dealer's service department for the 5,000-mile check-up the day before the accident.

When I opened the left door of the truck, there was a Kenworth Motors Dealer's sticker confirming the truck had been serviced the day before the accident. We walked over to his office and found the "paid" invoice. We got lucky because the invoice said "air brakes checked and in proper working order." Obviously, the Kenworth Motors service department failed to properly service the air brakes or possibly the air brake connectors failed to work and a mechanical defect and caused this accident. It would be up to a mechanical expert to prove the exact cause but it had to be either the Kenworth dealer's or the Kenworth manufacturer's responsibility for the air brake failure that caused Douglas Peterson's injury.

Suddenly, we had a client with a serious injury and financially solid defendants. I returned to my (warm) office and made out my report recommending a lawsuit be filed against Kenworth Motors (the dealer) and Kenworth, Inc. (the manufacturer of the connector valves).

But as usual, the lawsuit took its usual course of 12-16 months of expert testimony, depositions and discovery. Douglas Peterson had improved to the point where he could walk with a cane but his left arm was completely useless and his migraines continued.

Finally, the day came for the Mandatory Settlement Conference in Judge Ely's chambers. Martin Wortel thought the case should settle, as the facts were crystal clear. The air braking system had not been properly assembled and road tested the day before, despite the fact that the invoice stated it had been done. Martin could prove the connector valves were defective and he had evidence that 17 similar accidents had occurred in California alone. But, the defendant insurance company was represented by a law firm that prided itself on a string of defense verdicts and was just waiting to try a case against the renowned trial lawyer, Martin Wortel.

Martin prepared a settlement brief with medical, future medical, lost wages and pain and suffering for the rest of Douglas Peterson's life. The demand for the permanent injury to Douglas was a realistic $1,800,000. Martin entered Judge Ely's chambers and outlined the proposed settlement package. It sounded like a reasonable demand to Judge Ely and Martin gave his personal guarantee that the injuries suffered by Douglas Peterson were permanent and life-threatening.

Then it was the defense attorney's turn to argue on behalf of the defendant Kenworth Motors. He stood up and addressed Judge Ely and said they had undercover movies of Douglas Peterson mowing his lawn and playing softball with his young children. This proved Doug Peterson had no apparent injury of any kind and the lawsuit brought by Martin Wortel 45 minutes of film and proudly said they paid an investigator over $5,000 for the undercover movies in an honest attempt to show the court the suit brought by Wortel was without merit. Not only did these movies prove Douglas Peterson was a not injured but it put Wortel's personal reputation in question. This was just the case the defense firm was looking for to discredit Martin Wortel.

Martin came out of Judge Ely's Chambers roaring mad. He told me to go to Douglas Peterson's home and tell him he had just seen movies of him that proved he was not injured in any way. Wortel demanded his explanation or we would withdraw from the case immediately.

I jumped into my Pontiac and drove over to the Peterson home and, sure enough, there was Douglas Peterson mowing his front lawn! I told him about the movies and we were forced to dismiss his case. He just laughed and said "this happens all the time. My name is John Peterson, I'm not Douglas - I'm John, his identical twin brother." Just then Douglas came out the front door leaning on his cane. He told me that ever since the accident, his brother John would come over and mow his lawn and help around the house. When Douglas stood next to John, so help me, it was impossible to tell them apart. We three sat on the porch with cans of beer and laughed at the $5,000 the insurance company had spent on movies of John when they thought it was Douglas mowing the lawn and playing with the kids.

The next morning I told Martin about the twin brother mix-up. He grabbed the phone and called Judge Ely and explained Douglas had an identical twin brother. Martin asked for a second Settlement Conference and he agreed to have the twins present. The Settlement Conference was scheduled for the following Monday afternoon. I had the twins dress exactly alike and we sat on the hallway bench outside Judge Ely's chambers. Martin looked at the twins in disbelief and shook his head as he realized he could not tell which one of the twins was his client, as they sat together on the bench.

Now, it was time for the defense lawyers to walk down the hallway and into the Judge Ely's chambers. The twins just sat there and smiled. I sat next to them and wished I had a camera when Douglas Peterson waved to them with his cane and John just sat there and smiled. The Judge's chamber doors closed and within an hour the case settled for Martin's demand. Martin left the courthouse satisfied his reputation had been fully restored and the defense team was out $5,000!

A Lab Report Coverup

One morning an airline stewardess called our Century City office from a hotel in Santa Monica. Sally, our receptionist, referred the call to me because all the lawyers were either on the phone or with clients. A 23 year-old stewardess was stationed in New York and assigned to the New York-Los Angeles route. Usually, the crew would fly into Los Angeles, stay overnight and then fly back to New York the following day. They had standing reservations at a Santa Monica hotel that was close to the LAX airport.

It was one of those "turn around" flights that turned into a nightmare for this young stewardess. She told me her flight landed in Los Angeles at 11:23 p.m. and the crew took a cab to the hotel. They checked into their rooms and went to bed. Their flight was scheduled to leave for New York the next afternoon at 2:45. The stewardess awoke around 8:00 a.m. and went into the bathroom to take a shower. While showering, she felt a strange lump in her right breast. It was a round, hard lump and it hurt a little. She was scared and since she had almost seven hours before departure, she decided to go to the hospital and have it checked by a doctor in the emergency room. Her mother had died of breast cancer three years earlier so she was especially cautious and concerned with this lump.

A doctor examined her and ordered an immediate biopsy to determine if the lump was malignant. She went down to the hospital cafeteria and waited for the doctor to give her the lab report. She decided if the report proved the lump was cancerous, she would have emergency surgery done here in Santa Monica where the weather was nice and warm (not like the ice and snow in New York). And she would use her two-week vacation to recover from the surgery.

An hour later, the doctor met with her and said the lab report just came back and he had some bad news. The lump tested positive for malignant cancer of her right breast. He advised an immediate mastectomy because the lump was at stage #4 and there just happened to be an available operating room and staff available

She agreed to the surgery when the doctor said any delay could prove to be fatal. She was prepped for surgery and her right breast was removed. When she awoke in the recovery room, the surgeon was standing at the foot of her bed saying, "I've got great news for you! It wasn't malignant after all

After two days in the hospital, and just prior to being discharged, she became more and more angered by this most callous and shocking "mistake." She wanted to talk to an attorney and see if there was anything she could do to make the hospital and staff fix this nightmare. She called her home office and learned the Wortel Law Firm represented her airline. She called our office, told us the whole story and we filed suit against the hospital, the laboratory and the doctors for medical malpractice, emotional distress and general negligence.

The case never went to trial. It settled at a mandatory settlement conference for $180,000 when the lab admitted they gave the cancer report on the wrong patient to her doctor. To make matters worse, the doctor tried to cover up the lab's mistake by not telling our client of this horrific error. These types of "cover-up" stories do not happen too often (I hope) but this is one example of how the "medical family" takes care of its own…regardless of the cost.

Governor Brown Helps a Friend

Only a few of you readers will remember the agony of Pearl Harbor or when President Franklin D. Roosevelt declared December 7, 1941 as a "day that would go down in infamy." As a result of that tragedy, we had to start building aircraft to fight our battles in the air. One of the leading aircraft manufacturers at the time was Martin–Marietta who specialized in fighter planes, along with McDonnell Douglas, Lockheed and Boeing. Americans were mad…very mad. The demand for fighter planes kept Martin-Marietta working at full capacity for the next three decades. During that time, Glen Martin of Martin-Marietta and California Governor Pat Brown became close friends.

Pat Brown retired from politics after serving as Governor of California from 1959 to 1967 and joined a law firm in Long Beach. One day he called our office in Century City and told Martin Wortel he needed help in handling a case for the Glen Martin Foundation. Pat Brown's close friend Glen Martin had set up a trust fund for his mentally retarded daughter, Rita Martin. Before he died he named Pat Brown as the Administrator of the Trust. We agreed to meet with Pat at the Brentwood Country Club the following day for lunch and he would explain his "problem." I was excited because I had never met Pat Brown and it's not every day that an investigator like me got to dine at the Brentwood Country Club!

At lunch, Pat explained Rita Martin had been confined to a hospital in Hemet, California, for the last 20 years. Before his death, Glen Martin had set up a $1 million trust fund to ensure Rita would receive the best care possible for life.

The Trust Fund maintained a balance of $1 million and the president of the hospital could use the funds as he saw fit for any special care Miss Martin might need. Over the years, everything ran smoothly but four years ago, the hospital president died and his successor took charge of the hospital and Rita's Trust Fund. With the change in the hospital presidency, the Trust Fund was audited, revealing a balance of only $327,000.

Pat Brown wanted to know where all that money went. He brought this discrepancy to the new president's attention. To Pat's surprise, Rita's medical records indicated she had "violent tendencies." Two hospital psychiatrists recommended Rita be treated at facilities in Rome, Paris, London, even one month in the South Pacific Islands! All of the money for these trips came from Rita's Trust Fund with the rationale that it was for necessary medical reasons.

Pat Brown had been on the Board of Directors of the Hemet Hospital for years and did not want a conflict of interest claim against him. That is why he called our office for help.

It was decided I should look into the matter and see if there was enough evidence to prove the psychiatrists and the hospital were using the Trust Fund for their own personal use rather than any possible "medical or psychiatric" use that would benefit Miss Martin. It was a tall order but I promised to look into the matter and within two weeks I would report to Pat Brown and Martin Wortel on my findings.

My first stop was the Hemet Hospital where I introduced myself to the receptionist as a cousin of Rita, just stopping in to say hello. The young girl at the desk said she would have an attendant take me to her section. I sat and waited until finally a tall, expressionless young man, in his early 20's, with arms bulging from the short sleeves of his white uniform walked up to me and said dryly, "Visiting hours are over in fifteen minutes."

He led me down a long hallway and finally he stopped in front of a locked door with a glass panel where one could look inside the room but the patients could not see out. My muscle-bound attendant pointed out Miss Martin who sat quietly in a chair facing our entry door. She was heavy-set with short, cropped brown hair and she appeared to be about 40-45 years old.

It was then that I noticed her hands and arms. A leather strap was wrapped around both wrists and attached to a leather belt around her waist. She was staring at nothing in particular, but in my direction, with an expression I will never forget. It was a helpless yet hopeful look as though she was pleading with someone, anyone, to get her out of this nightmare of a room. I asked the attendant to open the door so I could talk to her. He said it would be useless because she was unable to speak and at times she would become violent...hence the restraining belt. However, he said he had never seen her act out.

She just sat quietly while the other six patients wandered around the room. But in her medical chart there were orders signed by the President of the hospital demanding Rita Martin not be allowed out of the closed ward because of her violent tendencies and that no visitors were allowed in the room with her. Terry Fox (I read his name tag) said he had been with the hospital for over six years and Miss Martin never had a violent outburst that he knew of, she never left the closed ward, and no-one ever came to visit her. The Martin family all lived in or around New York and, according to her medical chart, no one ever visited Rita after Glen Martin's death.

It was becoming clear to me, Rita Martin had been a prisoner in this hospital for many years and she was at the mercy of the doctors at the hospital who were spending her trust fund money on themselves. The look I saw on her in the closed ward was a plea for freedom and it was my job to do all that I could to see she would spend the rest of her life with the best quality of life possible. That was Glen Martin's intent when he set up the Trust and it was becoming quite clear the doctors were egregiously misappropriating her account.

I waved to the receptionist as I left the hospital and paused to write down the badge name Terry Fox, my muscular guide to Rita Martin's closed ward. I suspected Rita's medical records had been altered and would show she made those trips all around the world for medical reasons. If true, Terry would be a prime witness to the fraud that had been committed. I recommended that Martin Wortel issue a subpoena demanding all of her medical records in order to find other attendants who possibly would testify Rita never left the closed ward in the last four to six years.

The next morning, when I told Martin Wortel what I had found at the Hospital he called Pat Brown and told him my suspicions. Pat called a friend of his who just happened to be the head of the Psychiatric Department at UCLA Medical Clinic. He agreed to visit Rita Martin, review her medical records and give his expert opinion on her mental condition. He would submit his report within two weeks to Pat.

Three weeks later, we met with Pat again at the Brentwood Country Club. Pat had some good news: the President of the hospital had read the audit and my investigation report. He agreed to repay all the money taken from the trust fund if the Wortel Law Firm would agree not to file suit for fraud. We agreed. He also agreed to follow the report of the UCLA Psychiatrist who found Rita Martin to be mildly mentally retarded but not violent. It was also the psychiatrist's opinion that her inability to speak could be corrected in time. Pat Brown, as Administrator of the Trust, was a "silent partner" in all the negotiations and the final settlement was confidential.

Rita was taken out of the violent care ward and placed in a quiet little three-room cottage on the hospital grounds with her own private nurse and a speech therapist. She seemed to be happy in her new surroundings and was allowed visitors anytime. I stopped by about every three months just to say hello.

In 1983, Rita Martin died peacefully in her sleep, in the arms of her nurse and in the air-conditioned cottage decorated in her favorite colors. Glen Martin must have smiled down on Rita as she spent the last ten years of her life in peace and comfort.

A Dad & His Two Sons – Dead

It was in all the newspapers, the sad story of a father and his two sons who were killed when their private plane crashed near the Downey Airport yesterday afternoon. The article said they were returning from visiting relatives in Salt Lake and apparently the plane ran out of gas. The National Transportation Safety Board (NTSB) was investigating the accident. I finished breakfast and headed to my office in Century City.

When I got to the office there was a copy of the *L.A. Times* story with a note from John Dale saying, "See me." I walked down the hall to his office. John was on the phone talking to the NTSB Investigator who was confirming "pilot error" as the cause of the accident because the plane ran out of gas. John said the attorney representing the family's estate called and asked us to do an investigation on the true cause of the accident. I grabbed my briefcase and a camera and was on my way to Downey Airport.

About halfway to the Control Tower, I noticed a flatbed tow truck hauling away our plane! I drove my car across his lane and asked the driver where he was taking my clients' plane. He said the insurance company told him to pick up the plane and take it to the city dump. He demanded I remove my car and let him pass. Instead I made a Citizen's Arrest and demanded he take our plane back to our hangar where it could be examined by our own experts.

John called our expert who met me at the hangar and he began his examination of the wreckage. Meanwhile, I noticed a three-story building next to the parking lot where our plane crashed. I began knocking on doors hoping to find witnesses who saw our plane go down. On the third floor, I got lucky and found two men who were standing at their front bay window watching our plane do the usual "S" turns prior to landing. Both were pilots working for a missionary group flying medical supplies to South America. They both said as the pilot started his approach to the runway, he began his "S" turn. Suddenly, the engine stopped running; the plane crashed in their parking lot and caught fire. I asked them if they thought the plane just ran out of gas. They explained the gas tanks were in the wings and when the plane crashed both wings exploded proving there was gas in the tanks and causing the plane to catch fire. I took statements of both pilots who were never questioned by the NTSB. I planned to show the statements to the insurance company investigator to prove it was *not* pilot error and the plane did *not* simply run out of gas.

Back at the hangar, our expert had come up with the true cause of the crash. He explained there are baffles in the wing tanks to keep the gasoline from sliding away from the fuel ports and causing the engine to be without fuel. He found that the baffles in the right wing tank were defective and failed to operate properly, thus causing the crash.

Suddenly, we were in business. We had a reason the plane crashed and we could prove it. Two-and-a-half years went by before the case finally came up for trial. At trial, John presented evidence the dad was earning $120,000 a year and he believed the case had a true value of $1,200,000. The defense offered $25,000 (the cost of defense) and "...not a penny more!" They were relying on the NTSB report that pilot error caused the plane to run out of gas. The trial lasted three weeks and finally the jury came in with its verdict, a whopping $8,200,000.

End of story? Well, not quite...

The verdict hit all the newspapers and the *Los Angeles Times* had the story on the front page calling it a "run-a-way" verdict that the defense would certainly appeal. John and I remembered we left the courthouse when the jury went into the jury room to deliberate. In fact, we went over to Hollywood to interview a doctor on a malpractice case when the verdict came in. We talked to no reporters and wondered how the *Times* got the story.

The next day, I jumped in my car and returned to the courtroom. I asked the Bailiff if he had any idea who talked to the press. He told me the defense team contacted the *Times* reporter. The story sharply criticized the plaintiff lawyers who were getting these "run-a-way verdicts" and the poor insurance companies had to absorb the losses. Within a year, Aircraft Insurance went up 50% and the cost of a new aircraft rose 35% nationwide. By the way, we settled the case for $1,800,000 plus interest from the date of the accident.

My Adventure with Alligators

I always thought Florida was a state where old people went to relax in the sun and drink orange juice. I had never even heard of a place called the "Florida Everglades." Now, we in Los Angeles never get snow but we do get rain. And it was on a rainy day in January, when John Dale told me I was going to Florida to investigate an aviation accident where two doctors were killed in the Florida Everglades. He said I could read the National Transportation Safety Board (NTSB) report on the airplane. There was only one witness to the accident but the NTSB investigators were unable to find him. However the NTSB report concluded the plane simply ran out of gas (pilot error) and crashed in the Everglades. I packed a bag, threw in some sun screen and was on my way.

In Miami, I rented a car, grabbed a map and found the Everglade Highway. No one prepared me for the alligators. Until now, the only alligators I had ever seen were in the old Tarzan movies. I once read in a *National Geographic* that an alligator can outrun a human by the length of a football field but that was about all I knew of alligators. Alligators seemed to be ever-present in the Everglades, from alligator warnings posted near every body of water, to signs advertising "Alligator Wrestling" and my favorite, "Alligator Hamburgers"!

The "Alligator Hamburgers" sign got my attention. It was lunchtime and I was starving. The small café was set off the highway with customer parking next to an old abandoned garage. There were two or three other cars there and I parked next to them. I could see customers seated at the counter inside the café. On the outer wall of the garage were two drinking fountains. One had a sign above it that read "WHITES ONLY" and the other read "BLACKS ONLY." I had never seen signs like that before so I grabbed my camera, got out of my car and took a picture. Suddenly, the screen doors of the cafe opened and two men came running toward me. One was shouting, "Grab his camera!" The other was shouting something about me being a "n---ger lover." I got back in my car, slammed the door and raced out of the parking lot. In my rear view mirror, I could see the two angry men throwing rocks at my car. As I drove away I thought, "So this is Florida? And I thought all men were created equal!"

My quest for eating an Alligator hamburger quickly vanished as I drove further west into the Everglades. When I was about 30 miles down the road, I saw a general store with a small sign on the side of a flat-bottomed canoe which read: "Wind Machine for rent." The Wind Machine was nothing more than a flat-bottomed canoe with an airplane engine and propeller attached to the rear but it was intriguing.

I walked into the store and struck up a conversation with Steve, the owner. I told him I was investigating the plane crash near here that killed two people. Steve recalled the accident and said the plane crashed about two miles from his store. I showed him the NTSB report and it noted only one witness, an Indian named Ambrose Pennington. Steve just laughed and said he knew the witness only as "Moonshine Charlie." He lived on a small island about a mile from the Everglades Highway and very close to where the accident happened. He said Moonshine Charlie was working at a service station down the road but would be home in about two hours. The owner offered to take me for a ride in his Wind Machine to the scene of the accident. His wife could take care of the store and we would be back in time to meet the witness. We climbed aboard the Wind Machine and off we went. On our way to the scene, the owner told me Charlie hated "government men" and after the accident he hid out on his island until the NTSB men went away.

Our speed was around 35 mph as we skimmed over the marshes and shallow water. Then Steve stopped suddenly as a heard of tiny wild deer crossed in front of us going from one island to another. They were no larger than my Golden Retriever. At the same time Steve pointed to both sides of our boat and I could see probably 15 alligators sleeping in the sun on the sandy beach. I had a horrible thought: if the alligators were awakened by the deer or our boat, they could easily capsize us and we would be their lunch!

We arrived at the scene of the crash. Steve said the NTSB had the plane removed and taken to Miami for examination. Several trees were knocked down and badly burned, evidence that the plane glided into them. I reasoned if the plane simply ran out of gas it would have "nose dived" into the water and it would not have glided into the trees. I shot a roll of film and we returned to the store. On our way back, Steve pointed to the trees that overhang the water's edge. He said, "A Cottonmouth Moccasin is a very poisonous snake and they lay on these branches ready to strike anything that comes along. That's why we keep the boat in the center of the stream." I couldn't wait to get back to the store.

When we returned to the store, Steve called "Moonshine Charlie" and told him I was an investigator who represented the families of the two doctors killed in the crash. He agreed to meet me, "so long as he ain't no government man." He said for me to meet him in a parking area next to the highway just west of Steve's store. I drove down and parked my car as I watched him row over in his canoe to meet me.

"Moonshine Charlie" threw a rope around a tree and steadied his canoe. He didn't look like an Indian at all. He was 26-27 years old, tall, with a full head of blonde hair. He was about six feet tall and skinny, maybe 140 pounds. He shook my hand firmly and introduced himself not as Ambrose Pennington but as Moonshine Charlie. He said he saw the plane go down in the swamp. He was fishing when he heard the plane's engine roar past him. This told me that the plane was not out of gas and the props were spinning. He also said the plane was flying low and flames were coming from the engine. It crashed into a grove of trees and there was an explosion when the fuel tanks exploded.

This statement of Moonshine Charlie clearly proved the plane did not just run out of gas as claimed in the NTSB accident report but crashed in flames and burned. I grabbed a notebook and started taking his statement on the hood of my car. While I was writing, I looked over Charlie's shoulder and saw two huge alligators racing towards each other. When they hit, their jaws were locked in mortal combat. I let out a yell and my notebook fell to the ground. Charlie looked over his shoulder and said, "Aw, that's nothing. They are just fighting over the garbage bags we leave on the shore of the island. It keeps them from attacking the little kids who play on the island. " (I'll take California any time!)

I thanked Moonshine Charlie for the statement and I waved goodbye, turned my car around and headed to the Miami Airport. On the way home, I thought about those alligators hitting each other. They were within 15 feet from Charlie and me and knowing full well they could out run us. And then there were the Cottonmouth snakes…and those sleeping alligators on the beach. And I couldn't forget those angry men who threw stones at my car. It was hot and humid at the airport but I was glad to return my rented car and get on a plane to Los Angeles.

Soon, I was 15,000 feet above the Everglades and on my way home with an eyewitness statement that would at least help two widows and five children win their lawsuit. I should add, in checking the NTSB records nationwide, we found 92 cases where the planes caught fire because the fuel line went directly over the hot exhaust manifold. This is exactly what happened in our case. The case settled and the fuel lines in all current and future planes were re-routed to correct the problem.

Now, the years have flown by and this adventure is only a dim memory...thank God. But I will always wonder what an Alligator hamburger tastes like....

The Smell of Death in Samoa

Someone must have told someone in the Wortel Law Office that I was in the Naval Air Corps during World War II because every time an aviation case came into our office, I was elected to do the Investigation. Now, what that "someone" didn't know was I spent my two years (1944-1946) in the Naval Air Corps playing baseball at Great Lakes, Illinois and Pensacola Naval Air Station in Florida. After all, someone had to keep up the morale of our Navy fighting men. What better way than for them to watch a baseball game! To tell the truth, the only time I ever boarded a plane during my time with the Naval Air Corps was to fly from one Naval Air station to another to play a ball game!

The front page of the *Los Angeles Times* told the tragic story of a DC-10 that went down in Pago-Pago (pronounced "Pang-go-Pang-go") or more correctly, American Samoa. There were106 people on board and only eight passengers survived the crash by crawling out on the wing and jumping to the ground. When I got to our office in Century City, John Dale was on the phone with Chief Steven Lay, a lawyer who represented 67 Samoans killed in the crash. John motioned me into his office and I listened in on the conversation. The Chief agreed to act as the referring attorney for the 67 families and assist us in preparing the case for trial.

The Chief said at the time of the accident, the airport in Pago-Pago had been closed because of bad weather and the pilot had only about three hours' worth of fuel left in his tanks. Normally, he could land in Haiti, but the airport was closed because of a thunderstorm. In the alternative, he could circle the Pago-Pago airport and pray the weather would clear within the three-hour period. The pilot had no choice but to circle the island and after two-and-a-half hours, he attempted his landing in very rough weather with only limited visibility. He was 340 feet from the start of the runway when the right wingtip of his DC-10 struck a huge mango tree. The DC-10 spun around and caught fire. The Chief wanted an investigator to come to the island while the National Transportation Safety Board (NTSB) was investigating the accident. John looked at me and I was elected.

I placed a phone call to a good friend of mine at the local NTSB office in Santa Monica. He told me all of the bodies were shipped to the Coroner's office in Hawaii and then removed for toxicology testing to our Coroner's office here in Los Angeles. I placed a second call to a friend in the Coroner's office and she told me "off the record" that the bodies had just been examined and not one of them had any broken bones. Their deaths had been caused by a gas called Phosgene Cyanide that originated when the ceiling of the aircraft caught fire and the air conditioning system blew the deadly Phosgene Cyanide gas onto the passengers. My source told me the foam rubber that cushions the seats is also used to act as a sound deadener in the ceiling of almost every commercial aircraft and when it is ignited, it produces the lethal gas. I learned all of this before I left Century City.

The next morning I was on my way to an island halfway around the world. It was a 23-hour flight with a layover in Hawaii to fill our gas tanks for the long journey across the Pacific Ocean to Pago-Pago. As we prepared to land in Pago-Pago, I could see the tree limbs and the crash site. It was 4:30 a.m. Pago-Pago time, so I checked into the only hotel on the island. I took a nap and waited for the sun to come up. Then I had breakfast, rented a car and drove out to the scene of the crash.

While I was shooting a roll of film, I met an NTSB Investigator who told me we were standing on "sacred ground" where the DC-10 was buried 15 feet below. He said the aircraft was buried because it was a tradition among the Samoan people to declare the place where their people died "sacred ground" and therefore the plane was buried at the site. This made it impossible for the NTSB or me to examine the plane. He did tell me that when the bodies were removed from the DC-10, they still had their seat belts fastened. I learned later that afternoon, a team of investigators from Douglas Aircraft had ordered the plane buried before the NTSB arrived. I didn't volunteer the true cause of death was Phosgene Cyanide but I strongly suspected the Douglas team knew how the passengers died and it was one of the reasons they took advantage of the Samoan religious custom for sacred ground and had the plane buried.

I placed a call to Chief Steven Lay, who I learned was a Justice of their Supreme Court and his secretary said I could meet him when the Court recessed at 4:30 p.m. When the chamber doors opened the Chief greeted me…in a *skirt*! No one ever told me a skirt was a badge of honor in Pago-Pago. I learned the "skirt" is actually called a "Lava Lava" and it is the traditional form of businesswear for Samoan men. It is a sarong wrap-around skirt and is always worn with a jacket.

Anyway, we retired to the nearest bar and sat at a corner booth. The Chief said he was a recent graduate of Loyola Law School in Los Angeles and was admitted to the bar when he was forty-eight years old. He was immediately appointed to the Supreme Court in Samoa. While he was at Loyola Law School, he met Martin Wortel and John Dale at a Trial Lawyers Convention and he learned John's focus was on Aviation Law. Because of his position on the Supreme Court, when the plane crashed he immediately called John.

While he was talking to me, I noticed we never ordered a beer but the bartender kept placing glasses of beer on our table (at last count there were six glasses for each of us). It was raining very hard on the sheet metal roof of the bar and it was hard to carry on a conversation. But as each patron entered the bar they nodded to the Chief and me and apparently sent a complimentary beer to our table. Welcome to Pago-Pago. While we were trying to drink all that beer, I was introduced to several Samoan employees who worked at the airport. They assisted in removing the bodies and operating the Caterpillar tractor that buried the DC-10 where it landed. They confirmed the fact that the emergency exit at the front of the plane was frozen and failed to open. They were also present and overheard the Douglas people discussing the foam rubber insulation as the possible cause of death. Finally, there were three witnesses who overheard Douglas' decision to bury the plane to hide the evidence.

It was a long evening but it was exceedingly profitable. I had a briefcase full of information to prove Douglas Aircraft had a defective exit door that failed to open and they knew the foam rubber insulation produced Phosgene Cyanide when ignited. At around 7:00 p.m. we left the bar and the Chief invited me to his home for dinner (and more beer). His wife was glad to meet someone from the "mainland." She spoke perfect English without any accent and it was clear that she and her husband were highly educated. She was a big woman, probably 5'11" and at least 250 pounds and the Chief was about the same. We were served a great fish dinner by a Samoan girl who was also over 200 pounds and I learned it was a badge of beauty to be big and strong and heavy. After dinner, I excused myself because I was so tired from jet lag. I walked to the hotel and fell into bed.

This was my first (and only) visit to the famed South Pacific and I hated to leave. The next morning I had breakfast with the NTSB team, four guys, and learned they were upset with the Douglas people for making it impossible for them to examine the DC- 10. I listened and it became clear I knew as much or more than they knew about the accident. But they were working for the Government and they were taking their time with an unlimited expense account. I had finished my investigation and had some very good news for John Dale and those 67 families we represented.

We filed suit in Los Angeles Federal Court and a Mandatory Settlement Judge was assigned the case. John presented his case and defense counsel for Douglas admitted liability but argued the plaintiffs were all Samoans and unable to prove any substantial earnings. It became obvious the judge was very defense-minded. He listened to all of John's arguments with a frown on his face. Finally, the case was submitted to the judge for a decision. The case sat on his desk for a full nine months before he rendered his combined verdict for all sixty-seven families. It totaled $12 million. But it took another two years while Douglas took the case up on appeal (they lost) and all those families were paid...finally.

The Case of a Hit-and-Run Aircraft

They are called "Weekend Warriors" and on weekends they fill the skies of southern California with aircraft from every branch of the Armed Services. Army, Navy, Air Force and Marine pilots need the flying time to keep their licenses current, and could be seen taking off from air bases in California and Arizona. The pilots prefer to fly over the desert where the sky is clear and if you have to land (or crash) you will only disturb a few rattlesnakes.

In the dead center of the desert is the small mining town of Iron Mountain where a few hundred miners and their families live in almost total isolation. For food and clothing they must drive west to Indio or east to Blythe. But Iron Mountain does have two local bars to keep the miners from dying of thirst.

One Saturday morning in mid-August, two young mothers from Iron Mountain jumped into their Volkswagen "Bug" and headed east to Blythe for a day of shopping and errands. It was 68 miles across the desert with only a few cars on the two-lane road because of the 112-degree summer heat.

High up in the sky was a fighter pilot who was also going eastbound, at 10,000 feet. He thought it would be "fun" to do a bombing run on the little Bug on the highway. The aircraft dove from 10,000 feet to about 50 feet above the little Bug. The only warning the driver had was the terrible roar from the jet engine as it shook the little Volkswagen from side to side. Then the "hot shot" pilot spiraled into the sky and suddenly turned around for a second bombing run on the little car. Only this time, he was going westbound and the plane looked like it was going to hit the little car head-on. The pilot was so low a witness said the plane almost took off the car's antenna. The Volkswagen went out of control and rolled over as it went down a steep embankment to the desert floor. Both mothers were killed and the pilot disappeared into the sky. The deaths left five little children under the age of eight without their mothers.

I was in my office in Century City when John Dale handed me a copy of the Highway Patrol Report and said, "Lots of luck O'Brien. You're going to need it." I read the report and then reread it. I had to agree with John, I would need a whole lot of "Irish Luck" to find the hot shot, hit-and-run pilot who caused this terrible accident. As you may or may not know, if you sue the Federal Government for a negligent act, the Government will allow the suit *only* if a Federal Court first rules the case has merit. Our suit was submitted to the Federal Court for approval based on the California Highway Patrol Report that quoted an eyewitness saying it was a military aircraft that caused the accident, not a privately owned aircraft. The court granted approval.

We immediately filed our lawsuit and demanded all branches of the Army, Air Force, Naval Air Corps and the Marines to provide us with information on all the aircraft they had in the air on the day of the accident. It took John a month of prodding, but finally the government got around to answering the interrogatories. The Army and Air Force each had three planes in the air, the Navy had three and the Marines had one. Then I had an idea I believed just might work. I got on the phone and called the manufacturers of all ten aircraft. I made up a story that I was an Air Safety Investigator and I needed a photograph of each specific plane for a speech I was giving on Air Safety. Much to my surprise (and relief) it worked and within a week I had a stack of 8" x 10" photographs of all the planes in the air on the date of the accident.

The Highway Patrol Report had listed only one witness. He was a Mother's Cookie truck driver who was following the

Volkswagen. He was the one who said the plane almost took off the car's antenna. The Patrol Report showed a rural Post Office address for this man: "Route 3 Box 56, in 29 Palms."

Early one Saturday morning I drove out to 29 Palms and found the home of the only witness to this tragic accident. The Mother's Cookie truck was parked in the driveway. But I had one big problem: there was a Great Dane that apparently hadn't been fed and wanted me on his menu. Luckily, the yard was fenced but still, I just stood there like a dummy while this dog snarled, growled and barked at me and I hoped the noise would alert the occupants of the home that I was waiting at the fence.

Finally, the barking caused the owner to open his front door and calm down that giant of a dog. I introduced myself and handed him my card. He and his wife and children were just finishing breakfast. He suggested I wait for him in their living room. I spread the photographs out on the living room floor and waited.

Shortly thereafter, Jess Martin came in. He was a tall man, about 50 years old with premature gray hair. He said he retired from the Army Air Force after 26 years as an Aviation Mechanic and for the last two years he had taken the truck driver's job with Mother's Cookies. Of all the lucky breaks, this was one of the most qualified witnesses I could ever recall. He was intelligent and highly competent to identify the plane that caused this accident. He looked over the photographs I had laid out on the floor. He carefully studied each one and turned over the planes that were not involved. Finally, only one photo remained. It was an F-111 marine fighter plane out of the El Toro Marine Base in Orange County (north of San Diego). I asked him if he was positive it was this model aircraft. He said he was positive because he had worked on F-111's at March Air Force Base in Riverside before his retirement.

I gave John Dale the good news and told him I was on my way to El Toro Marine Base to see if I could identify the pilot.

The next morning, I drove from our home in Claremont to El Toro. I told the guard at the gate I was an investigator on an air crash near Blythe and was looking for any possible witnesses - well, it was almost the truth! The idiot at the gate treated me like a spy and turned me over to the Military Police. I was taken into their building and told to take a seat and wait for Master Sergeant Jim Thomas to see me. Finally, at 11:45am, he ushered me into his office. We sat down and I handed him my card. He said his tour of duty would end next month and he wondered what it would be like to be a Private Investigator. He wanted to know how much money he could make and whether it as exciting as it was on T.V.

This was just the opening I needed. I told him about the five little children who lost their mothers when a fighter pilot from El Toro did a bombing run on them and caused their Volkswagen to run off the road and rollover. I guess I laid it on a little thick because I almost had the Sergeant crying when I told him I represented the little children. I said it was my job, as an investigator, to identify the pilot and interview him if at all possible. He looked at his watch and told me to go over to the Canteen for lunch while he made some phone calls. He said he would join me in a few minutes.

Twenty minutes later, Sergeant Thomas joined me, all smiles. He told me the pilot who caused the accident was Lieutenant Jeffrey Reyes. He was a twenty-year career man in the Marine Corps. It was only a rumor, but it was said Jeffrey Reyes told the Commander at the base about the accident and he was immediately transferred to their base in Hawaii. I congratulated Sergeant Thomas on a fine piece of investigation and I promised not to reveal his name as the one who gave me the pilot's name. He said he would call me after his discharge and I agreed to help him get his Private Investigator's License.

I gave all the information to John Dale. He immediately set a deposition date for Jeffrey Reyes but was told he was in Hawaii on a top secret mission and was beyond subpoena range. However, defense counsel agreed to produce him for the trial although they continued to maintain none of their pilots were guilty of any wrongdoing.

Finally, the case came up for trial in federal court. John gave me a subpoena to serve on Jeffrey Reyes who had returned to El Toro for the trial. While John was picking a jury, I drove out to El Toro to serve the subpoena on Jeffrey Reyes. At the gate, I asked for the Officer in charge of the Military Police because I thought Sergeant Jim Thomas had been discharged months ago. I was told to park over in front of the M.P. building. Master Sergeant James Thomas's name was still on the door to his office and when I knocked, there was Jim Thomas. I told him I thought he was discharged. But he told me it was "too scary on the outside" so he signed up for another four-year hitch. His dream of being a Private Investigator had long since vanished.

I said I had a subpoena for Lieutenant Jeffrey Reyes to appear at the trial that was now going on in federal court in San Bernardino. He told me "all hell broke loose" after my last visit when someone told an investigator (me) it was Jeffrey Reyes who caused the accident. But luckily, no one had suspected *him* of leaking the information. He said Jeffrey Reyes was on the Base but I had to go through the Commanding Officer, Colonel Leon Marshall, to get permission to serve him. On my way over to the Commander's office, Jim told me the "boss" was a real pain who put fear into everyone below him in rank. He cautioned me to be very careful or I would end up in the brig.

Jim drove away as I walked up the steps to "the Boss's" office. I had the subpoena in my hand as I walked past several guards and into Colonel Leon Marshall's private office. There sat the Commanding Officer of El Toro Marine Base with a scowl on his face and glory bars all over his fat chest. He demanded to see my card and my Private Investigator's license. I told him I had a subpoena for Lieutenant Jeffrey Reyes to appear in federal court Wednesday morning at 10:00 a.m. The Commander stood up, pounded his desk and shouted. "Jeffrey Reyes is in Hawaii on a secret mission. He will not appear for any trial. Now get out of my office!"

I knew he was hiding something because defense counsel had promised the judge that Officer Reyes would be present for the trial provided he was subpoenaed. So, I gambled a day in the brig. I stood up and grabbed a pen from his desk. I crossed out Jeffrey Reyes's name and wrote in "Colonel Leon Marshall, Commander of El Toro Marine Base" and shoved the subpoena across the desk to the flustered Commander. I said, "If Officer Reyes is in Hawaii, then you are ordered to appear in Federal Court on Wednesday and explain his absence to the judge!" I fully expected one of the guards at the door to grab me and take me to the brig. But I just walked past them, past the Canteen, and into my car and drove away.

On Wednesday morning, I was in the hallway outside Judge Patterson's courtroom when I saw the Commander and Officer Reyes walking down the corridor dressed up in full military parade uniform. They didn't look in my direction but I wondered how they felt when they saw five little children seated next to me on a hallway bench outside the courtroom.

Anyway, by mid-afternoon, the case settled for over $5 million (one million for each child) and we all went home. John and I drove to our office in Century City; Colonel Marshall to his "kingdom" at El Toro; Lieutenant Reyes to the nearest bar to examine his conscience, and the five little children, without their mothers, went to a foster home at Eagle Mountain. But I'll bet every one of those children would trade their million dollars just to have their mother home again.

The Maher Oil Company Millions

If I had another life to live, I would handle only Will Contests. Contrary to what they teach you in law school, just about every will can be broken one way or another. Sometimes, an investigator will prove the person drawing the will (the "testator") was being unduly influenced to write a will giving the estate to the person or persons exerting the undue influence. Sometimes, the mental capacity of the testator is questioned at the time the will was drafted. The story I'm about to tell you is true, only the names and places have been changed to protect persons both living and dead.

It all began in 1925 when Dave Maher struck oil on Catalina Island. It was a real "gusher" and it made Dave an instant millionaire. He was married to Sarah Maher and they had a three-year-old daughter, Dorothy. They lived modestly in San Pedro but in part, due to Dave's newfound wealth, within a year Dave divorced Sarah and married Ruth, his personal secretary. Sarah agreed to the divorce on three conditions: 1) she would receive a monthly alimony payment of $4,500; 2) she would have sole custody of Dorothy; and 3) Dave would give to Dorothy, via an Irrevocable Trust, The Maher Oil Company upon his death. Dave agreed to these conditions and the documents were signed and witnessed in the Law Offices of Mayo and Fulton, a firm specializing in estate planning in Los Angeles, California.

Dave Maher had a home and cattle ranch on Catalina Island. Within five years, alcohol and drugs took their toll on Ruth and she was committed to a rehab center in Beverly Hills. Dave divorced her and was now one of the richest and most eligible bachelors in Southern California at just 58 years old! Ten years later, along came Olga Crawford, who became wife #3. She was divorced and had a grown son named Thomas.

Olga had been living in San Francisco when one day, she told her sister she was moving to Los Angeles with the goal of "marrying one of those Hollywood millionaires." Lo and behold, she packed her bags and moved to Hollywood. For weeks, she had her dinners at Joey's, the fanciest restaurant in Los Angeles. She made friends with the bartender and one evening, he pointed to Dave Maher and said, "There is one of the most eligible bachelors in town. Why don't you go over and introduce yourself?" So she did.

Within just a few months, Olga Crawford was staying at Dave Maher's Ranch on Catalina Island and poor old Dave was swept off his feet. Not long after, they were married in Santa Barbara and flew off in the Maher Company jet for a month-long honeymoon in Hawaii.

On their return to Catalina, Olga managed to talk Dave into writing a will giving her his entire estate and excluding his daughter Dorothy. But when Olga learned Dave had already executed a binding Irrevocable Trust in favor of Dorothy, she went ballistic. She hired a big law firm in San Francisco to try and bust the Trust agreement.

By this time, Dave had retired as CEO of Maher Oil Companies and he was virtually being held prisoner by Olga in his own mansion on Catalina Island. He did as he was told and Olga spent thousands of dollars trying to break Dorothy's Trust while at the same time, buying homes in Aspen and Paris.

Finally, it was decided by the "army" of lawyers in San Francisco that the Trust could only be broken if Dave Maher executed a new will specifically revoking the terms of Dorothy's Trust Agreement and naming Olga Crawford Maher, his wife as sole heir to his entire estate.

When his daughter Dorothy learned of this attempt by Olga to have her dad revoke the trust and sign a new will, she came to our law firm and asked us to protect her interests. She said she had learned from employees at her dad's mansion that a new will was about to be signed by her dad who, unfortunately had been admitted to the Good Samaritan Hospital in Phoenix. The doctors there said his condition was not serious but he did have a serious lung congestion problem (he was a cigar smoker). Doctors were running various tests to correct his breathing problem.

I was elected to make the trip to Phoenix to see if Dave Maher was in any condition mentally to make a new will and destroy Dorothy's Trust Agreement. Dorothy drove me to LAX airport. On the way, she told me all about Olga's complete domination of her father. Dorothy lived in a guest house on the Ranch and was in daily contact with her father. Now, it was going to be my job to prove Dave was in no condition to execute a new will. After all, he was in a hospital with doctors in attendance and he was mentally and physically very old.

When I landed in Phoenix, I realized I grabbed my briefcase when I left my office with Dorothy and it would be of no use to me if I was going to try to look like just another visitor at the hospital. I decided to store my briefcase with my coat and tie in a locker at the airport. I kept my camera just in case it would be needed.

At the airport, I told the cabbie to take me to the Good Samaritan Hospital. I only hoped I was in time and Dave had not already signed the new will. I learned Dave Maher was on the "Executive" 5TH floor where no visitors were allowed. Then I had a wild idea. I followed a male nurse into a dressing room and when he left, I "borrowed" his white jacket from the laundry (with his name tag...Juan Garcia!) and his clipboard, which he had left on the counter.

My camera fit nicely into the pocket of the jacket. I got onto the elevator and pressed the button for the 5th floor. When the doors opened, I smiled at the Security Guard in attendance and walked down the long hallway (as if I knew where I was going!). I have a vague recollection of seeing several men talking to the nurses at the nurse's station but my focus was on getting past the Security Guard and honestly, it never crossed my mind that they may have been the attorneys about to have Dave sign his new will.

Thank God, on the wall of each patient's room was the patient's name and medical chart. In room #6, the door was open and there sat David Maher all propped up with pillows in his bed reading the *Wall Street Journal.* Olga was sitting in a chair next to his bed and a nurse was pouring him a glass of water. The only problem with this scene was, the newspaper was upside down!

I walked past the room. I took my camera out of my jacket and adjusted the lens. Then I turned around, walked back to Dave's open door and took two pictures of Dave and the upside down newspaper. The nurse looked up, with the clicking of my camera, and ran to the open door screaming, "SECURITY!" I heard Olga shout, "Get him and get that camera!" I turned and ran down the hallway. I noticed a stairway and as I opened the door, I turned around and saw two Security Guards running after me.

I ran down the stairs two at a time. At the 3rd floor, I opened the door and saw a Men's Room just down the hall. I ran into a stall and closed the door. The Guards must not have seen me enter the 3rd floor and go into the Men's Room. All was quiet. I took off my "borrowed" jacket and placed it on a hook on the door of the stall. Then I stuffed my camera into a wastebasket because sooner or later, I knew I was going to be caught.

I gambled that later in the day, I could come back and retrieve my camera with photographs that would prove Dave Maher was being set up by Olga to show he was of sound mind and reading the Stock Market section of the *Wall Street Journal* when the attorneys came in to have him sign the new will. However, Olga made a huge mistake, because in her haste, the *Wall Street Journal* was accidentally placed upside down and I had the photographs to prove Dave was not reading the newspaper. He appeared to be sound asleep when the pictures were taken.

I walked slowly to the 3rd floor elevator and punched the basement floor key where a sign said "cafeteria." I was in luck, no one recognized me and no Security Guards were looking for me. My watch said it was 5:00 p.m. and I could tell, by watching the employees hurry to the time clock, it was a change of shifts. I had to retrieve my camera before some custodian emptied the restroom waste basket. I ran to the elevator and punched the 3rd floor key. In the men's restroom, I dug my arm down into a full waste basket of paper and found my camera! I calmly took the elevator to the 1st floor, caught a cab, headed for the airport, picked up my sports coat, tie and briefcase and caught the next flight back to Los Angeles. It was a whirlwind afternoon to say the least!

On Monday morning, Dorothy was in our office for a meeting with our attorneys and me. They showed her my photographs and she sadly shook her head because it confirmed her suspicion that her Dad was completely under the control of Olga. Dorothy told us Olga's attorneys did have Dave Maher sign a new will giving his entire estate to her.

Olga's attorneys were completely unaware that I had taken the photographs. Olga and the nurse had apparently failed to tell them I had been there. Dave was released from the hospital within a week. Dorothy said her father's personal wealth was at least $56,000,000 plus controlling stock in the Maher Oil

Company. The Maher cattle ranch was larger than downtown Catalina.

Dorothy gave me a list of Dave's closest friends who had known him over the last 40 years. My job was to contact them and learn Dave's true mental capacity and the extent of Olga's undue influence. Several of them had summer homes on Catalina but most of them were retired and lived around Santa Barbara. For the next year and a half, I spent my Fridays and Saturdays talking to these old friends (132 in all) of Dave Maher. About a third of them agreed to testify that Olga was in complete control of Dave Maher. Another third were undecided and the last third said Dave Maher was of sound mind and not being unduly influenced by Olga.

Three days before Christmas, Dave died in his sleep on his beloved ranch on Catalina Island. Olga wasted no time in filing his newly executed will in Probate Court and we filed our contest to the will. What followed were months and months of legal maneuvering and waiting for a courtroom. I was told there were 32 defense attorneys working on this case against only my office and me representing the plaintiff Dorothy Maher.

We were finally given a trial date. It dawned on me that I had seen 132 witnesses. We had picked the 17 best witnesses who were willing to testify that Olga exercised almost total control over Dave and he was virtually a prisoner in his own home. Our fear was if the defense had 32 attorneys working on the case, then how many investigators did they have?

We had to assume a team of investigators had interviewed all 132 potential witnesses. If they did, they could easily produce at least 60 witnesses who would deny Olga had exerted any undue influence on Dave Maher and testify he was mentally alert at all times before and after his stay at the Good Samaritan Hospital in Arizona.

I dropped everything about a week before trial and I interviewed all 17 of our best witnesses again. Not one of them had been contacted by the defense attorneys nor had they talked to any investigator other than me! Then I went through the list of witnesses and re-contacted the 60 or more who were angry at Dorothy for filing the Will Contest. I had to know if they had been contacted by the defense. Again, I was in for a big surprise. Not one of those potential witnesses had been contacted by anyone but me! It became apparent that the defense team of 32 lawyers had been more interested in billing their time on the file than doing any investigation on all possible witnesses.

We were assigned to Department 46 with Judge Eugene Watkins presiding. After opening statements, we put on 12 of our 17 key witnesses and rested our case. The Defense put on two doctors and two nurses who were present at the time the will was signed. They testified Dave was in complete control of his mental faculties and his medical chart showed he was even reading the *Wall Street Journal* just before the will was signed. The defense rested their case and it was clear that neither Olga nor the nurse had told them of my taking Dave's photographs. Then in rebuttal we showed Judge Watkins and the jury my photographs (enlarged to 3'x4') and they were admitted into evidence showing Dave "reading" the *Wall Street Journal* upside down.

The entire trial lasted three weeks and in three hours, the jury returned a verdict for Dorothy Maher. Damages were assessed of $51,000,000 and the original Trust Agreement was validated. The new will was thrown out and Olga was found liable for exerting undue influence over her deceased husband.

End of story? Well, almost.

I was seated on a bench in the hallway when the verdict was read. Then, the doors flew open and out charged Olga Maher. She was raving mad. She came up to me and shook her finger saying, "I'll get you for this O'Brien, just you wait and see." I smiled as she stomped out of the courthouse. Then a very strange thing happened and I am at a loss to explain, but I will try.

The verdict came in on a Thursday afternoon. I planned to take Friday off and rest. Then I learned there was an opening for a weekend retreat at the Manresa Retreat House in Azusa, California. I usually went on retreat once a year and this was a perfect fit. I signed in on Friday evening with 65 other men. We had dinner and a conference before retiring to our rooms. I was getting into my pajamas when I heard a knock on my door. I opened the door and there stood a young man about 35, wearing glasses and he was very thin.

He introduced himself as Tom Crawford, the only son of Olga Maher. He said he noticed my name and room number on the Retreat Register. He said his mother had mentioned my name many times during the trial. He had no idea I would be on the same retreat, but he did have some information for me that would prove to be quite interesting. He told me that during the trial, his mother put out a "contract" on me and paid a "hit man" $5,000.00 to break every bone in my body. However, the "hit man" happened to be an undercover detective for the Los Angeles Police Department. She was arrested almost immediately after the verdict came in. Her lawyers posted $100,000 bail and she was awaiting trial. He just thought I should know.

Now, it would be easy to chalk off this chance meeting with Tom Crawford and me at a weekend Retreat as accidental, OR was someone looking over my shoulder and protecting me? I wonder.

Now – End of story. And almost the end of me!

Baton Rouge in the Rain

One of the key witnesses in the Maher Oil Company case lived in Miami, Florida and the other lived in Baton Rouge, Louisiana. After seeing them, I planned to go to New Orleans and meet Cathy for a weekend of great food and maybe we could even catch Louie Armstrong somewhere on Basin Street.

I saw my witness in Miami and then boarded a Delta Flight going from Miami to Baton Rouge, where I planned to see my other witness. The plane took off at 7:00 p.m. and seated next to me was a real-life "pan handler." He explained the name by saying he sold pots and pans to the major supermarkets in the south. He was a nice guy, about my age. He was going on to New Orleans and I had a stop to make in Baton Rouge.

When the stewardess came by, he ordered a round of martinis for us and when we finished, I felt obligated to order a second round...of course. Well, we got talking baseball and soon both glasses were empty...again. When the stewardess came by, the "pan handler" tried to order us a third round of drinks but he was told she could only serve two rounds to a customer. Well, by then, I was feeling no pain. I told the "pan handler" if he was a real salesman he could talk the stewardess into a third round.

Now, I must confess, (as well as I can remember) he gave her a sales pitch that even had me crying. It had to do with something about us having to go to a funeral for our mother in Baton Rouge and we needed the martinis to strengthen us for the awful ordeal and it worked! She kept our glasses full all the way to Baton Rouge.

The plane landed in Baton Rouge and I said goodbye to the "pan handler." I tried to walk down the aisle but things were spinning in me and around me. I plopped down in an empty seat and stayed seated until all the passengers got off the plane. Finally, a stewardess shook me and said I had to leave. I grabbed my suitcase from the overhead bin and somehow I walked off the plane and into the pouring rain. I didn't care, all I wanted to do was get into the airport lounge and sit down until my head stopped spinning.

The next thing I remember was sitting in the lounge with my suitcase on my lap and I was soaking wet. Then someone placed his hand on my shoulder and said he was a Yellow Cab driver. He asked if I needed a ride somewhere. I asked him if he could help me find a motel so he picked up my bags and led me to his cab. He stopped at several motels but there were no vacancies. Finally, he found a motel with a vacancy sign in the window. I remember paying him, giving him a tip and wandering off to a nice clean warm bed.

The next morning, after a shower, breakfast and a gallon of coffee, the bells and whistles finally stopped clanging in my head. I paid my motel bill and grabbed a cab to take me to see my witness on the Maher Oil Company case. Then it was off to the airport to catch a Delta flight to New Orleans and meet Cathy.

At the Delta Airlines desk, I learned my flight was about an hour late so I bought a newspaper and sat down in the waiting area. Suddenly, I had the strange feeling someone was looking at me. I looked up from the Sports Page and saw a tall man wearing a Yellow Cab driver's hat walking quickly toward me with a serious look on his face. Then he started smiling and held out his hand. Instinctively, I stood up and he grabbed my hand, shaking it vigorously. "Mister, I thank you, my wife thanks you and my five kids thank you, for the tip you gave me last night!" I had no idea what he was talking about so I just smiled and thanked him for his help finding a motel for me. Fortunately, my plane was loading so I said good-bye and boarded my flight to New Orleans.

The whole way down the tarmac and up the steps to my plane, I scoured my brain to try and remember what he could have been talking about. After I was seated, a sick feeling gripped my chest. I counted the money in my money clip. Although I vaguely remembered paying the cab fare, I thought I'd given the driver a $5.00 tip. However, I had given him a $50.00 bill for a tip! No wonder the Cab driver and his family were so happy. Cathy met me in New Orleans, but for dinner that evening we went to McDonald's for a hamburger. Oh well, that's the price I paid for a few free martinis!

My Adventures in Claremont

Meet Syd DeVito

For over seventeen years, Syd DeVito was my secretary. She was from New York and moved with her daughter to Claremont, California after her husband died. She was a diehard baseball fan, especially when it came to her beloved "Brooklyn" Dodgers.

When I moved my office from Century City to Claremont, she joined me as my secretary, receptionist, bookkeeper and friend. She was barely five feet tall and she always wore four-inch heels. She never told me her age but I guessed she was at least fifteen years my senior – and I was fifty at the time. Syd was a chain smoker. We had to install fans and open all windows in the office just to see her through the haze at her desk! Her friends called her "Old Leather lungs."

She lived alone and never took a vacation. But about three to four times a year, her church would take a bus load of ladies to Las Vegas for a weekend of bingo and slot machines. She would tell me on a Thursday for example, that she would not be coming to work on Friday because she and the "ladies" from church were going to Las Vegas. But always, come Monday morning, she would be seated at her desk with a cigarette, a cup of coffee and a hundred stories about her adventures in Vegas. She followed this routine religiously (pardon the pun) year after year after year.

On one Monday morning, my son Mike and I came into the office and Syd was not there. We knew she had gone to Las Vegas for the weekend but she was *always* at her desk on Monday morning. We called her home...no answer.

At 10:30 a.m. our phone rang; it was Syd calling from Las Vegas. I asked her if she was sick or hurt. Her answer was, "Eldon, I'm winning and I'll be back tomorrow!" Well, at her age, we were just glad she wasn't sick or in an accident. So Mike went off to law school and I was saddled with the office phones for the rest of the day.

On Tuesday morning, there was Syd at her desk, smoking a cigarette as usual. She said she had won $135.00 on the slot machines and had a great time with the ladies from her church. There was a mountain of mail on her desk so I went back to my office. Mike was studying in the back office while I was meeting with a client.

About a half-hour into my meeting, my intercom rang. It was Syd in the front office, scared and out of breath. "Eldon, come quick! I think I'm having a heart attack!" I thought to myself, "Oh God, don't let her die right here in my office!"

I ran down the hall and told Mike to drive her to the hospital while I called Dr. Stryker, her doctor, and I told him to meet them in the emergency room. Mike left with Syd and I waited and waited. Finally, my phone rang. It was Dr. Stryker and he was laughing! He said "there is nothing wrong with this old broad, she just strained her shoulder muscles pulling the arms on those damned slot machines!"

Syd returned to my office much relieved she wasn't going to die. She went on working for me for the next ten years - cigarettes, high heels and all. We all loved "Old Leather Lungs."

She was a great secretary and a great person.

Please Find My Dad

My office in Claremont was a few blocks from the local grammar school. After school, some of the kids would walk down to the ice cream shop near my office. My secretary, Syd sat at her desk and could see the children from a huge bay window in our front office. One Friday afternoon she called me on the intercom and said, "Eldon come up here and look out the window, you have to see this." I saw the usual eight or ten school kids standing around with about half eating ice cream cones and the other half wishing they had the money to buy one. But Syd pointed to one boy in particular who just stood on the sidewalk looking up at my office window. Syd said for several days now, this boy just stands there on the sidewalk looking at our window. I decided to meet this young man and see if there was anything I could do for him.

I stepped outside and introduced myself. We sat on a wrought iron bench between the curb and the sidewalk. He said his name was Tommy Olsen; he was 9 years old and in the 3rd grade. I asked him why he came every day and just looked in our front window. He looked me straight in the eye and said, "Mr. O'Brien, Could you please find my dad? My heart went out for this freckle-faced young boy with blonde hair and a baseball mitt hanging out of his back pocket. He said he wanted to pay me but all he had was $32.23 in his Christmas savings account. I told him not to worry, sometimes I worked for free.

We walked into my back office and I grabbed a sheet of paper to take some notes. Tommy said every morning his dad would take him to school and then go to his accounting office in Upland. But on Monday, he dropped Tommy off at school and had not been seen since. His mom and his sister just didn't know what to do. He told me they reported this to the police but all the police said was to wait a few more days because missing persons usually come home within a week.

We called his mother, Anne. I introduced myself and told her I would be glad to make a few phone calls at no cost to the family. She gave me the address of her husband's office, his birth date, his social security number and offered to drop off a photo of him. Tommy and I shook hands as he left the office and he promised to come back tomorrow after school with the photograph of his dad.

It happened that my son-in-law's family owned the office building where Tommy's dad had his accounting business. I made a phone call to Jean, the secretary who collected the rents for the building, and I learned Tommy's dad had taken off with his secretary for a few days in San Francisco. Jean told me this sordid little story was supposed to be an office secret but everyone knew and they simply made excuses for Doug and Sarah's absence.

Now I had a problem...a BIG problem. How was I going to explain this trip to San Francisco to Tommy and his mother? Tommy was going to be in my office right after school Monday. I'm an investigator, not a marriage counselor. I talked to my wife Cathy, and Syd but we could not come up with an answer that wouldn't derail both the marriage and Tommy's faith in his dad.

Early Monday morning, Jean called to tell me that Tommy's dad, Doug, was back in his office and that Sarah had quit abruptly. I called Doug, told him who I was and told him to meet me at Denny's coffee shop. I said I had been hired by his wife and Tommy to find him. Now, he had a BIG problem. If he was to save his marriage and the respect of his children, he had to explain his absence.

Doug sat down and we ordered coffee. He just sat there clutching the coffee cup with two trembling hands. I asked him, how was he going to explain the "lost weekend" to his wife and family? Doug made no eye contact; he just tapped his coffee cup and shrugged. Still gazing into his coffee cup, he sheepishly confessed he did a stupid thing by sneaking away to San Francisco for the weekend with Sarah. They had a big fight there when he told her he wouldn't divorce his wife and Sarah quit the firm. Doug seemed to be sincere in wanting to save his marriage and retain the respect of his family and then he began to cry. Across from me sat a young accountant who was maybe 32 years old, very good looking (despite the fact he looked like he didn't sleep at all last night), who was now coming to grips with the fact that his entire future was at risk. I really wanted to help him but I remembered what Walter Ward told me years ago: Lies have a way of compounding on each other and it's always much better to tell the truth and hope for the best. He thanked me for the "wake-up" and told me he needed to figure out how he would handle this. We shook hands and went our separate ways.

A few hours later, Doug called me and asked if he could meet his family at my office when Tommy got out of school. I agreed, asked Syd to cancel my afternoon appointments, then called his wife and asked if she could come in around 3:30, that I had some news for her regarding her husband. She agreed, once I assured her that he was alive and well.

By 3:35 p.m., Tommy and Anne were seated in my office when Doug arrived. Syd and I excused ourselves while the family exchanged uncomfortable, bittersweet greetings. Syd and I waited out in the reception area and said a silent prayer.

In the months that followed, every once in a while I would see Tommy at a little league baseball game or when he'd stop by my office and we'd have an ice cream cone. Tommy and I never talked about his family's meeting in my office but I had a sneaking suspicion Walter Ward was right. Doug told the truth and our prayers were answered.

Ron Buys a New Mercedes

During the years I worked with the Wortel Law Firm, we lived in Claremont, a small college town about 50 miles east of our offices in Century City. We had a branch office in San Bernardino that we shared with the Reynolds & Golob Law Firm, a worker's compensation firm. Ron Golob ran the office and when he had a client who was injured by someone other than his employer, he would refer the client to our office for handling of the personal injury case. And since Claremont was only 24 miles from San Bernardino, I was elected to meet with Ron Golob on Fridays and he would usually have several potential new clients for me to interview (see, "A Good Turn For a Nice Lady"; "A Witness Risks His Life For a Friend").

When I met with Ron, we usually went down to the Arrowhead Bowling Alley for lunch. We were being seated at our usual booth in the corner when Ron said "hello" to the man in the next booth. He was a family law attorney with offices near the courthouse. He was seated alone when Shirley, our waitress, came to take his order. Then a strange thing happened: she sat down at his table with him and they talked for several minutes. Waitresses seldom, if ever, have the time to do this, especially at a busy time like the lunch hour.

Ron asked her, when she came to take our order, if he was her "boyfriend." She said, "No, he is my attorney. My husband was badly injured in a car accident last Wednesday and he is handling our case." Ron and I dropped the subject and wished her well, not wanting to pry into the confidentiality of her case with her attorney. A week later, we went back to the bowling alley for lunch. Shirley took our order and when she came back with her arm full of food she asked us if we were attorneys. Ron said he was an attorney and I was his investigator. She told us the attorney we saw her with last week had turned her case down because the driver who hit her husband was drunk and had no insurance. She asked us if there was anything we could do because her husband was paralyzed from the neck down. I told Shirley to meet me at our office after her shift ended at 2:00 p.m.

That afternoon, Shirley came to the office with a copy of the police report. It placed the responsibility for this accident on the drunk driver. Shirley said her husband was driving a Budweiser Beer truck and was on his way home at about 6:00 p.m. when he was hit head-on by a drunk driver who was on the wrong side of the road. The 5th Street Bridge had been narrowed from four lanes to two (one westbound and one eastbound lane) with 21 flashing red lights warning drivers of the lane change. The driver of the other car failed to see the warning lights and hit the beer truck head-on. The force of the impact caused a load of empty beer kegs to slide forward and pin her husband against the steering wheel. As a result, he was paralyzed from the neck down. The other driver was arrested for drunk driving and, adding insult to injury, he had no insurance.

I signed up Shirley's case because of the extreme injury. Walter Ward had always told me a severe injury case was always worth a good investigation. I explained to her that we would investigate the accident at no cost to her and then we would decide if her previous lawyer was correct in turning her case down.

On my way home that evening, I decided to go over the 5th Street Bridge and see if they still had the two lanes closed for repair. It was getting dark when I noticed a San Bernardino City car parked on the bridge and a man with a clipboard drawing a diagram. I parked my car next to his and asked him if there had been another accident on the bridge. He said no, he was drawing a diagram showing only three flashing lights were working and 18 had dead batteries when the drunk driver hit the beer truck. He said the city would contact the independent lighting contractor in the morning and lodge another complaint.

I told him I had been contacted by the driver of the Budweiser truck who was hit head-on by the drunk driver last week. He said he remembered the accident and this lighting problem had existed for at least a month before the beer truck accident. Numerous complaints had been made to the lighting company but the batteries kept burning out on the flashing lights. They were supposed to warn motorists that the four lanes of traffic narrowed to two lanes.

He was a nice guy, a young safety engineer for the City of San Bernardino, and it was his job to inspect the street repairs to the 5TH Street Bridge while Southern Pacific was making repairs to the 5th Street Bridge over the railroad tracks. Suddenly, we had three solid potential defendants: (1) The City of San Bernardino, responsible for the traffic safety on the street when the two lanes had to be closed; (2) The independent lighting company for defective batteries; and (3) Southern Pacific Railroad who owned the property. These three potential defendants each played a role in the accident that resulted in our client's injury. Suddenly, we had a valid lawsuit.

To make a long story short, Ron Golob handled the workman's compensation claim; the Wortel office settled the case against the City, the lighting company and Southern Pacific for $989,000. The attorney's fee was $320,000 and Ron Golob's firm got a 1/3 referral fee. Ron's cut was $56,000 and he went right out and bought a brand new fancy Mercedes Benz.

A week later, Ron took me to lunch at the bowling alley in his new car. When Ron drove into the parking lot, he saw the family law attorney who turned down Shirley's case. He was just getting into his car so Ron parked right next to him and got out. The lawyer took a long look at Ron's fancy new Mercedes and said, "Ron, where did you ever get the money to buy such an expensive car?"

Ron's answer was a classic. He said, "Let me tell you, some idiot lawyer here in town turned down a beer truck accident on the 5th Street Bridge and we took it on. The case settled for $989,000 and part of my cut was this new Mercedes!" The lawyer never said a word; he just shook his head, got into his old car and drove away!

A Good Turn for a Nice Lady

On Fridays, it was my job to open our San Bernardino branch office for Wortel & Dale. We shared office space with the Reynolds & Golob Law Firm. Their practice handled Workman's Compensation claims with Ron Golob running the office, and I interviewed new clients who had personal injury claims as well as Workman's Compensation.

One Friday morning, a lady was waiting for me as Ron and I opened the office. She had been in an accident where a cleaning truck had rear-ended her brand new Chevrolet Impala. She was not injured but I could see her car through my office window. It had about $500 damage. Mary Clark was a pleasant lady in her early 50's. It was a simple claim for her to present to the insurance company representing the cleaning company. I photographed her car and had her get an estimate of the damage. Then I told her to return and I would write a demand letter for her to send to the insurance company. It was no big deal. Within three weeks, she received a check for the full amount demanded. She wanted to pay me for my help but she was a pleasant, nice lady and I was glad to help her so I told her there would be no charge.

About three weeks went by and while Ron and I were having breakfast one morning, we noticed the headlines in the newspaper saying an Alaskan Airlines plane had gone down in Canada killing all 105 passengers and crew. We finished breakfast and drove to our office. Waiting for us, at the front door, was Mary Clark. She said her daughter had been a stewardess on the Alaskan Airlines plane and was killed. She wanted us to investigate the accident and handle her daughter's case. It was a very sad morning but she trusted us to do all that we could to determine the cause of the crash. She had with her a passenger list of all occupants on the plane. This allowed us to contact all the other parties and/or their attorneys and offer our services. We ended up with 34 cases.

Eventually, all of those cases settled and we even were able to take home a much-needed bonus...and all because we did a favor for a nice lady.

60 Years in a City Dump

At the turn of the century, Los Angeles County was a sleeping giant with a great climate, a strong agricultural base and a harbor in San Pedro that shipped its produce all over the world. But it was the discovery of oil in the early 1920's that awoke the giant and changed orange groves into oil drilling rigs and refineries. By 1924, most people owned automobiles and a billion dollar gasoline industry was born. Little towns like San Pedro, Wilmington, La Brea and Huntington Beach suddenly became boom towns with drilling rigs, refineries and gasoline stations everywhere.

Signal Hill in San Pedro was the site of many oil strikes creating oil giants like Standard Oil and Shell Oil. They built huge refineries and storage tanks along the beaches and cliffs between Huntington Beach and Newport Beach to process the liquid gold coming out of the earth. Even during the Great Depression there were "Help Wanted" signs for drillers, welders, truck drivers and general labor needed to turn the oil into various grades of aviation, gasoline and diesel fuel. The tar residue was used for asphalt roofing shingles and asphalt roadways. But unfortunately, there was the remaining residue which had no practical use, called "Gunk" that the big refineries had to get rid of somewhere. The "Gunk" was often disposed of close to the refineries lining the coast from Huntington Beach and Newport Beach.

In the spring of 2004, a lawyer from Huntington Beach called me and said he represented a General Contractor who was building a 200-unit apartment complex on a ten-acre site known as the Bolsa Chica. It was a choice parcel of land overlooking the

Pacific Ocean and about halfway between Huntington Beach and Newport Beach. But the lawyer said when the Contractor started to dig the foundations for the apartment units, they found "Gunk" under two feet of soil throughout the ten-acre site. The building inspector shut down all construction until the "Gunk" was removed. The lawyer said his client was not told the Bolsa Chica site was once used as a city dump during the Depression years and that it was later closed to the public in 1951. It was only after a two-foot layer of topsoil was placed on the dump site and the area was made into a park that the land was re-opened to the public.

The lawyer reached a nominal settlement with the realtor for failing to disclose to our client the Bolsa Chica was once a city dump. The City of Huntington Beach claimed they had no knowledge of the oil companies dumping "Gunk" on their property in the Depression years and during World War II. It was clear the responsible parties for the Bolsa Chica soil contamination were Standard Oil and Shell Oil. And the burden of proof would rest on finding truckers willing to testify that 50-60 years ago they deposited "Gunk" from Standard and Shell refineries into the Bolsa Chica dump.

To tell the truth, I was not at all excited about accepting the assignment. This was the first time I ever worked with this lawyer and finding truckers who were now in their 70's and 80's was going to be quite a task. I made up my mind I would turn down the assignment. Then the lawyer offered me a $5,000 retainer. I reluctantly agreed to take on the case provided the retainer was non-refundable and with no promises on the outcome.

I drove out to the 10-acre site, which was at the end of a cul-de-sac. It was all roped off with "No Trespassing" signs everywhere. The neighborhood was old and the housing tract was probably built in the late 1930's, before World II. There was a sliver of a chance at least one of these homes was still occupied by the original owner. It was a long shot but I started ringing doorbells anyway. There were about thirty homes on the block and no one was at home. Then, I got lucky. I rang the doorbell of one of the last homes on the block and an elderly lady answered. I guessed her age at 75- 80 years old.

She was hard of hearing so I had to raise my voice to get her to understand that I was trying to find someone who may have lived here when truckers used the old Bolsa Chica dump. She just kept shaking her head saying she had moved into her home in 1993. But then she opened the screen door and there was a lady standing behind her listening to our conversation. This lady said *she* was the original owner and the woman who answered the door was her sister. She invited me into her living room and introduced herself as Barbara North. She said she remembered when she was a young girl, trucks were always driving by her parents' home with *"that foul smelling stuff"* and dumping it into the Bolsa Chica dump. She said the name on the side doors of the trucks was "Graham Trucking." Amazed at her memory, I asked her how she remembered these things so clearly.

I saw a faint blush on her cheek as she told me she had a crush on one of the truck drivers for Graham Trucking and although they were both in their "teens" they were madly in love. His name was Richard Wheeler and with the bombing of Pearl Harbor, he joined the Marines. When the War was over, he came home with a Filipino war bride. She was devastated and never married but she exchanged Christmas Cards with the Wheeler's every year. She gave me his address as 220 Florida Street in Hemet, California. Barbara was unable to tell me where *"that foul smelling stuff"* came from but she assured me that Richard Wheeler could identify the source.

The next morning I got up early and drove to Hemet. The address Barbara gave me turned out to be a huge trailer park. The community mail box showed Richard Wheeler was living in a trailer at space D-34. I parked my car and noticed an elderly man seated on his porch with a can of beer in one hand and *Sporting News* in the other. I asked him if he was Richard Wheeler, he nodded as he sat down the *Sporting News* and offered me a beer. I declined and told him Barbara North had given me his name. We talked baseball for awhile and then finally we got around to his working for Graham Trucking.

The years had been kind to Richard as he sat there tall and erect with silver grey hair and a smile that made you feel quite at home. He said he was employed by Graham Trucking in 1940 and 1941 and then he joined the Marines. He said all of that time he hauled "Gunk" from Standard Oil and Shell Oil to the Bolsa Chica dump. In fact, he was one of six other truckers who drove the same route every day, six days a week. I asked him if he kept in touch with the other drivers. He said only one was still alive, Roger Wyatt, who moved to Green Bay, Wisconsin years ago.

I took a long detailed written statement for Richard Wheeler and it included the possibility that Roger Wyatt was a possible second witness who could confirm the statements made by Mr. Wheeler. I left him with the promise I would keep in touch with him as the case progressed.

The next morning, I met with our Contractor client and his lawyer. I gave them the signed statement of Richard Wheeler and I said we should consider a trip to Green Bay, Wisconsin, and find Roger Wyatt because he could confirm the statement of Richard Wheeler. They both agreed and I was on my way to Green Bay Wisconsin with Cathy on what we called a *"paid, mini-vacation."*

I rented a car and found a motel in Green Bay, Wisconsin. In the local phone book I found a Roger Wyatt listed with an address and phone number. I called the number but there was no answer. I decided to drive by the address and saw a Cadillac parked in the driveway. I rang the doorbell and a young man answered who identified himself as Roger Wyatt, Jr. He said his father was the truck driver I was looking for and he was now retired and living on Mackinac Island. He phoned his dad and told him I was an investigator from California, then handed the phone to me. We agreed to meet for lunch the next day at The Grand Hotel on Mackinac Island.

Roger, Jr. explained there were no cars allowed on the Island and the Grand Hotel was one of the ten most famous hotels in the world. The next morning Cathy and I caught a ferry crowded with tourists going to the Island to sight-see and buy their world famous fudge (the locals called them "Fudgies"). We arrived at The Grand Hotel in a horse-drawn carriage and were greeted by Mr. & Mrs. Roger Wyatt. It was a beautiful day as we talked and ate lunch on the veranda.

Roger Wyatt proved to be an excellent witness and re recounted in detail dumping "Gunk" from Shell Refineries to the Bolsa Chica dump for over two years. Roger was now 84 years old, distinguished-looking and he said he worked those two years and saved enough money to pay for his college education. I took a long detailed statement from him and explained that we may need him to testify if the case ever went to trial. He agreed to make the trip if necessary.

We now had a solid case so it was time to celebrate! At the registration desk, we were told there was space available for us to stay at the Hotel for the next two days. And now looking back on those two magical days, it filled us with memories that will last a lifetime.

When we returned home I met with the lawyer and his client and presented them with Roger Wyatt's statement. They said a Settlement Conference had been set for the next morning with both Standard Oil Company and Shell Oil Company attorneys. They suggested I meet with them for lunch tomorrow after the Conference.

Now either they were late or maybe I was early, but it was the strangest lunch I had ever been to in my life. I was seated in a booth where I could see everyone entering the restaurant. Finally, the lawyer and his client entered and walked slowly to my table and sat down never saying a word. Something was wrong but I couldn't figure out what it was. Then the lawyer said, *"We no longer need your services, Mr. O'Brien. The case was settled this morning."* I asked them how much was the settlement but they said it was confidential and if any news of the settlement or the amount was made public the entire agreement would be null and void.

For years, I had worked with dozens of lawyers who trusted me and we became a team and with that trust we won most of our cases. But Walter Ward had warned me about some lawyers who treat an investigator not as a trusted member of the team, but as just another employee. So I was mad - *real* mad, because I was the one who found the witnesses who confirmed the extreme negligence on the Oil Companies and I did not even get a thank you, or a *"job well done"* - nothing!

In looking back on this case years later, there was never a trusting relationship with this lawyer (whose name I have chosen to forget) and for me it was probably just my "Irish ego" that was bruised anyway! I learned later (from a court clerk) the case settled *"in the millions,"* so I guess that $5,000 retainer was well spent after all.

A Witness Risks His Life for His Friend

A huge storm drain was under construction in San Bernardino at the intersection of 40th and Waterman. It was 18 feet deep and 12 feet wide with two men at the bottom of the ditch clearing the way for the crane to drop in an eight-foot-long cement storm drain pipe. At street level, the foreman and a City Inspector were watching the operation. The Inspector had been warned not to stand at the very edge of the ditch but it was too late - he accidentally kicked a large rock, about the size of a football, into the ditch. It hit one of the men at the bottom of the ditch on the head with great force. His metal helmet was crushed and he fell to the ground unconscious.

The injured man's name was Tommy Cruz, husband and father of three young children. Jake Summers, the other man with him in the ditch climbed out of the ditch in a blind rage, swearing he was going to kill the idiot who kicked in the rock. The Inspector hid behind the foreman, or probably, he would have been killed. The City Inspector apologized profusely for standing so close to the edge of the ditch while crew members summoned an ambulance. Tommy was rushed to the hospital but he never regained consciousness and died two days later.

Tommy's widow hired Ron Golob to file a claim for Worker's Compensation death benefits. My job was to prove the City of San Bernardino was responsible for the wrongful death of Tommy Cruz. I grabbed my camera and drove to the scene. When I arrived, construction was still going on. I shot a roll of film and asked to see the foreman. He was reluctant to talk to me for fear he would anger the City of San Bernardino and cost the Inspector his job. He did give me the address of Jake

Summers who quit his job in anger after Tommy, his best friend died.

I drove out to Oak Glen to see Jake but all I had was a rural box number. I stopped at the post office and learned the box number given to me by the foreman belonged to a "Carl Richardson," not Jake Summers. The clerk at the post office said he knew Carl Richardson and that he owned an apple orchard next to the old grammar school.

I made my way to the Richardson home, parked my car, walked up to the front door and rang the bell. A tall grey-haired man about 60 years old opened the door and said he was Carl Richardson. He shook his head when I asked if he knew Jake Summers. But when I told him I was an investigator representing the widow and three children of Tommy Cruz he sheepishly admitted Jake Summers was his son-in-law who lived in a small cabin behind the barn. He apologized for misleading me but he said Jake was very suspicious of strangers. As we walked out onto the driveway, Carl explained Jake was a former member of a motorcycle gang and he did not want anyone to know he was living at the orchard.

Just then, Carl waved to someone in the barn. The barn door opened and Carl whispered to me, "That's Jake." He walked toward us carrying a hunting rifle on his arm. When we were introduced Jake told me he had the rifle trained on my head as Carl and I walked from the house to the driveway. He only lowered the rifle when Carl waved "OK" to him. I quickly gave Jake my card and told him I was representing the Cruz family. Suddenly, the scowl left his face and he started to smile. Jake said he was glad to meet me and he would do everything he could to help the Cruz family.

As we walked into Carl's kitchen, Jake put down the rifle and Carl poured us a cup of coffee. Jake appeared to be about 26-27 years old with a tattoo on his left arm of a skull and cross-bones. He was very good looking, about 5'9", jet black hair, well built and quiet. He reminded me of Paul Newman when he smiled. But why did he have that gun pointed at my head and why was he so suspicious of strangers? I needed to know the answers to those questions but right now they had to wait. We finished our coffee and I took a written statement from Jake covering the Inspector admitting he was at fault and the foreman warning the Inspector not to stand so close to the edge of the ditch. His answers were clear and concise, his choice of words excellent and there was no doubt in my mind, Jake would make a great witness if and when, the case ever went to trial.

I agreed to keep Jake Summers' location confidential. Jake said he was planning to "move up north" soon but Carl Richardson would always know how to reach him if he was needed to testify. I thanked both Carl and Jake for seeing me and I would let them know if the case settled or had to go to trial.

The insurance company interviewed the foreman and the Inspector who both claimed it was just an "unfortunate accident." The Inspector "forgot" he admitted to Jake and the foreman that he was at fault for standing so close to the edge of the ditch despite the foreman's warning. The insurance adjuster went to Oak Glen to interview Jake Summers, but the postal clerk denied knowing a Jake Summers. Consequently, Jake was never interviewed nor was his deposition ever taken. Sixteen months later, the case was set for trial. The lawyers for the City of San Bernardino relied on the Inspector and the foreman saying it was just "an unfortunate accident" and no one was at fault.

Our whole case depended on Jake Summers' testimony and it was my job to find Jake and have him ready to testify. I drove back to Carl Richardson's apple orchard and Carl told me Jake was no longer at the orchard. The "Gang" had somehow learned Jake was hiding at the orchard and he had to move because now there was a price on his head. I told Carl how important it was for Jake to testify. He agreed to make contact with Jake and have him call me at my home on the weekend before trial. I agreed to pay all of Jake's expenses and put him up in a motel under an assumed name. This was a life and death risk for Jake to return to San Bernardino County with the 'Gang" waiting to kill him. But Tommy Cruz was his best friend and I knew Jake would take the risk for Tommy's widow and her three kids.

On Sunday evening, Jake Summers called me at home. I told him the trial was set for Monday at 10:00 a.m. in Judge Noonan's courtroom in San Bernardino however it would take a full day to pick a jury and Tuesday morning would be opening statements for plaintiff and defense attorneys. Jake agreed to meet me at the Ontario Airport at noon on Tuesday. He refused to tell me what airline he'd be on or where he was coming from. He just said for me to meet him at Norm's Coffee Shop across from the airport at noon on Tuesday.

When I walked into the coffee shop, Jake Summers was already there with a lunch bag for each of us. We walked to my car and headed to the San Bernardino Court house. I told our trial attorney, for some unknown reason Jake Summers had a price on his head and a motorcycle "Gang" wanted to kill him. I said we would enter by a side door of the court house and go up the back stairway to the fourth floor and wait on the stairs next to Judge Noonan's chambers. Then when Jake was called to testify, the bailiff would take Jake into the courtroom from the Judge's chambers and have him seated in the witness chair. Our attorney told the Judge of our plan and he agreed to allow the witness to enter the courtroom from his private chambers.

Jake and I sat on the back stairs of the fourth floor opposite Judge Noonan's chambers. We had our lunch and waited. It was 12:45 p.m., and a perfect time for me to ask Jake about this "price on his head" and why the Gang wanted him killed. We opened up our lunches and Jake told me an amazing story. Jake never knew his father, who "took off" when Jake was born; his mom died when he was in eighth grade. He went to live with "Aunt Tessie" in Riverside, California. In high school, Jake got in with a bad crowd and before long he ended up in reform school.

He was 18 years old when he got out but by then Aunt Tessie had died and he had no place to go. He ended up picking apples at Carl Richardson's orchard in Oak Glen. When the season was over, Carl asked him to stay on as an orchard hand. Jake agreed, partly because he liked the job and partly because Carl had a beautiful young daughter named Julie. It wasn't long before they got together and Julie was pregnant. They were married in the small chapel in Oak Glen and they lived in the guest house behind the barn. Eight months later, Jake was the proud father of a son Jake, Jr. For the next three years, Jake worked on the orchard with Carl while Julie took care of their young son. Jake said it was the happiest time of his life.

Then Jake said he bought a Harley Davidson and soon he joined a motorcycle gang called the "The Pythons." Within a year, Jake quit working at the orchard and was travelling all over California with the Pythons. Jake and Julie split up with Julie keeping Jake Jr. at the orchard. Jake told me it was the biggest mistake he ever made when he left Julie and his son to join the motorcycle gang.

The "head man" was Charlie King. He had a young, wild, 18-year -old sister, Ellen, who soon fell madly in love with Jake. She was homely and unkempt, and had been expelled from high school in her junior year for using drugs. Jake never told her or Charlie he was married and had a young son. He never told anyone. Soon, Ellen wanted to get married and Charlie King thought it would be a good idea because Charlie had terminal liver cancer and his days were numbered. He trusted Jake and knew he would take good care of Ellen when he was gone. Jake feared Charlie King who had a terrible temper.

Charlie was a big man, 6'4" and at least 230 pounds, with a full beard and eyes that pierced right through you. Only Ellen and Jake knew Charlie's cancer was terminal and his plan was to have Jake take over the gang when he died. Jake feared him and knew it was fatal to cross him. He reluctantly agreed to marry Charlie's sister and one day take over the Pythons.

Finally, a wedding was set for Ellen and Jake in Yosemite National Park. The entire gang was in attendance and Charlie officiated at the solemn ceremony. Afterwards, Charlie said he wanted to give the couple a wedding present, so Jake and Ellen got on their motorcycle and followed Charlie on an old dirt logging road that led out of the park. When they were about 17 miles down the road, Charlie turned onto a dirt trail. It was a steep climb and when the road ended, they parked their bikes in a small cave where the bikes would be safely hidden. Then, they walked another four miles along the edge of a cliff with a creek roaring below. Charlie stopped in a small clearing where they pitched their tents, one tent for the bride and groom and the other for Charlie. He had brought along food, water, champagne and strangely two 100-foot lengths of rope.

The next morning, before the sun came up, Charlie woke Jake and said they were going for "a little hike." They got dressed and took the ropes and some water with them. Ellen was sound asleep in their tent. They walked another seven miles along the edge of the cliff with the creek roaring below. Charlie was looking intently down at the creek bed. Finally, he said, "This is the place" and he wrapped the end of his rope around a large boulder and told Jake to do the same. It was around 10 a.m., the sun had come up and it was very hot. Both men were dripping wet with sweat as they lowered themselves down the cliff and into the cold water below.

The Creek was only about 20 feet wide as it wound around huge granite boulders and roared down the canyon. Charlie and Jake both let go of their ropes and fell into the ice cold water.

They swam to shore and sat on a small sandy beach. Charlie had hardly said a word since they left their camp. But now, he was talkative. He said they were standing on the secret treasury of The Pythons. He said there was gold beneath their feet...lots of gold! It was a secluded beach and only Charlie and his treasurer knew its exact location - and now Jake Summers was added to the elite list.

Charlie started kicking in the sand and soon he was kicking up gold nuggets about the size of marbles! Jake did the same and within a half- hour, they had pockets full of gold!! They sat on a big granite rock to dry off and then they both started laughing. There was a fortune beneath their feet and it was there for the taking! Then Charlie explained the gold nuggets could be converted into money by a jeweler in Glendora. The money was used to post bail and pay fines for gang members who got in trouble with the law. And the gold in Jake's pocket was his wedding present.

It was time to climb up the ropes from the roaring creek to the hills above. Jake had no problem pulling himself up the 80-foot-side of the canyon wall, but Charlie got only about halfway when his arms gave out. Jake had the task of pulling Charlie up the rest of the way--all 230 pounds of him, to dry land. But he made it with blisters and blood on both hands. Charlie was doubled over with stomach pain. Finally, after a short rest, they made their way back to camp with pockets full of gold. They headed back to where their motorcycles were hidden then returned to their tents. Ellen was angry.

All this I learned while Jake and I sat on the stairs waiting for court to convene. But the worst was yet to come. Jake took a deep breath and said it was almost a year to the day when Charlie King died and a member named Jimmy Cato became president of the Pythons, not Jake, as Charlie had promised. Jimmy never liked Jake and the next year proved to be living hell for Jake and his bride. She was drunk all the time and spent most of their "wedding present" on drugs and wild parties.

One day, Jake jumped on his motorcycle and headed home to his wife, Julie and his son in Oak Glen. Jimmy Cato was wild with anger because he knew Charlie had told him of the "wedding present" given to Jake and that Jake knew the location of the Treasury. Jake admitted he had been on the run ever since with a price on his head.

Just then the doors of the Judge's chamber door opened and the Bailiff took Jake into the courtroom. Our attorney said Jake made a great witness. The jury believed him and the jury eventually came back with an award of $1,450,000! But just as soon as Jake got off the witness stand, he joined me on the stairway and we ran down the stairs to my car, making sure we were not followed. I paid Jake in cash for his out-of- pocket expenses and headed for the Ontario Airport. It was then that Jake surprised me (again). Once we were sure we were not being followed, Jake told me to drive to the John Wayne Airport in Orange County.

When we got to the airport, Jake suddenly said good bye and he jumped out of my car when I stopped at a stop sign. That was the last I ever saw of Jake Summers. He was a great guy who risked his life to protect his best friend's family. Where he is now, I doubt if even Carl Richardson knows. But of this, I am certain: Jake is with Julie and Jake, Jr. and he knows he risked his life for his friend.

A Snow Cone and Greed

A case came into my office where a five-year-old girl was hit by a car while she was buying a snow cone from an ice cream truck. The little girl was still in a coma when I got the case three weeks later. I picked up the police report and it cited the driver of the car that hit her for speeding. The police diagram showed the ice cream truck on the right side of the road and yet the little girl was hit in the middle of the street. As if that weren't curious enough, the ice cream truck driver was not even listed as a witness.

The parents' home was in a middle class neighborhood of small tract homes in Long Beach. It was a nice home with new paint, a white picket fence and a beautiful lawn with flowers all around. I went to their home on a Saturday morning to talk with the family. At the same time as I rang the doorbell, the father opened the door with a golf bag over his shoulder. I introduced myself and handed him my card but he said he was late for a golf game and asked me to talk to his wife.

We sat down in the living room and she told me how the accident happened. She said the ice cream truck would come by every afternoon about 3:00 p.m. and always parked in the middle of the street. She gave her daughter two quarters and wanted to teach her daughter how to accept the change for her snow cone. Mom said the ice cream man was serving children on both sides of his truck with his red lights blinking and music blaring from his loud speakers while she waited on the curb.

Her daughter stepped off the curb, walked out to the middle of the street to the truck and she bought a snow cone. The driver gave her change then she turned around and started walking to her mother who was still waiting at the curb. Out of nowhere a car swerved around the ice cream truck on the wrong side of the road and struck the little girl.

Despite my first impression upon meeting the dad, I was greatly impressed with the parents. Mom was about 30 years old, happy and intelligent. They also had a seven-year-old son. Dad was a little over 30 years old, good-looking, polite (despite our hurried introduction). His wife told me he was the dispatcher for a large trucking company. Their home was immaculate inside with maple furniture and cut flowers everywhere.

The sad reality was the hospital expenses were mounting and the motorist who hit their little girl had no insurance. This family was facing financial ruin but the case had one big problem: who to believe - the mother or the police report? Was the ice cream truck on the right side of the road or in the middle of the road? And why was the snow-cone driver not listed as a witness?

I decided to ring some doorbells in hopes that maybe someone saw the accident. Then I got lucky - I talked to a neighbor who said he was mowing his lawn when the accident happened. According to this neighbor, the ice cream truck was in the middle of the road when the little girl was hit by the passing car. He heard the ice cream man say he was sorry for not parking his truck on the right side of the road. The police had warned him several weeks ago of the danger posed to the children by his parking in the center of the road.

I showed the witness a copy of the police diagram showing the ice cream truck on the right side of the road. He just laughed because when the police officer arrived at the scene, it was obvious the ice cream man and the officer knew each other. Evidently, this was the reason the ice cream man was not listed as a witness and the truck was shown on the right side of the road.

If this witness' testimony held up, we now had a case and a very good one against the ice cream truck business for parking in the middle of the street. I went back to the office and shared the good news. Suit was filed and depositions were taken. The deposition of the investigating officer was a classic. He had to admit he not only knew the ice cream man but the guy was his brother in law! A police log proved the driver had been warned by the police not to park in the center of the street. At the Mandatory Settlement Conference, the case settled for $1,420,000. The little girl was still in a coma and required full-time nursing care. The medical bills to date were over $300,000.

As with all Minor's Compromise Settlements, court approval is required. The court approved this settlement as being fair to the little girl and the money was deposited in a special savings account to be used only as needed for medical and special care expenses for the minor child. All expenses had to be approved by a Superior Court Judge. I was given the job of having the parent's sign the court-approved settlement papers and endorse the $1,420,000 check so it could be deposited in the court-approved savings account.

I drove out to their home and was surprised to see a "For Sale" sign on their front lawn. We sat down in their living room with the parents seated on their couch and me in a chair facing them. The little girl was lying in a recliner chair and appeared to be asleep (but she was still in a coma). I asked the mom and dad why they were selling their beautiful home. The father said the home was too small and now that they had the settlement money, they could afford to move into a bigger home in a better neighborhood. The mother sat and nodded her head but it was clear to me she did not want to move. It was also eerily apparent that her husband couldn't wait to get his hands on his daughter's money. Greed had consumed him.

I explained the strict requirements of a Minor's Compromise Settlement. The money could only be withdrawn from the savings account for their daughter's medical bills and expenses that were approved by a Superior Court Judge. Now, it was the father's turn to be shocked. He shook his head in disbelief. He said, "What happens if she dies? Do we get the money then?" He turned and looked at his daughter with an evil look unlike anything I had ever seen before. It made me sick. Anyway, they signed the settlement papers and the Settlement Draft and I walked out to my car with a sick feeling in my throat for the safety of the little girl.

Now, to this day I wonder every once in a while, if that little girl is still alive. And like the old Irishman once said, "There is only one thing worse than being broke…and that is having money you can't spend!"

A Doctor's Conscience is Calmed

M att McLewis had his Law Office just down the street from mine in Claremont. He heard I was planning a vacation to Ireland and wondered if I could stopover in London and check on a doctor who was practicing medicine there. Of course, I was happy to let Uncle Sam help me with the air fare and expenses. I agreed to meet Matt for lunch and review his case.

We sat outside at Walter's Café and Matt told me about a case he tried nine years ago. He represented a young college student, Tom Blake, who was riding his bicycle to a class when a medical student by the name of Charles Anston hit him (his brakes failed). Tom was badly injured and is now paralyzed from the neck down. Charles Anston was from London and he was in his last year of Medical School at UCLA. The jury came in with a verdict of $1,600,000. The insurance company paid their policy limit of $100,000. Then Matt Lewis had a judgment against Dr. Charles Anston for $1,500,000. He knew the young man was now a cardiologist with his medical offices in London. Matt wanted me to do a financial asset check on Dr. Anston in hopes of collecting some of the money owed to his client. Matt said his judgment had a time limit of ten years and he had only one more year to collect any money from this doctor.

I agreed to do the investigation in London. I thought it would be a simple asset check like it is here in the States. All you have to do here is make a "connection" with a Credit Bureau person and usually you can learn bank account balances, credit card payments and property owned. But in London, I was in for a big surprise!

Cathy and I landed at Heathrow Airport and checked into a hotel in Piccadilly Square. I figured it would take me a few hours in the morning to make a "connection" and do the assets check, then we could go and see London – particularly, the Sherlock Holmes Exhibit at 221 Baker Street and maybe even have dinner at the Waldorf-Astoria Hotel.

I let Cathy sleep off the jet lag and I went down to the Lobby to call a Credit Bureau office. There were four Credit Bureau offices in the phone book but they all demanded an account number, which I didn't have, so I looked up Private Investigators in the yellow pages. I talked to all nine investigators listed with London addresses. Not one of them did asset checks because in England it was considered a violation of privacy to do such investigations. Most of them even told me they would not work for an investigator from the States because they never got paid. Then I had an idea. I would pay a visit to Scotland Yard and maybe I could talk to a detective and get the information I needed. Scotland Yard was in many of Conan

Doyle's stories with Sherlock Holmes and Doctor Watson – surely they would be able to get me the information I needed.

I almost believed Lieutenant Lastrade would greet me at the front door but I was not so lucky. Instead I was introduced to Lieutenant Starkey who turned out to be a really nice Detective and willing to help me if he could. I told him my need to do an asset check on Dr. Charles Anston, a cardiologist, with offices somewhere in London. Starkey recognized the name and said he was a young and very successful Cardiologist with offices on prestigious Gaffney Lane near the Big Ben Clock. But that is about all he could tell me.

All the Banks and Savings and Loan records were highly confidential and his office could only get the information with a valid court order. He said he would call me at my hotel if he learned anything that could help me. I was hitting brick walls at every turn...but we were in London and there was so much to see!!

Cathy and I caught a cab to 221 Baker Street and walked thru the Holmes and Watson apartment and had a cold Guinness at the Sherlock Holmes Pub. Conan Doyle was a master at bringing his characters to life. Now, 100 years after Sherlock Holmes had his adventurers, 1000's of people still visit their apartment that never really existed, except in Conan Doyle's imagination. We had dinner at the Waldorf Astoria and returned to our hotel.

All night long, I tossed and turned, trying to find a way to learn the assets of Dr. Anston but I was stumped. Finally, I had an idea that just might work. I reasoned, since there was no chance of doing an asset check, why not just go over and see him in his offices and tell him what Tom Blake had been doing these last nine years, confined to a wheelchair and having someone feed and care for him. Perhaps, Dr. Anston would realize how fortunate he was as a successful cardiologist here in London. It was a gamble but one worth taking.

Right after breakfast, I put on a coat and tie and caught a cab to Gaffney Lane. Big Ben was just striking 10:00 a.m. Gaffney Lane was a block long with brass plaques on each door announcing a doctor's office. The cab driver told me the very best doctors in London had their offices here on Gaffney Lane. I said a little prayer and walked into his waiting room. The receptionist asked my name and I gave her my card. She gave it to a nurse who walked into Dr. Anston's office and closed the door. I sat down and grabbed a magazine.

Suddenly, the Doctor's door burst open and out came Dr. Charles Anston, all smiles as he shook my hand vigorously. He said, "Please come into to my office, Mr. O'Brien, I've been expecting you." I was dumbfounded, I had no appointment but he was expecting me? Then it dawned on my thick head, Lieutenant Starkey must have called him last evening and warned him that I was in town.

I sat in a leather chair as Dr. Anston told his nurse to hold all his calls. There was silence for a moment and then Dr. Anston spoke up. "How is Tom Blake doing after all these years?" I told him, what Matt had told me; Tom had graduated with a degree in Political Science and was now working for a newspaper part-time in San Bernardino, California. Of course, he was still in a wheelchair and barely able to move his arms. Dr. Anston took in every word and it looked like he was about to cry. Here he was a successful Cardiologist and there was Tom Blake confined to a wheelchair for the rest of his life!!

I told him about the $1,500,000 judgment pending against him after the verdict nine years ago but before I could go on, Dr. Anston interrupted me. "That accident has been on my mind ever since it happened. I am so sorry for Tom, I only wish I could do something for him but I certainly do not have $1,500,000. I'm so sorry but I just can't help him," he said sheepishly.

Then, I made a proposal. I suggested to Dr. Anston, if he agreed, he should write a letter to Matt Lewis and make an offer to settle the case for, say, $1 million with payments monthly of $1,000 or more. I told Dr. Anston this would be a "win-win" because not only would it help Tom, it would help ease Dr. Anston's conscience. Now, I had no idea if Matt would accept the offer, so I suggested Dr. Anston keep our meeting confidential and he agreed.

Cathy and I left London and caught a plane to Ireland. After a two-week stay on the Emerald Isle, we returned to Claremont. I ran into Matt Lewis at the courthouse and he said, "O'Brien, it was too bad the asset check didn't work out but a strange thing happened: Dr. Anston sent me a letter proposing we lower the judgment to a million and he would pay us $1,000 a month until paid in full. It's sure better than nothing so I agreed to take it!" I said it was a surprise to me but it seemed to be a win-win proposal that would end a very sad situation.

P.S. ...And Matt paid my bill!!

A Lost Briefcase Leads to Murder

W e were just finishing a BBQ-swim party on a hot summer afternoon at our home in Claremont when the phone rang. It was John Stevenson calling from Hemet, California. He was primarily a criminal attorney but occasionally he would come up with a good personal injury case. This time his call was personal but he didn't want to talk about it on the phone. He said he and his partner, Larry Doyle, would fly over to Bracket Airport and meet me around 7:00 p.m. I agreed, put on some dry clothes and drove to the airport. I waited in the coffee shop and watched the planes come and go.

Finally, Larry's 310 Cessna touched down and parked in the visitor's space and Larry and John got out. We sat down and ordered some iced tea while John told me how he lost his $500.00 briefcase. I started to laugh but soon realized they didn't fly all the way from Hemet to have me find his $500.00 briefcase. I sat back and listened as John told me an amazing story of a $5,000,000 will that was in the briefcase when it was stolen and how his own daughter was the primary beneficiary. It began like this:

For years and years, John Stevenson and his daughter, Helen would celebrate Christmas and New Year's in Santa Monica with his old maid Aunt Jessica Wilson. She lived in a beautiful home in the old part of town just off Pico Blvd. She was a great cook and loved to go to the opera and stage plays. John, being a lawyer, was aware the old girl (74 years old) had become quite wealthy but she had never written a will. Her key to success was buying (she never sold) foreclosed property that went up for sale in Santa Monica and she always paid cash. She bought her first property in 1956 and now 30 years later she owned over 60 homes. All were rented and free and clear of any mortgages. Jessica never married and had no children. John would always remind her that she had to write her will. Her answer was always the same, "Some day John...some day."

Finally, the day came when she called John and asked him to drive up on the weekend because she finally decided to take his advice and draw up her will. John and Helen drove up from Hemet and had lunch with Aunt Jessica. She appointed John as the Executor of her estate and after a few small bequests, she bequeathed her entire fortune to Helen. It was a very big surprise because John always thought she would leave all her money to either the Catholic Church or a charity. John had the will typed up, signed, and witnessed. He kept the original will in his safe at his office in Hemet and he gave a copy of the will to Jessica. John told me that when times got bad and bills were piling up, he would open his safe and read Aunt Jessica's will. It assured him at least Helen would always be financially secure with an estimated value of Aunt Jessica's estate of over $5 million.

On Jessica's 77th birthday, Helen and John drove to Santa Monica planning to take Aunt Jessica to dinner and a play at the Dorothy Chandler Pavilion. Reservations were made for three but John was surprised when Jessica greeted them at her door, all decked out in a beautiful evening gown. At her side was a tall, good looking young man in his early 50's. Jessica introduced Fred Bowman to John and Helen. Fred said he sold Jessica a new Mercedes several months ago and their friendship had grown into a serious relationship. Jessica was plainly taken by this tall, handsome car salesman. Over dinner, Fred mentioned he lived on his 41- foot yacht in Long Beach Harbor with his 22-year-old son Michael who was a senior at UCLA. It was indeed a strange relationship but John was pleased to see Jessica so happy. John and Helen bid the couple goodbye after the play and returned to Hemet.

Seven months after this visit, John received a phone call that sent shockwaves through his spine. It was a Homicide Detective calling. He said Jessica's body had been found off Catalina Island. She had been strangled. Michael Bowman (Fred's son) told the detective his father had taken Jessica to Las Vegas for the weekend. Jessica caught him forging her name on a Deed of Trust he had found in her purse. There was a big fight and his father strangled Jessica and put her in the trunk of her Mercedes car. Michael said he planned to drive back to Long Beach and put Jessica's body on his yacht and dump the body overboard beyond Catalina Island. The Detective said Michael admitted being with his father and Jessica in Las Vegas but he was at a floor show when the murder took place. According to Michael, Fred said he would claim Jessica committed suicide. Michael wanted no part of the scheme and returned to Los Angeles by Greyhound Bus. On arrival he turned himself into the Sheriff's Office and made a full confession. His father was arrested in a rented cabin in Lake Arrowhead and was now in custody without bail.

Now, I'll bet you have been wondering what this tall tale has to do with me and John Stevenson wanting me to find his $500.00 lost briefcase. Well, hang on and I'll tell you. The Detective said the reason for his call was he and the County Assessor went to Jessica's home and found among her personal effects stacks of Deeds of Trust, and a will appointing John Stevenson as Executor of her estate. This murder came as a complete surprise to John but suddenly he realized his daughter Helen would inherit Jessica's Estate and would soon become a very wealthy woman. The Assessor made an appointment with John for Tuesday morning. They would meet at Jessica Wilson's home at 10:00 a.m. and he told John to bring along the original will.

By 6:30 on Tuesday morning, John was showered, dressed and he had Jessica's original will packed safely away in his brand new alligator-skinned ($500.00) briefcase. He got into his car and was on his way to meet with the Assessor. It was a good two-hour drive but with traffic he didn't want to be late. John drove down Pico Blvd at 9:15 a.m. and was within a block of Jessica's home when he realized he had time for breakfast. On the corner was a Del Taco drive-thru and it was open. A taco is a little hard to handle for breakfast but John was hungry and he reasoned he could sit outside at a table with his briefcase by his side. From his vantage point, he could see Jessica's home and would be able to see the Assessor's car when he turned onto Pico Boulevard.

He ordered two chicken tacos and a cup of coffee. He sat and waited. It was now 9:45 a.m. and no sign of the Assessor. 10:00 a.m. … 10:15 a.m. … nothing. Finally, John decided to call the Assessor's office. He noticed a payphone on the corner next to the Del Taco. He walked over, placed his briefcase on the ground next to the payphone and reached for some change to place the call. Just then, he noticed a County of Los Angeles car make the turn on Pico Blvd. It was the Assessor! John raced into the street and flagged the driver down. He stopped, John got in and they drove to Jessica's home. It was only three doors down the street from the Del Taco.

When John got out of the car, he remembered his briefcase with Aunt Jessica's will in it, was left beside the payphone at the corner. John ran to the corner but the briefcase was gone! Someone had apparently seen the expensive briefcase on the ground and stole. John questioned everyone at the Del Taco but no one saw anyone steal his briefcase.

John told me we had to find the briefcase because the Probate Court will not allow a *copy* of a will to be submitted; only the *original* will is allowed. I cancelled several appointments and left the next morning for Santa Monica in search of the missing briefcase that contained an original will worth over $5,000,000!!

I beat the early morning traffic and was at Del Taco before 7:00 a.m. I questioned the owner and his employees but they were of no help. I questioned at least a dozen customers and told all of them there was a $1,000 reward for the return of the briefcase and its contents. Still no luck. Then I noticed a large dumpster sitting next to the alley behind the Del Taco stand. I reasoned that whoever stole the briefcase might have emptied the contents in the dumpster, not ever realizing it contained a valuable will. The dumpster had not been emptied overnight so I climbed into all that garbage searching for the lost will. I ruined a new pair of slacks and a pair of shoes but still no luck...no will.

On a hunch, I returned on Thursday and questioned the Del Taco employees again and the customers hoping the $1,000 dollar reward would lead to the briefcase and the Will. I even put an advertisement in the *PennySaver* but no luck. I checked the pawn shops in the area looking for the briefcase - no luck. I had to return to John's office and tell him the bad news. I did my best but it wasn't good enough. That $500 briefcase was too tempting for the thief.

End of story? Well, not quite.

Larry Doyle, the attorney who flew John Stevenson to Brackett Air field to meet me, practiced Appellate Court work and when the copy of Aunt Jessica's will was submitted to the court it was immediately rejected. Larry then had me submit a sworn statement on how the briefcase was stolen and my diligent search for the original will. The court allowed the copy of the will to be submitted because of the "unusual" circumstances of the murder of Jessica and the briefcase being stolen. Helen went on to law school, passed the bar and bought a shopping center in Hemet with her money. John retired and bought a farm in Indiana.

The Curse of the Kensington Pearl

When we moved from Eureka to Los Gatos, it was like coming home all over again. My Mom and Dad built their home on Middlefield Road and after they died, we decided to

242 In The Shoes of an Investigator: The True Life Adventures of a Private Eye

move into the home. It was in a great neighborhood with young adults like us, busy raising our families, and it had an excellent grammar school. It was a magical time for our family to live in the sun and not the fog and rain of Eureka. Our kids were on summer vacation and by September, they had all made close friends and were (almost) ready to start school. I had a briefcase full of interesting files to work and Eureka was quickly becoming a dim memory.

My son, Tim, went to school with a kid named Mark Conti, who was also in the 7th grade. Every morning, I would pick Mark up at his home and take Mark and Tim to school. Mark lived in one of the nicest homes on the block, a classic Cape Cod. He lived with his parents Gerri and Joe and his three-year-old sister Mary Anne. Joe had owned a small casino in Reno and when he sold it, the family semi-retired to Los Gatos. Now, Gerri and Joe ran sixteen bingo parlors from San Mateo to Salinas, as well as a very successful Jewelry Mart in San Jose. They were obviously very wealthy because there was a new Mercedes parked in their driveway every year and Mary Anne had her own nanny.

One morning, Joe called and said he would like to meet me for breakfast at the Los Gatos Grille, after I dropped the boys off at school. Joe was an excitable thirty-six year-old Italian who always had some wild scheme to run by me. This morning, he was all excited (as usual) because he had read in the *New York Times* that the world-famous Kensington Pearl, the largest and most perfect pearl in the world, was being auctioned in London by the Earl of Kensington who was in dire need of money to pay his taxes. The article said the Pearl was worth around $750,000-$800,000 at auction but based on estimates Joe received from experts at his Jewelry Mart, the Kensington Pearl was worth at least $3.5 million here in the United States. Joe suggested we go to our bank and float a loan for $800,000 and attend the London auction. I thanked him for the offer but it was *way* out of my league and anyway, I had a big family to feed. Joe shrugged off my decision and mentioned he had an uncle in Las Vegas who might be interested in loaning him $600,000. Joe said he had $200,000 in a savings account to make up the difference. When Joe reached for his wallet to pay the bill for breakfast, he stammered, exclaiming he must have left his wallet at home, so I picked up the tab (as usual) and we headed to our cars.

Gerri Conti told my wife Cathy, her husband went to Las Vegas to see his uncle about "some kind of loan" for their jewelry mart and he would be home in four or five days. After a week and a half, with not a word from Joe, Gerri and her family were worried sick. I suggested she file a missing person's report, which she did but still, no sign of Joe.

I had a "friend" with many contacts in Vegas. I called him and asked if he knew "Joe Conti" who had owned a small casino in Vegas several years ago and whose uncle owned it now. He said, "Of course, I know Joe. I helped him set up those bingo parlors." I asked my "friend," to do me a favor. I told him that Joe had been missing from his Los Gatos home for almost two weeks after telling his family he was going to Vegas to meet his uncle and that he would be gone only about five days. I asked my "friend" if he could help us find Joe. He said he would talk to a few people and he would call me the next morning.

At noon the next day, my phone rang. It was my "friend" calling. He said, "I have quite a story to tell you about our friend Joe Conti…" and he proceeded to tell me how Joe made a mistake that could cost him his life. My" friend" said he learned Joe came into town last week all fired up about a deal he was working on in London. Joe met with his uncle and told him about the auction of the Kensington Pearl. A deal was made and Joe flew to London with a $600,000 letter of credit from the "Family" and a cashier's check of his own for $200,000 which Joe had borrowed from his bank (without telling his wife). Joe said he planned to tell her of the loan after the Pearl had been sold here in the United States. He told his uncle the Pearl would sell for around $3 million in the U.S. with 60% of the profit to his uncle and 40% to Joe.

My "friend" said Joe landed at Heathrow Airport in London and went directly to the auction house when it opened. It was packed with onlookers and there were at least six buyers interested only in the Pearl. Joe sat in the back row and watched the bidders. The bidding started at $250,000 and quickly rose to $425,000 when all but two bidders dropped out. Both seemed determined to buy the Pearl. Each bidder raised the other by $10,000 until a final bid was made at $510,000 and the auctioneer said, "Going once . . . going twice . . ." Then Joe raised his hand and bid $525,000. The other man threw his arms in the air and swore, as the auctioneer sold the Kensington Pearl to Joe Conti who promptly wrote out a check for $525,000 (U.S. dollars) on the letter of credit account that had been cleared by the Bank of London. Joe left the auction house with the Kensington Pearl safely placed in a jeweled case and a notarized Certificate of Authenticity in his pocket. Joe was on cloud nine. He got his Pearl without using any of his loan money and he could return $75,000 to his uncle and the "Family."

It had been an exciting and profitable day for Joe Conti but the jet lag was finally catching up with him. He checked into the Savoy Hotel in London and made a United Air Lines reservation (first class…he could afford it!) for his return flight to Las Vegas and home. Then he went upstairs to his room and took a nap.

When he awoke he still had a four-hour wait for the airport shuttle so he walked into the Savoy bar. He ordered a Scotch and sat on a bar stool. He was already packed and checked out of the hotel so all he had to do was wait…and drink. He was about to order his second Scotch when he noticed an attractive young woman in her early twenties sitting at a table alone. She smiled at him and he noticed she also was packed and apparently waiting for the same United Air Lines flight. He raised his empty glass and nodded to her to see if she would like a drink. She smiled and nodded "yes." Joe ordered two Scotch and waters from the bartender and took the drinks over to her table. Not since his college days had Joe made a "conquest" on a pretty girl and here he was in London, far away from his wife and small children and now he was about to become extremely wealthy so it was time to celebrate, right? Who would ever know? He sat down with her and she thanked him for the drink.

He introduced himself, "My name is Joe Conti, I'm just killing time waiting for the airport shuttle and the United flight to Las Vegas." She smiled and said her name was Sally and she was on the same flight but getting off when it made the first stop in New York. They learned they were both on business trips and returning home. The hours flew by and Joe was indeed celebrating. He lost count after the fourth Scotch but he reasoned he could sleep all the way to Las Vegas on the plane. He failed to notice that Sally had been ordering just water after she finished her first drink.

Unfortunately, the Scotch had loosened Joe's tongue and he began bragging to Sally about having bought the Kensington Pearl. He went on about his uncle with whom he was splitting the profits 60/40 when the Pearl was sold in the U.S. Just then, the hotel concierge called all passengers leaving for Heathrow Airport to board the awaiting limousine.

At the airport, Joe and Sally checked their luggage and proceeded to the first-class section of the aircraft. Within minutes, the plane was airborne and they settled into their seats. They both sat quietly as the plane finally leveled off at 40,000 feet. It was probably a combination of high altitude and too much Scotch, but Joe resumed talking to Sally when he should have kept his mouth shut. Then he said, "Sally I'm thinking, maybe I'll get off in New York and meet with Alexander

Claypool, an expert on pearls. He may be interested in buying my Pearl."

"But doesn't your partner in Las Vegas own 60% of it? You can't sell it without your friend's permission, can you?" inquired Sally.

Joe, thinking out loud, said "One of my employees at the Jewelry Mart showed me a book Mr. Claypool had written and one of the chapters was on the Kensington Pearl. He said he had seen the Pearl on two occasions and he valued it at $2,800,000-$3,400,000. Now, suppose I sold the Pearl to Mr. Claypool for around $3,000,000. Then, I'll return the $600,000 to my uncle…I mean *partner*, in Vegas and tell him I was outbid at the auction and couldn't buy the Pearl. That would leave me with a clear $2,400,000 profit!" The thought grew more enticing as Joe kept talking. Sally just shook her head in disbelief.

She said, "That would be pretty dishonest, wouldn't it? Anyway, you shouldn't be talking about such personal things with me, I don't even know you. "After a moment, Sally said, "Look, we have a long flight ahead of us. I'm going to get some sleep now, if you don't mind." Sally eased back in her seat and turned her head away. Joe did not agree with Sally but he nevertheless stuffed a pillow between his head and the window and succumbed to an intoxicated slumber.

Joe and Sally awoke as the Boeing 747's wheels hit the pavement at John F. Kennedy Airport. Sally asked if Joe was going on to Las Vegas. Obviously, the sleep did not change his mind and he replied groggily, "No, I think I'll stop over in New York and pay a visit to Alexander Claypool." Joe stretched his arms to the ceiling, yawned and tried to clear the cobwebs from his head.

"OK, Joe but I think you are making a big mistake. But it's your life not mine. Goodbye." They collected their luggage and went their separate ways. Joe figured he would never see Sally again, and then it dawned on him, he didn't even know her last name. He did all the talking and all she did was listen. But maybe it would be a blessing not to see her again because he was afraid he was becoming a bit too fond of her.

At this point, I interrupted my "friend" and asked, "How do you know so much about Joe and what he did in London?"

"I'll get to that in a minute," my "friend" replied.

Joe had the address for Alexander Claypool at one of the high-rise buildings in the financial district. He hailed a cab and was on his way. The building directory showed The Claypool Group was on the 11th floor. Joe rode the elevator up and walked into the office. He proudly introduced himself to the receptionist as the new owner of the Kensington Pearl. She immediately pressed the intercom button and Mr. Alexander Claypool entered the waiting room. He was a tall man, bald and pale with thick, wire-rimmed glasses that he peered above as he stooped to shake hands with Joe. "So you're the proud owner, are you?" said Mr. Claypool, eagerly pumping Joe's hand. "I read about you in the paper. Congratulations."

Joe smiled with confidence and said he had the Pearl with him along with a Certificate of Authenticity. "I'd like to get your unbiased opinion of the Pearl's true value, if you would be so kind." Mr. Claypool ushered Joe into his private office. Joe handed him the jeweled case with the Pearl inside. Mr. Claypool opened it and gently placed the Pearl under the microscope on his desk.

After what appeared to be an intense inspection, Claypool started to laugh. "Ha! It's a *fake*...and not a very good one at that!" Joe fell back into his chair in utter agony. He pulled the Certificate of Authenticity from his shirt pocket and Claypool again scoffed. "This is an obvious forgery; it doesn't even have the Notary stamp across the signature!"

Joe's whole world was imploding right there in Claypool's office. What was he going to tell his uncle at the casino? He was a dead man for sure. He asked Mr. Claypool how much he thought the fake Pearl was worth. He said, "Nothing, but I will give you $1,500 for the jeweled case." In desperation, Joe handed him the case with the allegedly worthless Pearl inside, took Mr. Claypool's check and left the office in defeat. Mr. Claypool took the box and placed it in his desk drawer.

It was raining when Joe hailed a cab to take him to the airport. The flight to Las Vegas was three hours late because of the storm, which gave Joe time to collect his thoughts and prepare an explanation for his uncle. He landed in Vegas at dinner time but Joe had no appetite. He called his uncle and asked if he could see him right away. The uncle agreed. Joe had made up his mind the only thing he could do was simply tell the truth. He had spent $525,000 of his uncle's and the "Family's" money on a worthless, fake pearl but somehow, he would find a way to repay his uncle for his stupidity. He caught a cab and in minutes he was going up the outside elevator with a fantastic view of the city, to the top floor of the casino as the lights were coming on all over Las Vegas.

The doors to his uncle's office suite were wide open and Joe was ushered into a high-backed leather chair. There were three tall men in black suits standing behind his uncle. They neither spoke nor took their eyes off Joe. His uncle was seated behind a huge mahogany desk. Behind him was a floor-to-ceiling window looking out over the city. Joe just sat there with his head in his hands. Finally, he told his uncle the whole story: how he out-bid the antique dealer and won the Pearl with a bid of $525,000 and how he planned to sell the Pearl to the expert in New York and return the $600,000 loan to the "Family" telling them he was out-bid at auction. He admitted he planned to keep all the profit for himself, confessing his greed and stupidity. He was so engrossed in purging his soul, he failed to notice the door to the uncle's office slowly open and close behind him.

Silently, a figure crept up behind Joe's high-backed chair and waited. With a nod from his uncle, the figure stepped out in front of Joe and there stood Sally. The blood left Joe's face and pooled in his legs. She was holding the jewel case with the Kensington Pearl inside. Thoughts raced through his mind: How did Sally get here? Who is she? How did she get the Kensington Pearl? He could only guess that Sally was a trusted member of the "Family." She stood in front of Joe, not saying a word. But there was something about her face that was strangely different. No longer did Sally have the pleasant, innocent look of the young lady he met in London. She looked older. Her smile was gone, her teeth clenched in anger and her eyes - her eyes, sent chills down Joe's spine. He thought for sure he was going to die.

Finally, Sally spoke. She told him she was on the plane with him when he flew to London. She was in the audience when he bought the Kensington Pearl. She sat next to him on the flight to New York when he was drunk and told her how he planned to cheat his uncle out of the profit by selling the Pearl to Alexander Claypool. She said she followed him to the Claypool office where she just missed him as he was leaving in the elevator. She stood at the partially-open door to Claypool's office and overheard Claypool bragging to his receptionist about how he just bought the Kensington Pearl from a "fool" for only $1,500, when the actual value was at least $3 million. Suddenly, Claypool noticed her standing in the doorway and realized she had overheard the entire conversation. She introduced herself and said she had a personal matter to discuss with him.

Sally explained, rather dryly, how he ushered her into his private office and she told Mr. Claypool she represented "investors" in Las Vegas who sent Joe Conti to London to buy the Kensington Pearl. They would be most upset if they learned Joe Conti had been cheated out of the Kensington Pearl by an expert in New York. Mr. Claypool sat at his desk for a full two minutes before he came to a wise decision. He reasoned this young woman represented "investors" in Las Vegas who would probably kill him if he did not return the Pearl. He knew what she meant by "investors" and realized he should sell the Pearl to her and save his life.

Finally he said, "Give me $1,500 for the jeweled case and the Kensington Pearl is yours." She told him he was a very wise man not to anger her "investors." She handed him cash, put the Pearl and the case in her purse and was on her way back to Las Vegas.

Joe just sat expressionless as he heard the good news and the bad news. The good news was the Kensington Pearl was real and back in the hands of the "Family" at a bargain price. The bad news was the "Family" would never forgive him for trying to swindle them out of the Pearl. Joe finally found the strength to stand up, shake hands with his uncle, nodded good bye to Sally and head for the airport.

My "friend" finally explained to me that he was one of the three men standing behind Joe's uncle when Joe came to him empty-handed and pleaded for forgiveness. And after all, the uncle was not a fool who would send Joe with over a half-million dollars to London without following his every move. That was Sally's job.

On the flight to San Jose, Joe decided he had to close up his bingo parlors, sell the Jewelry Mart and sell his beautiful home in Los Gatos. He was certain a contract would be put out on his life. In desperate defeat, he decided to disappear with his family to some remote place where they would be safe and never be found.

All of us neighbors who lived on Middlefield Road noticed a security company installing a state-of-the art alarm system on the Conti home. Then we saw several plumbing trucks parked out in front, so we figured they were remodeling their kitchen. All was seemingly normal for about six months when one Saturday morning as we were having breakfast, a giant explosion rocked the whole neighborhood. Joe's entire kitchen and breakfast room ended up in his swimming pool! Fortunately, Joe and Gerri had taken Mark and Mary Anne to Mark's soccer game so they were not home at the time of the explosion. The Los Gatos Fire Department came and determined it was a faulty water heater connection that caused the explosion. But Joe knew better. It was a "calling card" from the Family. Probably, one of the plumbers set the bomb and timer underneath the kitchen, with enough explosives to wipe out the entire Conti family. Joe was certain a contract had been issued and it now was imperative they disappear...and soon.

Joe listed the home for sale at a reduced price while the kitchen was being repaired. In thirty days, the home, the Jewelry Mart and the bingo parlors had all been sold. The Conti's moved away, never to be seen again by any of us on Middlefield Road.

End of Story? Well, not quite.

About a year later, I happened to be in Los Vegas on *"A Doctor Goes Fishing"* case and was having lunch with my "friend." I asked him what ever happened to the Conti's after they moved away from Middlefield Road. He laughed and said," No one ever cheats the "Family" and lives. But Joe was one of the very few lucky ones because he did confess his stupidity to his uncle and the explosion was just a warning to Joe never to lie again. My "friend" and I hoped Joe and his family would live a long and happy life...but wherever they are, Joe will always be looking over his shoulder in fear. Maybe *that* is the curse of the Kensington Pearl.

The Case that Couldn't Be Won

This is the very last case I ever worked as an investigator. My son Mike, an attorney, called one morning and asked me to come by his office. He said he had an interesting case and he needed my opinion. I reminded him I was retired and working on this book. Anyway, he promised to buy my breakfast, so I agreed to meet him.

Mike said he was referred a case by a businessman in Chino whose close friend's son had been badly injured. His 14 year-old son was riding his skateboard when he was hit by a motorist driving a van. The boy was airlifted to the County Hospital with a severe head injury. The medical bills for the first month alone totaled over $123,000. The driver of the van was a local contractor with a two million dollar insurance policy.

Over our second cup of coffee, Mike admitted to me, it looked like "a case that couldn't be won." But the referral was from a close friend, we had to at least take a good look at it before turning it down. Mike had talked with the boy's parents and learned the following facts:

(1) The boy was on his skateboard at night;
(2) The boy was wearing dark clothing;
(3) He was on the wrong side of the road;
(4) He was talking to a friend on his cell phone and on his way to meet the friend at a city park nearby;
(5) He cut across the intersection and hit the left side view mirror of the van;
(6) There were eight witnesses on the police report who said he was on the skateboard and caused the accident;

(7) The local police cited him for failing to wear a helmet.

I had to agree with Mike's evaluation. It was a case "that could not be won."

But I remembered Walter Ward telling me long ago that if the injuries were substantial, (and they were) and there was sufficient insurance, ($2 million); and if you worked hard enough and used a little imagination, you could find a way to win. And if there ever was a case where all the cards were stacked against a young boy this was it. I agreed to take a look, because I wanted to test Walter Ward's theory. But the logical side of my brain told me, this was a case that could not be won.

Mike obtained a copy of the Chino Police Report. It was 72 pages long! In my 60 years of being an investigator (1948-2008) I had never read a police report this long! It took an entire morning just to read and try to understand the report. It became clear the Chief Investigating Officer had delegated the entire investigation of this accident to a young police Cadet and it must have been his first automobile case. The Chief Investigating Officer did nothing but gloss over the Cadet's work, but hidden in the report were several valuable facts that could help us with our "impossible" case:

(1) The driver of the van admitted he was drinking wine with his daughter at dinner...drunk driver?
(2) The driver of the van drove 412 feet after impact before stopping...Hit and run?
(3) The van was impounded after the accident for defective brakes. ...Cause of the accident?
(4) His driver's license required he wear prescription glasses but he failed to wear them on the night of the accident - The driver's fault?
(5) The Cadet placed the point of impact in the crosswalk, where pedestrians have the right of way.

(6) A traffic light was burned out near the crosswalk.

Before I questioned the eight witnesses, I went to the scene and made a scaled drawing so I could position each witness in reference to the point of impact. It was something the Cadet failed to do in his lengthy 72-page report. Since we were faced with an almost impossible case, I decided each witness had to be carefully interviewed and just maybe I'd find a way to transform this case from a loser into a winner.

I talked with witness #1 and learned at the time of the accident, he was walking home after playing tennis with his brother. It was totally dark at 9:05 p.m. and he did not actually see the accident. He only heard the impact and when he turned around our client was on the pavement "near the crosswalk." But the most important thing I learned from this witness was no Adjuster from the Contractor's insurance company had come out to interview him. In addition, the Cadet only interviewed this witness on the telephone. I gave him my pen and asked him to position himself on my drawing of the scene. When he did, he placed himself and his brother 460 feet west of the crosswalk. I took a written statement and told him if someone came around to question him, just let them know his statement had already been taken by me. Adjusters and defense lawyers hate knowing a witness has given a signed statement to the (enemy) plaintiff.

Witness #2 confirmed he was walking home with his brother, Witness #1. He placed his initials next to his brother at 460 feet west of the crosswalk. His written statement was the same as his brother's.

Witness #3 was a jogger who was standing on the northeast corner of the intersection waiting for the pedestrian signal to change to "Walk" so she could run south across the intersection in the crosswalk. She said she saw our client get hit by the van in the crosswalk and land about 34 feet east of the crosswalk but she said the light was still red for her and our client. I went with her to the scene because she seemed to be confused about the red/green signal for her to cross the intersection and she wasn't sure if the boy was on his skateboard or just carrying it when he was hit in the crosswalk. There was no doubt she was a key witness but because of her confusion, she could help us by putting our client in the crosswalk when he was hit. However, she could hurt us by claiming the signal was red when our client attempted to cross the intersection. I recorded her statement anyway.

Witness #4 was the friend of our client who was talking to him on his cell phone. He admitted talking to him but our client was at least 300 feet from the intersection when they both hung up their phones. The witness turned around and walked from the tennis courts. He did not see the accident; he only heard the impact and saw his friend's body land on the pavement. I took a short statement from him.

Witness #5 had been playing tennis with his friends (Witnesses # 1 and # 2) but he was picking up tennis balls and was at the southwest corner when our client was hit. He was positive all of the blame was on our client. I took him to the scene with a camera and a recorder because his testimony could ruin our case. Once again, I was the first and only investigator to question him and he was eager to place all the blame on our young boy.

He placed himself at the southwest corner of the intersection when he shouted to our client that it was dangerous to skateboard at night I photographed him pointing to his position at the intersection and pointing to where our client was when he was hit. Then I got the break of a lifetime - call it Irish Luck or a Magic Key but when I asked him to point to the exact point of impact (when the van hit our client), I photographed him pointing to the exact center on the Eastern crosswalk! Suddenly, the most dangerous witness was our key to the bank because now we could prove that our client was a pedestrian and according to the Vehicle Code he had the right of way because he was in the crosswalk when he was hit! With this key witness, I took his statement, a recording and photographs. Unfortunately, he was "unsure" if the stop signal was red or green when our client was hit.

Witnesses #6 and #7 were a husband and wife who were returning home after dinner at a friend's home. They were travelling westbound approaching the intersection when the accident occurred. The husband said he clearly saw the accident but his wife said she did not. He said our client was hit "at or near" the crosswalk and when the van continued on, he was about to make a "U" turn and catch him as a hit-and-run driver. But the driver stopped about 400 feet down the road and walked up to the scene. I took a recorded and written statement from both husband and wife. They were a young newly married couple and most cooperative. However, months later, an Adjuster questioned them and suddenly the wife clearly recalled the whole accident and placed the entire blame on our client. Her husband was of no help to either party. But I had a written statement from both of them in case they ever testified against us.

Witness #8 was a retired Police Officer who lived on the northeast corner where the accident happened. However, he told the Cadet he only heard the impact and called the police. He moved to South Carolina within a week of the accident and had not been contacted by the Cadet or me.

Our client was a 14 year-old junior at Chino High School. He was a strapping 6'2" and 195 pounds. He suffered a cranial fracture and somehow survived the accident. He was released from the hospital after only two weeks in intensive care and his medical bills were $230,000. But then we learned he was on the high school football team and returned to playing immediately after being released from the hospital, we only prayed the insurance company would not find out about his amazing recovery or how dangerous it was for him to be playing football after such a serious injury.

Mike filed a lawsuit for $1.5 million. It was based mainly on the lucky breaks we had in questioning the witnesses but we had to be realistic. With our client on the football team, the value of our case was cut in half and we knew we had less than a 50% chance of winning at trial. Our case had to be settled if at all possible.

Months later, after depositions and discovery were complete, Mike somehow convinced the attorneys at the Settlement Conference the case had substantial settlement value. After Mike let the defense lawyers read the statements and hear the recordings of the witnesses, the defense attorneys offered a confidential settlement. The exact amount will never be made public but it was a wheelbarrow full of money. Not bad for a "case that couldn't be won!"

But it was Mike who must have had a "Magic Key" in his pocket because he was able to convince the defense attorneys of this case's settlement value. It was certainly a job well done and his old dad can only sit back proudly and wonder....

The Final Chapter

The Magic Key

Thank you for taking the time to read my book. All the stories are true with just some of the names and places changed to protect people living or dead who for reasons known only to them may take exception to the "facts" as I have written. Just remember, I'm an old retired investigator (87 years old) recalling stories that happened over 50 years ago. And if I have ruffled some feathers along the way, I apologize.

Now we come to the final chapter and, I must admit, I have agonized over what I should say. By all means, I don't want these stories to give the impression to the reader that here is an investigator who won all these cases and now is just blowing his own horn. That is simply not the truth. And one day when I was writing *Burned Beyond Recognition*, it dawned on my thick head to just tell it like it is and let the chips fall where they may. So here goes:

First of all, I'm no great investigator. Sure, I made enough money to raise ten kids (five boys and five girls) but most of the money came from real estate investments and the sale of the *Verdictum Juris* newspaper. Walter Ward was my teacher and without his help I would probably still be an Adjuster living in Eureka. He was the one who convinced me to move the family from San Jose to Los Angeles and join a big law firm.

The years flew by and I semi-retired with a small office in Claremont where I founded *Verdictum Juris* ("Jury Verdicts") and later *O'Brien's Evaluator*. It was then that I started thinking about writing a book of my "Adventures." As I remembered a story, I would write it down on a 3"x 5"index card and put it in my pocket. I spread the cards out on our pool table and the

"Table of Contents" started to take form. My life was in chapters, as an Insurance Adjuster in Chicago and San Francisco and Eureka; and then my "Adventures" in San Jose, Los Angeles and Claremont as an investigator. Then I started placing the cards in the proper locations and it suddenly dawned on me most of these stories had a happy ending with losers becoming winners. This just couldn't be true. No one would believe me. It was the lawyers who won all those cases, not me. I knew from the verdicts reported in *Verdictum Juris* that almost half of all jury verdicts were defense verdicts. So I took that set of 3"x 5" cards and put them in a shoe box and forgot them.

Then along came a day when Cathy and I sold our home in Claremont and we moved to Lake Arrowhead. Buried in the stacks of boxes, I found the old shoe box. It started me thinking: Maybe there was a message hidden in these stories that had to be told and it wasn't just about me being a great investigator. It was bigger than that and much more important.

I used to tell my kids (and eventually, my grandkids) bedtime stories about a "Magic Key" that was found in an old oak tree in the forest in Lake Arrowhead. The key opened a magic door that led to a magic room filled with candies, milk shakes, cookies and toys of every kind. Many times, the Key led them to different places/times where they would have all kinds of exciting adventures. The kids would fall asleep dreaming of the "Magic Key" that opened the magic rooms.

Suddenly, all of my stories had a new focus. Maybe I had a "Magic Key" that opened all those impossible cases and changed losers into winners. But what was the "Magic Key" and how (why) did it work? In fact, when I started writing I felt the title of the book should be "The Magic Key" because it would explain, for example, how a nurse who had the most critical information would appear in *The Case that Refused to Die;* or how I came upon the aircraft mechanic who witnessed the crash in the *Hit and Run Aircraft;* or locating the two pilots who witnessed the crash in *A Father and Two Sons...Dead*. The "Magic Key" must have been someone or something that opened all those doors on all those cases and I was just the Irishman with a briefcase who took down the witness' statements.

Now, remember in *The Case That Refused to Die*, I awoke in the middle of the night and my conscience was yelling at me to look into what happened after the automobile accident. It led me to the pregnant nurse and the emergency room doctor that uncovered a powerful medical malpractice case. Anyway, when I visited the Snyder boy in the hospital and looked in his eyes, that screaming conscience of mine was repeating over and over, "What you do to one of these the least of my brethren, you do unto me." It was at that exact moment I realized I had a duty to fight for the Snyder boy because I was working not for the money but my Magic Key enabled me to work for God Himself. Now, I know a statement like this will convince you that I'm out of my mind. Well, consider the words of St. Bernadette of Lourdes:

FOR THOSE WHO BELIEVE IN GOD, NO EXPLANATION IS NECESSARY AND FOR THOSE WHO DO NOT BELIEVE, NO EXPLANATION IS POSSIBLE.

As I look back on my life as an investigator, it is the only rationalization possible to explain the reason for all of these victories. Someone (God) must have been looking over my shoulder and my "Magic Key" was a deep concern I had for the injured parties and not for just the money. I've learned a lesson: It's not how much money you can make in this life that makes you a success...It's how many people you can help.

It's all over now, the stories have been told and I've tried to explain as best I could how these cases were won. And now I have a proposition for you. My proposition is this...If the "Magic Key" worked for me in all these cases, just maybe it will work for you. No matter what your profession or job, consider working not just for the money you are getting paid, but how much you can help other people. I'm convinced the "Magic Key" will work for you just as it did for me.

May God Bless You!

THE END

INDEX OF CASES

EXPLOSION – *A Bowling Alley Blows Up; Burned Beyond Recognition; My Adventure With Alligators; The Curse Of The Kensington Pearl*

FRAUD – *Governor Brown Helps A Friend; Maher Oil Company Millions; A Lost Briefcase Leads To Murder*

FREIGHT TRUCKS – *The Richardson Grove Cameraman; A Case Of Mistaken Identity; Lew Buys A New Mercedes*

GAMBLING – *A Gambling Debt Turns Fatal*

GUNS - *Hold-Up At Mike's Liquor Store; "Boom-Boom" Gets Wet!; Murder At The Monte Carlo Hotel*

INSURANCE BAD FAITH – *A Bowling Alley Blows Up*

LIFE INSURANCE – *Burned Beyond Recognition*

MISCELLANEOUS – *When She Had To Go – She Went!; The Strange Case Of Raymond Nelson; The Case That Couldn't Be Won*

MEDICAL MALPRACTICE – *A City Bus…On The Sidewalk?; How Many Have You Killed?; The Case That Refused To Die (Part One…San Jose); The Case That Refused To Die (Part Two…Los Angeles); Death Plays Baseball; A Lab Report Coverup*

MISAPPROPRIATION – *Governor Brown Helps A Friend*

MISSING PERSONS – *Please Find My Dad; The Curse Of The Kensington Pearl*

Author and family in summer of 2010

CPSIA information can be obtained at www.ICGtesting.com
Printed in the USA
BVOW08s2043031013

332706BV00001B/93/P